AMARONE AND THE FINE
WINES OF VERONA

THE CLASSIC WINE LIBRARY
Editorial board: Sarah Jane Evans MW
and Richard Mayson

There is something uniquely satisfying about a good wine book, preferably read with a glass of the said wine in hand. The Infinite Ideas Classic Wine Library is a series of wine books written by authors who are both knowledgeable and passionate about their subject. Each title in The Infinite Ideas Classic Wine Library covers a wine region, country or type and together the books are designed to form a comprehensive guide to the world of wine as well as an enjoyable read, appealing to wine professionals, wine lovers, tourists, armchair travellers and wine trade students alike.

The series:
Port and the Douro, Richard Mayson
Cognac: The story of the world's greatest brandy, Nicholas Faith
Sherry, Julian Jeffs
Madeira: The islands and their wines, Richard Mayson
The wines of Austria, Stephen Brook
Biodynamic wine, Monty Waldin
The story of champagne, Nicholas Faith
The wines of Faugères, Rosemary George MW
Côte d'Or: The wines and winemakers of the heart of Burgundy,
    Raymond Blake
The wines of Canada, Rod Phillips
Rosé: Understanding the pink wine revolution, Elizabeth Gabay MW
Amarone and the fine wines of Verona, Michael Garner

AMARONE
AND THE FINE WINES
OF VERONA

MICHAEL GARNER

infiniteideas

Infinite Ideas Limited
www.infideas.com

A CIP catalogue record for this book is available from the British Library

ISBN 978–1–908984–80–7

Brand and product names are trademarks or registered trademarks of their respective owners.

All web addresses were checked and correct at time of going to press.

Front cover photo courtesy of LOOK Die Bildagentur der Fotografen GmbH / Alamy Stock Photo. Back cover photos (top left and bottom) Charley Fazio / Consorzio Tutela Vini Soave; (top middle) © Archivi Masi; (top right) Consorzio Tutela Vini Valpolicella.

Maps and illustrations adapted and drawn by Nicki Averill. Source map of Soave courtesy of Consorzio Tutela Vini Soave. Source maps of Valpolicella courtesy of Consorzio Tutela Vini Valpolicella.

Typeset by Suntec, India

Printed in U.S.A.

CONTENTS

AUTHOR'S NOTE

I should make clear from the outset my use of the word Verona and its derivatives. As well as being a city with a population exceeding a quarter of a million, Verona is also a province of the north-eastern Italian region of the Veneto. The vast majority of references below are, however, to the city and not the province. The word has two main derivatives, the first of which, 'Veronese', comes in two forms – as a noun and as an adjective. On the few occasions it has been used as a noun, this has been as an alternative way of identifying the area composed of the two DOC territories of Soave and Valpolicella and refers, in other words, to the 'viticultural' Veronese where the vineyards are planted within easy reach of the city. The use of Veronese as an adjective is far more frequent, and means simply 'of' or 'from' Verona. The context should make entirely clear which is which. The second derivative is the word 'Veronesi': this is the plural form of Veronese and is used to identify the people of Verona. Hence it could be said that 'The Veronesi inhabit the Veronese and their mindset is typically Veronese!'

ACKNOWLEDGEMENTS

It is of course the Veronesi to whom I owe a huge debt of gratitude for providing the material for this book which I am pleased to dedicate to them. They are too numerous to mention by name, but I feel I know most of them well enough to be forgiven for not doing so and am confident in any case that they know who they are. I cannot, however, fail to single out the people from the two growers' consortia. At the Consorzio Tutela Vini Soave, Aldo Lorenzoni has helped enormously, as have his staff and in particular Giovanni Ponchia (now responsible for marketing, promotions and administration at the Consorzio of the Colli Berici) and Chiara Mattiello. At the Consorzio Tutela Vini Valpolicella, Olga Bussinello has been a useful sounding board for many of the ideas expressed below – despite her extremely demanding position – and I would like to thank her staff too, and especially Greta Turrini for all the help she has given me. I must also mention Alberto Brunelli and Amedeo Bazzani who coped admirably with all my questions.

Finally, and most importantly, my thanks go to my family for their constant support and inspiration, and above all to my wife Trudy whose calmness at the eye of the storm is beyond measure.

INTRODUCTION

I would have no hesitation over my selection of desert island wines. Providing, of course, that I was allowed one white and one red for the duration of my stay, I would choose Verona's best known wine couple: Soave and Valpolicella. To be more precise, that would most likely be an example from the 'Classico' or geographical heartland of each denomination, from a good recent vintage and from one of the many small to medium-sized growers who have in recent years taken overall standards of quality to an entirely new level. An unconventional choice, perhaps, for someone who has spent most of his working life in the wine trade and has been lucky enough to taste fine wines from all over the globe, but my selection has nothing to do with the bargain-basement wines that the two denominations were once associated with. Such wines – bought and sold on price alone – may unfortunately still be found but it is a schoolboy howler to assume that they continue to be truly representative.

The iconic Piedmontese producer of Barolo and Barbaresco, Angelo Gaja, once expressed the view that the average consumer perceives a wine-producing area in the form of a pyramid. Taking Bordeaux as his example, Angelo argued that the 'lesser' wines bask in the reflected glory of those at the apex. In other words, the consumer has positive expectations of the humble AC Bordeaux wines at the base simply through their association with Chateau Margaux and the other first growths at the top. The problem for many Italian wines has long been that the consumer's perception is reversed and the least interesting examples of the denomination are seen as prototypical. Expectations of quality for the wines higher up the scale are correspondingly low as a consequence.

The Soave and Valpolicella I'm referring to are made by producers who, tapping into an intimate knowledge of their vineyards and local traditions, have all but closed that dog-eared page in history by following the production process from bud through to bottle and attempting to make the best possible wines from their own lovingly nurtured grapes. While the beauty of Soave and Valpolicella can be found to a large degree in their deceptive simplicity, their true value – as largely inexpensive wines – lies with their enviable versatility. They are the *ne plus ultra* of everyday wine. So my desert island choice is a highly pragmatic one. To worry the conceit a little further, my diet would no doubt be based on fish cooked over wood embers and accompanied hopefully by a few foraged vegetables or leaves. I really would be hard put to find a wine more ideally suited to such honest, nourishing and tasty food than Soave. There would be little or no meat but, if I was really fortunate, wild pig might occasionally be on the menu and maybe even some wildfowl every now and then: I'm in luck once more! Valpolicella is already one of my favourite wines to go with pork-based dishes and works superbly with feathered game too. Chilled down in a cool stream, it would also make an interesting and worthwhile alternative to go with fish. Furthermore as both wines are generally fresh, light and well balanced they could easily serve as an early evening aperitif when many other still wines are in reality not particularly refreshing. The reason my two choices would work so well is quite simply that they have been selected on the basis that they not only perform the fundamental role of accompanying food to perfection but are also an absolute pleasure to drink.

The key issue behind this point of view is of course one of balance, or the measure of how the component parts of a wine stand in relation to each other. On the whole, the most typical examples show a subtle, somewhat understated structure based on low to medium alcohol, highish acidity and light to medium body. This even combination of elements, lightly seasoned by that extra palate-cleansing twist of acidity, goes a long way towards explaining the versatility so vital to their success. Furthermore, flavour profiles are well proportioned and yet expansive enough to carry on delivering when other more 'obvious' wines have begun to tire the palate and lose interest and appeal. Tim Hanni MW, wine educator and professionally trained chef, is a guru of the food and wine experience and an astute observer of the effect food and wine have on each other. He points out that 'Primary taste interactions have the same effect on wines across the spectrum of styles, from delicate and sweet to dry and intense. The more intense the wine is in terms of primary attributes (sweet, acidic, bitter, tannic) the more the interactions will be exaggerated. This has given rise to the concept of "food wines" that typically are overall less intense and therefore are much less reactive with most dishes.' When applied to Soave and Valpolicella, this does not necessarily make a virtue of what their detractors (who might simply be drinking the wrong examples) refer to as an inherent neutrality but recognizes the part that flavour and structure characteristics play in arriving at a judicious food and wine pairing.

Because of their long association, the food and wine of a particular area seem to develop in tandem and this is certainly the case not just around Verona but also in Venice, not much more than an hour's drive eastwards along the *autostrada*, where Soave and Valpolicella are the default wines to accompany much Venetian cooking. In both areas it is extraordinary to see this very versatility (the ability to pair with a wide range of foods) in action. Classic local dishes in the Veronese – whether based on fish, such as *polenta e renga*, where the polenta (a thick maize porridge frequently cut into slices which are then fried or grilled) is dressed with salted herring and the fragrant local extra virgin olive oil; meat, as with the aromatic local salami Sopressa, or vegetables, such as *pasta e fasoi* (a hearty soup based on borlotti beans which also contains slivers of pasta) – seem to sit equally well with either wine. Apply a similar formula to some of the mainstay dishes of Venice – *polenta e baccala*, where the polenta is served with a ragu based on salt cod; *fegato alla veneziana* (calf's liver with onions) or *riso e bisi* (rice and peas) – and you can only come to a similar conclusion. The two are, however, not always interchangeable: on the whole, Soave is a safer choice with most vegetable-based dishes and Valpolicella with meat, and yet the affinity they have with the wide array of dishes typical of the Veneto remains the most natural fit imaginable.

Just as there is so much more to the local cuisine than the selection of the few relatively simple and well-known dishes above, so there is a far greater range of wines than might first seem apparent made in the hills that border the beautiful city of Verona to the north and east.

While Soave and Valpolicella are the best known and most widely available of them, they are, along with several sub-categories of the two denominations, made in the customary manner from the fermentation of freshly harvested grapes. However, the vineyards also give rise to an entirely distinctive range of wines that represents, in the view of many pundits, the pinnacle of a very particular variation on the wine-production process.

Most European wine-producing countries, and in particular those that flank the Mediterranean, have a strong tradition of concentrating grape juice in order to make a fuller, richer and often sweet or semi-sweet wine by the simple expedient of reducing the water content in the liquid through various 'natural' means. This is especially true of the Italians who, from the Alpine regions of the north down to the tiny island of Pantelleria lying between Sicily and the coast of North Africa, produce different examples of the style in pretty much every one of the country's twenty regions. The scale on which the operation is carried out reaches a whole new level in these hills where, every year in the last couple of decades, around 50 per cent of the red grape harvest in the Valpolicella has been set aside for the process of *appassimento* or grape drying; while there is a parallel tradition in the Soave area, this happens on a much-reduced scale. The tradition in Verona of using partially shrivelled grapes to produce a full and intense style of wine stretches back over more than two millennia, though it is perhaps surprisingly more popular now than it has ever been. The original model was the sweet red or white wine which came over the course of many centuries to be known as Recioto. However, it is the modern dry version of the red, Amarone, that seems to have captured the imagination of the wine-drinking public. Still widely considered as an unwelcome aberration until beyond the end of the Second World War, Amarone's reputation has risen to such giddy heights that it is now spoken of in the same breath as Barolo and Brunello di Montalcino, and is hailed as the third member of Italy's triumvirate of great red wines. The lesser known white version (Recioto di Soave) continues to be produced as a richly-flavoured and sometimes magical dessert wine. A parallel can be drawn with the original sweet Recioto della Valpolicella, to give the red wine its full title. Made in much smaller quantities than Amarone, Recioto was customarily produced from the grapes that formed only the ripest extremities of the bunch: the 'wings' or tips. The name is thought to be a corruption of the Italian word *orecchie* or ears.

The recent success story of Amarone has furthermore breathed new life into another local custom whereby the sugar-rich lees remaining after the first racking of the new Amarone or Recioto are given a second lease of life. Young Valpolicella is added in the spring following the vintage to start off a secondary fermentation designed to bring extra body, richness and alcohol to the new wine. If the production of dry red wines from the *appassimento* process is in itself an uncommon practice, the *ripasso* technique, as this secondary fermentation is known, is a strictly Veronese speciality.

The term 'Veronese wines' is frequently applied on a broader scale than the variations on Soave and Valpolicella outlined above. It is important here to distinguish between the province of Verona, which is vast, and Verona itself. As the provincial capital, the city of Verona represents the seat of local government for ninety-six different *comuni* or municipalities. These are bordered by the provinces of Trento to the north, Vicenza and Padua to the east, Rovigo to the south and Mantua and Brescia to the west. The city and its immediate surroundings lie right at the heart of the *provincia*. The scope of this study will exclude the wines from the north and west of the city: these include Bardolino and its rosé version Chiaretto, and Bianco di Custoza and Lugana which are more closely associated with Lake Garda these days. Indeed Lugana is primarily produced within the neighbouring region of Lombardy, while the others can be described as the wines of the right bank of the Adige. Similarly the 'catch-all' denomination of Verona IGP (*Indicazione Geografica Protetta*) will only be referred to where producers of the Soave and Valpolicella areas have chosen to use the category to cover interesting or unusual wines which do not correspond to the composition of varieties or other requirements stipulated by the local *Denominazione di Origine Controllata* (DOC) and *Denominazione di Origine Controllata e Garantita* (DOCG) rules, though which are still produced in those areas.

The subject can therefore be defined as the wines produced within the two delimited, contiguous and partly overlapping vineyard areas of Soave and Valpolicella. The vineyards are situated on the southern slopes of Monti Lessini, or Lessinia as it is also known. This area can be seen as almost an island in itself and is a particularly distinctive territory. Lessinia is a karst area formed of a plateau sloping gently to the south with a network of parallel valleys, aligned for the most part from north to south, that stretch down towards the course of the river Adige. Vines have been planted along the slopes of these valleys for more than two thousand years. These are the wines of the left or northern bank of the Adige as it veers to the south and east below the lake and onwards to its mouth on the Adriatic Sea at Rosalino Mare. There is also a surprise in store. Along the eastern reaches of Soave, a much lesser-known denomination, producing as yet tiny quantities of sparkling wine made from a rare local white grape, lies waiting to be discovered. When made by the *metodo classico*, Lessini Durello is capable of hitting heights of exceptional quality and adds a further element to the already diverse and plentiful history of wine production in the hills. Add Lessini Durello into the equation and all the bases for the wine lover can be covered from aperitif to dessert or cheese and even postprandial 'meditation' wine. For this author at least, these are the true wines of Verona.

1

HISTORY

FROM PREHISTORIC BEGINNINGS TO THE DECLINE OF ROME

Many visitors begin their tour of Verona with a short stroll across the Piazza Bra past the pavement bars, cafés and restaurants that line the north-western edge of the vast square. On the opposite side, across the public gardens, lies the town hall, the Palazzo Barbieri; behind is the imposing Palazzo Gran Guardia, finally finished in 1843 almost two and a half centuries after construction was originally approved. Directly ahead lies the Arena, built in the first century AD and lying just outside the city walls at the time. At the northern tip of the arena, the popular choice is to head up Via Mazzini, with its marble pavements and designer shops. (Until the nineteenth century the streets would turn to mud after heavy rains and were lined with warehouses and barracks reflecting the city's long history as an important military garrison.) Mazzini connects Piazza Bra with the important Roman square of Piazza Erbe, much the smaller and more beautiful of the two meeting points. The adjacent Piazza dei Signori, dating back to medieval times, is another essential stop on the itinerary but beyond, heading northwards through the narrow overhanging streets and away from the main tourist honeypots towards the Ponte Pietra, it is even easier to imagine that you are wandering back in time. Charles G. Bode, the author of *Wines of Italy*, which was one of the very first books in the English language on the subject when published in 1956, clearly felt the same way: 'I find the town still essentially Roman in character, much more so than any other town in Italy – Rome included … I could easily imagine the people of Verona walking about in togas …'

One of the great authorities on the cultural history of Verona was Lamberto Paronetto, and for wine lovers he remains the most important chronicler of Veronese wine. Born in 1915 in Quarto d'Altino just north of Venice, Paronetto was a widely respected technical director for major Italian wineries in both Tuscany and the Veneto. He worked for Bolla throughout the 1950s and remained in the area for much of the rest of his life. He was also a prolific author, writing and editing many books on wine. Three in particular stand out: *Viti e Vini di Verona*, *Verona Antica Terra di Vini Pregiati* and (with Antonio Calo and Giampiero Rorato) *Veneto*, the first volume of the *Storia Regionale della Vite e del Vino Italiano* ('History of the Vine and Wine in Italy'). All three have been invaluable sources of reference for the current study. Sandro Boscaini, President of the Veronese house of Masi, said of Paronetto, 'He taught me that there is more to a wine than its nose and its palate: it is the living memory of the culture and place which produced it.'

According to Paronetto, fossils found near Bolca provide evidence that plants since shown to be the antecedents of today's *Vitis vinifera* were present in the area some 50 million years ago in the Paleogene period. He confirms the conclusions of local palaeontologist Abramo Massolongo who was working during the middle of the nineteenth century. Massolongo hailed from the village of Tregnago in the Val d'Illasi, part of today's so-called 'extended zone' of Valpolicella, and his exhaustive description – reproduced in *Verona Antica Terra di Vini Pregiati* by Paronetto – of the fossilized leaf and stalk shows a painstaking attention to detail. The fossil in question was discovered in the Alpone valley, one of the main production areas of today's Soave Classico.

The area has been populated since the Stone Age. In the early 1960s, the father and son team of Giovanni and Alberto Solinas, both keen palaeontologists themselves, discovered the Grotta di Fumane (a.k.a. Riparo Solinas), a cave system in the Vajo di Roncomerlo above the town of Fumane which was found to contain extensive evidence of the presence of Neanderthals. The remains of prehistoric villages have also been found in the Vajo dei Falconi (Falcon valley), in the Archi area of Castelrotto and near the classic stone village of Molina, also in the Fumane valley. However, it is not until the Bronze Age that a connection between man and vine first becomes evident when traces of the fruit as part of the human diet can be ratified. A high-concentration grouping of grape seeds (in excess of one thousand), identified as *Vitis vinifera silvestris* and found close to Lake Garda, is believed to have been left by the pile- or stilt-dwelling peoples who inhabited the area at the time. There is no conclusive evidence to assume, though, that the grapes were consumed in the form of a beverage, fermented or otherwise. Confirmation that grapes were being processed into wine comes much later, in the centuries leading up to the birth of Christ, with the discovery in Rivoli Veronese and Valeggio of vessels dating back to the eighth and sixth century BC that were used for the storing or serving of wine.

Before the arrival of the Romans, the area was populated largely by the Reti or Rhaeti peoples. Dedicated hill dwellers, they inhabited the lower slopes of the Lessini mountains. They are known to have had, at the very least, trading contact with the Etruscans; some hold that their origins are Alpine while others argue that in fact the Rhaeti may have been the Etruscans' direct descendants. The Etruscans themselves had broken with the Greek method of training vines in the form of small bushes or 'alberelli' (little trees) and brought in a new approach of training vines high on support systems – poles, trellising or even onto the branches of other fruit trees. Thus other crops could be grown on the ground below the vine canopy – a method of farming that became known as 'promiscuous cultivation' and was to continue in the area at least until the first half of the twentieth century. Their system of high-training, introduced first into central Italy, was to leave an indelible imprint on the face of Italian viticulture – modified versions are still widely used throughout the peninsula and rely on a pergola as the support frame. Most of the vineyards of Valpolicella and Soave today are a classic example of the legacy. The Rhaeti were followed by the Arusnati, also dedicated farmers, who gave their name to the *pagus arusnatium* which corresponds roughly to the heartland of today's Valpolicella area (the Classico district). Fragments of stone tools and other artefacts from the time of the Arusnati are on show in the small museum located to the side of the church of San Giorgio di Valpolicella, a sleepy hillside village in the commune of Sant'Ambrogio di Valpolicella in the western part of the area. It seems highly likely that the Vino Retico for which the area was soon to become famous was named after the Reti.

Similarly, the origins of the city of Verona are thought to date back to the times of the Reti and Euganei and possibly even the Etruscans.

While the etymology of the name is uncertain, the city seems to have been founded on the hilltop site, a location typical of Etruscan settlements, where the present-day Castel San Pietro sits overlooking a loop in the Adige. It is almost impossible to overestimate the significance of Verona's geographical position as a vital intersection of trade and military routes: to the north, Central Europe; to the east, Venice and onwards to Byzantium; to the south, the heart of Etruscan civilization (lying just north of Rome in the area we know as Tuscany), and to the west via Genoa towards Gaul. This access to potentially important markets has played a fundamental role in the development of the local wine trade.

Indeed it is in Roman times that Veronese wine begins to establish a clear identity for itself. Whereas Vino Retico may feasibly have originated from almost anywhere among the sub-Alpine hills of north-eastern Italy, it becomes clear that the Romans held the local wines of Verona in great esteem. References to their growing fame abound. Amongst the first to write on the subject was Marcus Porcius Cato (known as Cato the Elder) who used the term Vino Retico to refer to a wine of great prestige; Emperor Augustus was also known to be an admirer. Columella, who wrote extensively about agriculture during the first century AD, reports that the great Roman poet Virgil considered Vino Retico second only to Falerno (from present day Campania) in status. Columella's contemporary Pliny noted that Augustus's successor Tiberius was served semi-dried grapes from the vineyards around Verona at table. The author of *Naturalis Historia* also recorded that the Retic varieties had found their ideal home in the temperate climate of the area. Similarly, Martial attributes the origin of Vino Retico to the land of his fellow poet Catullus, a native of Verona. There can be little if any doubt that the origins of the Recioto-style wines of Soave and Valpolicella made from semi-dried fruit are the direct descendants of this ancient tradition.

The area's vineyards were mainly confined to the lower hillside areas of the *pagus arusnatium* and under Roman rule extended into the territory now covered by the neighbouring communes of Mezzane di Sotto[1], Illasi, Colognola ai Colli, Soave and Monteforte d'Alpone. They

---

1 Mezzane di Sotto is the name of both a village and the commune which surrounds it, lying within the valley of Mezzane.

are thought to have been surrounded by woods, meadows and pasture land and below, along the flood plain of the Adige itself, areas of marshy land left behind from the original course of the river. The average size of a fruit-growing estate was probably no more than around 5 or 6 hectares owing to the high levels of manual labour required to tend the crop; any larger estates may possibly have been manned either by slaves or prisoners of war. Fruit growing had become quite a sophisticated affair, with the use of organic (dung) or mineral (ash-based) fertilizers and green manure common. Wine was often stored in clay amphoras which also allowed for the possibility of transport. The local wine was apparently sent as far afield as Illyria (modern day Albania), possibly via the Adige, which was navigable to the south of the city, and north towards settlements along the Danube via what were originally pack-animal tracks, gradually converted for use by wheeled traffic.

The Via Claudia Augusta linked the Po Valley with the Alps of southern Germany, and the even older Via Postumia connected Genoa to the west and the important military frontier town of Acquileia to the east. Soave, some 20 kilometres to the east of Verona as the crow flies, was a strategically important town along the Via Postumia. Originally a market town where people from the local hillside settlements would trade meat and dairy produce for grain, its history is more sparsely documented than that of Valpolicella, although tombs dating back to Roman times have been discovered in the Castelleto area and at Carniga which lies just north of the town close to the famous Calvarino vineyard. The well-known castle, which dates back in its current form to the time of the Scaligeri family, is thought to occupy the site of an earlier fort, quite possibly a *colombara* or watchtower of Roman origin when the settlement would no doubt have been a military outpost of the larger town.

The wine of these times, certainly the prized Vino Retico, was in all likelihood similar to either *mulsum* – sweetened with honey and flavoured with pine resin and herbs – or *passum*, a so-called 'raisin wine', one made from dried grapes, a practice known to have originated in ancient Carthage. While flowers may also have been macerated in the wine to boost fragrance, other flavourings – perhaps rather less appetizing to the modern palate – included pepper, dates, mastic, pitch and even seawater! The addition of seawater is neither as bizarre nor distasteful as might first appear: a small amount of added saline solution makes a wine taste fuller-flavoured and seemingly more mature. Salt is an important flavour enhancer and releases certain taste molecules which bring out intensity of flavour. Furthermore salt both suppresses bitterness and increases the perception of sweetness. In a similar way, highly seasoned food can have a correspondingly positive effect on the accompanying wine. Of course the addition of sodium chloride to wine is not allowed today, though the Romans were happy enough to embrace the practice.

The importance and prosperity of Verona during Roman times can still be seen today through the various surviving monuments of Roman rule; among the most notable are the famous amphitheatre, parts of the Piazza Erbe and the Ponte Pietra, the stone bridge which spans the Adige river at the northern tip of the *centro storico* (historic town centre). Wine culture enjoyed unprecedented popularity thanks to the city's position as a distribution centre, and numerous wine-related artefacts of pottery and sculpture from this time are preserved in Verona's Archaeological Museum. By the time that the Roman Empire was in its final stages, the wines of Verona were already well known for being produced by the *appassimento* process with grapes being dried on racks or *stuole* of fibre matting; they were commonly referred to then as *acinatico* wines (or 'acinaticum' in Latin, meaning derived from grapes). By the fourth century, Zenone had become the eighth bishop of the city. He was later sanctified and became Verona's patron saint; indeed the city's famous Basilica is named after him. Zenone is celebrated for the many sermons he delivered, one of which was addressed to the local *viticoltori* (grape growers), providing further evidence of the burgeoning importance of wine in the area. In his sermon, the 'smiling bishop' outlines as an allegory for 'treading the right path', the various operations carried out in the vineyard over the course of the growing season in order to realize a successful crop at harvest time.

THE MIDDLE AGES TO THE RENAISSANCE

As Roman rule declined, the Ostrogoths occupied and ruled over Verona, though Theodoric the Great chose to make Ravenna the capital of his kingdom. His 'magister ufficiorum', the learned Flavius Aurelius Cassiodorus Senator, dedicated most of his life to preserving various elements of Greek and Roman culture as well as keeping the peace between the Romans and the Barbarian masters he served. Cassiodorus was a great champion of the wines of Verona and in particular Acinatico. As Scipione Maffei reports in his famous eighteenth-century work *Verona Illustrata*, Cassiodorus describes in fine detail how the wine is produced from fruit gathered in the autumn and which is then hung upside down to dry until December before fermentation can begin. He marvels at the wine's freshness and smoothness, referring to the red as 'crimson nectar' which is both 'drinkable and suave' while the white is 'pure as if it had been born of lilies'. The practice Cassiodorus refers to of suspending grapes upside down to dry until the winter months was widely in use until superseded by wooden racks stored horizontally for reasons of space. It was no doubt a well-thought-out system: turning the grapes upside down opens up the bunch to permit the passage of air, allowing it to circulate around the fruit and affording some protection against the onset of rot.

Theodoric's rule began the period of Gothic domination over Italy. He was followed by Alboin whose kingdom was to last until Charlemagne drove the Lombards from the area in the mid 770s. It is conjectured that during this period the Barbarians introduced their love of eating horsemeat to the Veronese, a culinary tradition that lives on in specialities like *pastissada de caval*, one of the city's most famous and popular dishes. It is, however, probable that the simple modification of stewing the horsemeat in the local red wine was of later Christian inspiration.

Contemporary documents show that the area we know now as Valpolicella was called Pruviniense or Pruviniano; the name served to describe an administrative area which excluded the valley of Negrar, then commonly referred to as 'Veriago' or 'Veriaco'. Other local names, familiar today, begin to appear, such as the mention in 810 of vineyards in Monteclo (Montecchio), in 832 of Valle Paltenate, the present-day Valpantena, and Castorupto (Castelrotto) in 955. Following the break up of the Frankish empire, Verona was ruled over by various 'Kings of Italy' including Carolingians, Carinthians and the rest over the next couple of centuries, a period of great instability (often described as 'feudal anarchy') until the arrival of Holy Roman Emperor Otto I of Germany in the latter half of the tenth century. During these early and high middle ages, the clergy – as elsewhere throughout Europe – was mainly responsible for keeping the culture of wine alive thanks to its use for sacramental purposes in celebration of the Eucharist. Monks tended vineyards often reclaimed from the lower-lying land closer to the river, which had remained as marshland through the cool and wet climate that characterized the latter half of the first millennium. Ninety different vineyard locations in the hills of Soave and Valpolicella were recorded over the tenth and eleventh centuries according to Gloria Maroso and Gian Maria Varanini's 1984 study of vines in the Veronese during the medieval period. It was not, however, until the twelfth century that the name Val Polisella appears in official documents and the area's boundaries were broadly defined. There are many theories as to how the name was coined but none have been shown to be conclusive, and certainly not the familiar story that it is somehow a version of 'valley of the many cellars'. Soave, on the other hand, has followed a much clearer path to the current form of its name. Where the papal bull issued by Eugenio III in 1145 refers to Suavium (or the land of the Soavi), the name clearly relates to the Svevi people present in the area around King Alboin's time. Svevi was written as Soavi in medieval Italian.

In the first half of the thirteenth century the noble della Scala (or Scaligeri) family gradually assumed total control over the city. Following his election as *podesta* (chief magistrate), Mastino della Scala converted the so-called *signoria* (self-governing city state) into family ownership and his descendants were effectively to rule Verona until the end of the fourteenth century. This was a difficult time for Verona with outbreaks of the plague in 1348, 1362 and 1371, a serious earthquake in 1367 and widespread flooding in 1386. Nonetheless, the Scaligeri legacy of beautiful palaces (such as the Castelvecchio) and monuments (like the Lamberti Tower), aqueducts and bridges, many of which were constructed under such conditions, continues to this day. In 1353, nearly half a century after his father, the poet Dante Alighieri, had first spent part of his political exile from Florence in Verona, Pietro Alighieri bought a villa with surrounding vineyards. The villa remains in the hands of his direct descendants, the Serego Alighieri family. The city expanded rapidly, far beyond the original confines of the loop in the Adige it had occupied since pre-Roman times, to include new territory on both banks of the river. As the population grew, so did the thirst for wine and we see recorded progress in the management of the wine industry: harvesting times were being set by individual communes and the price of wine became fixed along with laws controlling the movement of grapes and wine throughout the city. Meanwhile the Garganica grape (today's Garganega) was first documented by the Bolognese writer Pietro de' Crescenzi in his manuscript 'Ruralia commoda', the first modern text on agriculture to appear in print, though a century and a half after it was written. However, despite their fame as patrons of the arts, the end of the Scaligeri family's domination was irreversibly tainted with fratricide and corruption and the city became a part of the Republic of Venice in 1405. The city was to remain under Venetian rule (apart from a brief occupation by Maximilian I – son of Frederick the Third, 'The Peaceful' Holy Roman Emperor – at the beginning of the 1500s) for several centuries.

The Renaissance years under La Serenissima were a time of great prosperity thanks to the nobility and the rise of a new middle class of wealthy merchants. Fifteenth-century records show Veronese wines being sold at 120 lire per *carro* (cartload) or 300 denari per litre, a high price reflecting no doubt its correspondingly high quality, and being sent as far as Rome. Licensing laws in the city's plentiful *osterie* even extended to the washing of drinking vessels to ensure that any water was being used for the correct purposes! A similar concern over 'authenticity' prevented innkeepers from stocking more than one red or white wine on the premises. Many of the countryside villas also date back to this time (Villa Sarego, Villa Santa Sofia and Villa Giona are all sixteenth-century constructions). Grape growing became an increasingly widespread activity throughout these landed estates as owners sought to exploit the area surrounding their villas. Farming was founded on either the Veronese version of the *mezzadria* system, whereby landowners – the church or noble local families – would agree a contract with the *contadini* (agricultural workers) on the basis of sharecropping or, alternatively, simple rental systems. Under the former, an agreement usually lasting between three and five years and known as the *'lavorencia'*, the workers were often granted foraging rights for their animals and, as with the fruit and vegetables harvested, payment was made in kind.

Verona was to become a political football for a brief period at the end of the fifteenth century after the House of Habsburg under Maximilian I acquired the city. The city was soon restored to Venice, however, and the Venetians lost no time in strengthening its fortifications. Verona became a major military stronghold (indeed the republic's most important garrison) and remained a city of considerable military significance until Italian unification over three centuries later. In the meantime Giovanni Francesco Tinto, in 'La Nobilita Di Verona' which was published in 1590, reminds us that there is at least one lineage that remained unbroken: 'the *vini Rhetici* which are born in Valpolicella occupy third place amongst noble wines'. Even though they may have dropped down the pecking order since Roman times, they are nonetheless 'strong, generous and excellent', he maintains.

The growing value of wine during these times is illustrated by the burgeoning presence of 'Saltari' or vineyard guardians in the hills of Valpolicella and Soave, though the practice dates back much earlier (probably to the beginning of the thirteenth century). Their principal role was to protect the ripening fruit of the summer months from pilferage. Such was the importance of their duties that the Saltari would even have their meals brought out to them in the vineyards so that their vigilance was not compromised. However, even they were powerless to intervene in the summer of 1626 when a plague of locusts decimated the local grape crop. The following year saw the publication of Alessandro Peccana's book on what he refers to as 'natural philosophy': *On the Problems of Cold Drinks*. The timing of the book is in itself of particular interest on two counts: firstly, it predates Verona's worst ever natural disaster (see below) by just a couple of years, and secondly it reflects a shift in focus in the use of wine at the time. Literary and historical manuscripts from previous centuries compile a continuing trend away from the symbolic importance of wine – in a religious context – towards more practical considerations, and in particular its use for medicinal purposes as well as a beverage. Peccana's book deals with the subject of mixing wine with water (and even snow!) and proposes various formulas (proportions of wine to water), listing the various benefits which accrue from them. The arrival of the book pretty much coincides with the end of the Renaissance period and the flourishing of the 'scientific revolution' which most historians agree began with Copernicus in the mid to late sixteenth century. This time bears witness to the waning power of the clergy as secular thought and philosophy became more entrenched in the lives and thoughts of ordinary people.

Peccana's book also refers to many of the grape varieties planted at the time; indeed, certain admixtures are applied to particular varieties either singly or in combination. Some of them are no longer familiar. Hence we find referenced Malvatico (also written as Malvasia), Luiatico (also written as Leatico), Lacrima, Trebiano (also written as Tribbiano), Vernaccia, Marzemino, Marcirolla, Cagaroza, Tramarino, Cremonese, Tripergo, Garganego and Corvino. These last two (as Garganega and Corvina) were to become the mainstay grapes of today's Soave and Valpolicella over the course of the next four hundred years. The book remains one of the earliest and most comprehensive records of the area's grape varieties to be found until the appearance of Guglielmo Marani's 1755 work, the wonderfully titled *Practical Observations on Keeping Horses and Planting Vines*, when varieties such as Rossetta, Cagnetta and Tirodola are added to the list.

The final years of the Renaissance carried a deadly sting in their tail and a natural event of catastrophic proportions was to follow when the bubonic plague ravaged northern and central Italy. During the worst outbreak, which lasted between 1629 and 1633, some 33,000 people (over 60 per cent of the population) died in Verona. The only remaining survivors in the village of Mazzano in the valley of Negrar were seven women. The population of the area would not return to pre-plague levels until the end of the eighteenth century. The brutal irony of the timing of Peccana's book becomes apparent where he advises his readers that the consumption of cool wine (along with bread, milk, eggs and oil) has the additional benefit of being a useful means of helping to fight off the plague.

THE EIGHTEENTH AND NINETEENTH CENTURIES

During the Age of Enlightenment we see Verona and its wines at, ironically, their lowest ebb. The beginning of the eighteenth century witnessed the War of the Spanish Succession which was often played out close to Verona at the foot of the Adige valley. The turbulence of the times is mirrored in the agricultural crisis which affected the whole of the Republic of Venice and was clearly evident in Verona. Even the usually indefatigably positive Paronetto records that contemporary local viticulture was geared up to produce quantity and the quality of the wines showed little to be recommended. This pattern was to be repeated until the latter half of the next century: a sorry mix of military skirmishing and wines of questionable quality.

We have a fairly clear picture of what the 'wines of the times' would have tasted like thanks to a famous abbot/academic turned poet and a native of the Valpolicella area. Bartolomeo Lorenzi's poem 'Delle coltivazione dei monti' was published in 1778 and deals with hillside agriculture including the cultivation of the vine. The work is split into four *canti* or songs, one for each season, and details the various tasks carried out in each. The plant should be nourished over the winter, replanting is undertaken in the spring, while summer is devoted to pruning. Preparation for the vintage occurs in the autumn including the cleaning of barrels and other tasks. Lorenzi recommends mixing a Corbin with some Lambrusco to bring a little more finesse and colour to the brew. Fermentation should take place on the skins for around eight days and the wine be racked once in April before it is ready. The abbot also advises concentrating (cooking) the must. Around the same time, the letters of the well-known Veronese priest and man of letters Benedetto del Bene, who also had a keen interest in agricultural matters, show that the traditional practice of drying grapes was still alive and well in the area. He describes how the harvested fruit is laid out on *arele* (this local word for a cane or bamboo screen is still in use) under the eaves and left open to the passage of air. The drying period, however, would only last for a matter of weeks. Unlike Lorenzi, Del Bene also experimented with prolonged fermentation (up to six months) with apparently gratifying results: he describes the wine as having bright and lively colour and a pleasing flavour, showing both maturity and lightness on the palate.

By the end of the century, Napoleon Bonaparte had occupied Verona but in 1797 under the Treaty of Campo Formio, it was handed over to Austria. More than fifty troublesome years passed before Verona was finally united with the rest of Italy in 1866. During these years of instability, uncertainty and Austrian oppression, wine production was to play an increasingly important part in the local economy. Land previously used as pasture, for growing mulberry bushes or grain, was turned over to vineyard: the silk industry was in slow but inexorable decline and world markets were saturated with cereal crops. Farmers had, however, little or no incentive to upgrade the quality of their wines and, in any case, grapes were just one of the many different crops to be harvested. While promiscuous or mixed cultivation was still widely practised, the choice of grapes in itself was huge. Between 1818 and 1823, the botanist Ciro Pollini recorded fifty-five red and twenty-five white varieties found in the province of Verona alone. Many have disappeared off the radar since though others, such as Bigolina and Pomella, are in the process of being rediscovered.

Inevitably winemaking leaned more towards the Lorenzi school of thought than the more ambitious approach of Benedetto del Bene. Grapes were harvested early in order to avoid the more difficult climatic conditions of the autumn and processed quickly; the wines were cloudy, acidic and short-lived and the producers' only aim was an empty cellar. By now, a clear structure of the wine trade in Verona had evolved. Growers or their landlords would sell to merchants who would then sell on the wines for consumption above all in local *osterie* (inns). Verona is still famous for its plentiful *osterie*: they have represented the traditional local outlet for the wines of the area since Roman times. These *negozianti* would continue to dictate the structure of the wine trade until the cooperative cellars established in the twentieth century gradually began to make their presence redundant. Sadly there was little call for anything other than simple and straightforward product. Local writers like Giuseppe Beretta, an agronomist and member of the Veronese Academy, identified 'a quality crisis', though the famous botanist Antonio Manganotti went one step further, declaring many of the wines to be simply 'undrinkable'. There was also a quantity crisis as production fell into substantial decline owing to the arrival of oidium in the middle of the century: output practically halved during the 1850s. Following unification, and with a new-found self-confidence, laws were passed to set up agrarian committees with the idea of reviving the flagging fortunes of Italian agriculture.

The wine trade in Verona clearly needed a major shot in the arm and found an unlikely hero in the first president of the Comizio

Agrario, which was founded in San Pietro in Cariano (a village in today's Valpolicella Classico area). Gaetano Pellegrini was a geologist and paleontologist as well as an agronomist but for some pundits he is, despite his brief three-year tenure, a key figure in the story of Veronese oenology. Pellegrini showed an unshakeable belief in the potential of the Veronese hills to produce great wine. The basis of his argument was the unique growing conditions that the area had been blessed with thanks to its geological origins and his ambition to usher the wines away from the limitations of the local market and on to a much broader stage. Free at last from the yoke of Austrian rule, farmers were offered a glimpse of a brighter future. Pellegrini's new methodology was based on scientific principles rather than tradition and inherited knowledge. This began with a selection of the most suitable varieties, favouring Corvina over other popular grapes like Gropella in the case of red wines, and targeting the finer soils of hillside vineyards. Similarly the cultivation of other fruits, wheat and mulberry trees (although in constant decline, silkworm farming was still a common way of life well into the twentieth century) were more appropriate for lower-lying land. He encouraged the movement away from 'promiscuous cultivation' and the introduction of lower training methods off shortened trunks. A selection of mature fruit from lower-yielding vineyards at harvest time would bring better results. In the cellar, closed vat fermentation pointed the way towards a more stable product along with more careful management of the fermentation process, including a better understanding of the use of sulphur. Such ideas may appear straightforward now, and indeed many of them were of course already in circulation, but Pellegrini brought them together into a cogent plan of action. He was in the right place at almost the right time and, though his ideas did not come to immediate fruition, the foundations for a new wine culture based on quality had been laid.

Finally the first oenological society was established in 1872 under the then mayor of Verona Giulio Camuzzoni, though it lasted no longer than ten years. Four years later – and shortly before the first outbreak of peronospera in the area in 1880 – wine production in the Veneto took a giant step forward with the founding of the School of Viticulture and Oenology at Conegliano. This institution remains at the forefront of oenological and viticutural science in Italy: at the time as a centre for the diffusion of knowledge it was revolutionary, prompting not only a better understanding of the theories and practices of modern wine production but also the arrival of essential agricultural and oenological machinery, such as presses, pumps and early filtration systems. In 1881, Stefano de' Stefani attempted the first classification of Veronese wines including three categories which have major relevance here: Vini della Valpolicella, Vini della Valpantena e del distretto di Verona and Vini dei colli di Mezzane, Illasi, Soave e Monteforte.

A further major setback occurred in September the following year when Verona's worst-ever flood devastated the city. Following prolonged heavy rains, combined with melting snow from the Alps, the Adige burst its banks. Verona was once more compromised by its position at the bottom of the valley and there were horrendous consequences. Many of the mills and landings which occupied the edge of the river were swept away. The Ponte Pietra was under threat and the Ponte Nuovo destroyed. New banks were constructed subsequently which changed the face of the riverside area of the city forever. But, as ever, the Veronesi bounced back and in 1888 the Agricultural Academy made the encouraging announcement that the wines from Cantina dei Signori Fratelli Bertani of Valpantena were being appreciated as far away as Switzerland, Holland and even England. Local wines were also beginning to find favour in the important market of Milan (approximately 150 kilometres to the west). Not everyone was quite so enamoured, and there were complaints that the 'new' style of Veronese reds was too 'softly sweet' (there is no simple translation of the Italian word *abboccato*). It is tempting to speculate that the red wines must have tasted similar to some of the lower alcohol (less than 10% abv) lightly sparkling reds produced in the Oltrepo Pavese today where wines from denominations like Sangue di Giuda and Buttafuoco fit that description perfectly.

In fact local wines were still classified by style under the broader designation of their simple origin; for example, Verona Agricola (the contemporary specialist farming newspaper) published a wholesale price guide for local wines in March 1898. Listed are 'Vini Da Valpolicella' comprising vini comuni da pasto (simple everyday wine), Buono (good quality), Buono quasi fino (good, almost 'refined'), Rechiotto fino ('refined' Rechiotto) and 'Recchiotto'. Similarly under (Vini) Da Soave, the categories are Bianchi torbolino (cloudy whites, quite possibly partially fermented grape must – a Venetian favourite), Bianchi bollito (literally 'boiled' whites) and Bianchi filtrato (filtered whites). By this time, the grape varieties behind Soave were firmly established as Garganega and Trebbiano, a fact corroborated by the famous engineer and agronomist G. B. Perez in his important reference work *La Provincia di Verona ed i suoi vini*, which was published in 1900.

Producers had enough reason to believe though that a corner had been turned: the first cooperative in Soave was founded in 1898, followed a year later by the first in Valpolicella at Sant'Ambrogio with a second in Fumane soon after. Transport systems were also improving and by the end of the century a new railway finally linked the Valpolicella valleys with the city of Verona. On a new tide of optimism, the years around the turn of the century saw the structure of the wine trade consolidated with the foundation of many of the (originally) merchant houses famous today: Bolla, Masi, Montresor and Sartori for example. Contemporary records also show the presence of families of vineyard owners who are still very much active: in Valpolicella Classico, Serego, Fumanelli, Rizzardi, Speri and Quintarelli; in Soave, Pieropan, Visco, Pra and Bogoni, while in the 'extended zone' of Valpolicella lying between them, names like Dal Forno and Mosconi can be seen.

THE TWENTIETH CENTURY

Sadly, though, another natural disaster threatened to derail this progress entirely. Phylloxera was first discovered in the Veneto at Treviso in 1900 and by 1909 had spread to the vineyards of Verona. It was not until the Second World War was coming to an end over thirty years later that the work of grafting the vines on to resistant American rootstocks would eventually be completed. At the same time, thanks also to work undertaken by the Stazione Sperimentale di Viticultura e di Enologia at Conegliano, the research arm of the wine school, planting systems would be rationalized – promiscuous cultivation was finally to fall out of favour as a result – and the choice of grape variety, for the Veronese, came down on the side of those local varieties identified as capable of delivering the right quality to their burgeoning markets. The pergola system was also confirmed as the preferred training method alongside the affirmation of those varieties that continue to dominate today's vineyards.

Following the First World War some form of regulation of the wine industry, and in particular the sector producing 'quality wines with a recognized history', had become an important enough issue to be debated at ministerial level. Growers' consortia were formed to sustain the impetus – Soave in 1924 and Valpolicella the following year. By 1930, Arturo Marescalchi, who had founded the Associazione Enotecnica Italiani (Association of Italian Winemakers) at Conegliano in the 1890s, had conceived of the idea of 'Vini Tipici' or typical wines and this would form the basis of the first attempts to classify Italian wine production at a national level. In 1931 studies carried out at Conegliano came to fruition when the area now known as Soave Classico became one of the first in the country to be mapped out in terms of the territory where 'Vino Tipico Soave' could be produced (alongside wines like Orvieto, Barbaresco, etc.). But once more plans had to be put on hold while Europe ushered in the madness of another world war. From the 1940s onwards, wine production in the Veronese was to become more streamlined: more and more small growers joined the cooperative movement as laws governing the *mezzadria* system were tightened up (it was finally abolished as recently as 1982). Smaller-scale grower/bottlers were still few and far between and the option of selling off grapes to merchant houses remained the preferred and traditional option for other smallholders.

There is a clear record of how a typical Veronese wine was being made at this time in Charles G. Bode's 1956 book: 'Concrete cisterns have been introduced in recent years; they are of course much easier to empty and to clean. But for maturing and ageing the wine needs oak around it. Therefore the producers have arrived at a compromise between old custom and technical progress. They use the cisterns only for the young wine in its first stages of fermentation. During that time it is transferred from one cistern to the other at intervals so that the deposit which comes to rest at the bottom is gradually left behind. The process is repeated until the wine becomes step by step crystal clear and ready to be transferred into oak.' Clearly the formula could be applied to either red or white wine.

A new rush of vineyard plantings in the 1950s and 1960s aimed to capitalize on a growing Italian trend of seeking new markets further afield, a move that had begun towards the end of the previous century, though it had suffered many interruptions. What started out as a trickle had become a deluge, so much so that Paronetto (Veneto) claims that in the absence of any legal status for the term, a quantity double that which the vineyards were capable of producing was being exported as 'typical Veronese wine'. In 1968 a greater semblance of order was brought to bear on the problem with the introduction of the DOC (*denominazione di origine controllata*) system to the area. This mapped out the geographical boundaries and the regulations which governed production, belatedly affording the burgeoning industry some right of legal protection against fraudulent practice. By that time the vineyards of Soave and Valpolicella had far outgrown their historical heartlands, or so-called 'Classico' areas, to include much of the territory lying in between the two.

Demand threatened to outstrip supply when, in the 1970s, Soave overtook Chianti to become the biggest selling Italian wine in the US and by the end of the decade approximately 10 million bottles a year were being imported. Interest in Valpolicella was also blossoming thanks at least in part to American author Ernest Hemingway, whose novel *Across the River and into the Trees* was published in 1950. The book, set in Venice, recounts the last days of Colonel Cantwell, a wounded war veteran with a seemingly insatiable thirst for Valpolicella. His passion was clearly matched by that of the writer who, according to the newspaper *Gazzettino Sera* on 24 March 1954, '... announced he will stay in Venice to recover from the injuries incurred in the well-known African accidents, with a powerful cure based on scampi and Valpolicella'. However, claims that he would regularly drink up to 8 litres a day seem far-fetched even for someone of Hemingway's legendary propensity for the consumption of alcohol! Meanwhile, during his first 'voyage of discovery' in August 1968 and in search of Hemingway's Valpolicella, Mario Soldati reported (in *Vino al Vino*, published in 1970) that he could not find a close match; of the dozen he tried the 'least distant' was the wine made by Quintarelli.

While another American, the chef, restaurateur and oenophile Robert Carrier, was convinced that Soave could never be a great wine – though he was happy to admit it was a very good one – in an episode of 'Food, Wine and Friends' made by HTV in the early 1980s, he writes more tellingly about Veronese wine in the 1981 book which accompanied the series. Referring to Valpolicella he suggests that the wine is 'a rich, ruby red with a soft, delicious bouquet'. He goes on to point out that '… today the artisan approach to winemaking in this region has changed. Now it's big business with huge modern vats and completely scientific installations that shows just how important winemaking has become in Italy today'. It is ironic that the wine he was filmed tasting in the grounds of Hintlesham Hall was Soave Classico Bolla, the leading brand in the US at the time. This 'very good wine' was the epitome of the big-business approach he outlined. His written description in fact charts the course away from the specific wine that typified 'recipes handed down from father to son' – as he portrayed the artisan approach – towards the generic version in vogue in his homeland.

Closer to home a different story was unfolding. Domestic consumption of wine dropped by around 25 per cent over the latter half of the 1970s and new markets were desperately required to take up the slack. However, to say that Italian and Veronese wine in particular had an image problem in many European markets at that time is a huge understatement. Nicolas Belfrage, in his ground-breaking *Life Beyond Lambrusco,* published in 1985, exposed the flip side of the supply and demand issue. Talking of Valpolicella he argued: '… the world buys quantities of them but only because they are cheap. These potentially zingy, zippy, cherry-reds with an almond twist at the back are deprived of their personality by overproduction in the vineyards, rendered lifeless by pasteurization and – most mysteriously of all – sold when they are past their prime.' And everyone must take their share of the blame: 'As long as the supermarket customers buy them cheap, so long will the Veronese industrialists make them cheap and sell what they want to sell when they want to sell it.' He continues 'but it's not Valpolicella, not as it ought to be, and can be'.

Recent years have seen the Veronese rethink their proposition, setting their sights on producing quality wines which reflect the nature of their singular terrain. It is a move that recalls Gaetano Pellegrini's aspirations and one which Belfrage was still so passionately concerned about over a century later. The perception of what makes a fine wine lies in its detail: generally speaking, the more precise the information the label gives about precisely where the wine comes from, the higher the wine lover's expectations will be. The process of mapping out the vineyards of a denomination is known in Italian as *zonazione viticola* and involves a study of growing conditions in order to identify a wine's defining style, usually undertaken through the combined efforts of consortia and educational institutions. The amount of work required to undertake a *zonazione viticola* study is of course prodigious (and frequently beset by the many obstacles of political manoeuvring, etc.), but the findings can eventually become embedded in production disciplines.

The concept is already quite advanced in the Soave Classico district where the *consorzio* has mapped out the principal historic vineyards that make up the production area and clarified how growing conditions have come to influence the defining characteristics of the wines. Examples of, for instance, Soave Classico Foscarino, one of the most prestigious sites, are now available commercially. Of course the name of the producer still remains paramount: Soave Classico Calvarino from Pieropan owes its renown as much to the excellent reputation that Nino Pieropan has built up over the course of several decades as to the name of the vineyard, but an important start has been made. The process has not progressed quite so far in the Valpolicella area though most of the work has been done, and for now even more depends on the producer's reputation: Masi's Amarone della Valpolicella Classico Mazzano made from vineyards in that village is a good example among the plethora of lesser-known names.

Despite the desire to put their house in order, the growers' lack of ability to work together holds back vital progress, such as the fact that bottling both Soave and Valpolicella is still permitted outside of the production area. Such an anomaly tends to keep prices artificially low and both authenticity and quality are inevitably compromised. Many of the larger wineries, such as the main cooperatives, have in recent years introduced a premium selection of wines sourced from grapes in some of the most prestigious vineyard sites – for example, both Cantina di Soave and Cantina di Negrar (in Valpolicella Classico) have appropriate ranges. Growers' wines are at present very much in the ascendancy following the successful pioneering work of smaller-scale grower/bottlers like Gini in Soave and Romano Dal Forno in Valpolicella. Historically important wineries like Pieropan and Quintarelli have assumed almost legendary status, given a track record in producing fine wine over a number of decades, and a profusion of smallholders have taken the plunge and begun making and bottling at least some of their own wine instead of selling their grapes off in the hope of emulating their heroes' achievements.

In the cellars, improvements have developed exponentially. There is no denying the giant leap forward in the overall standards of excellence throughout the area, from the hand-crafted approach of the smaller operations through to the technical expertise of the medium- to larger-scale wineries and the proficiency of the cooperatives. For the consumer the best news is that premium Veronese wines are still incomprehensibly undervalued. Excellent examples of Soave and Valpolicella still cost far less than they are worth and are not difficult to find, while at the higher end of the scale great bottles of Amarone are far more widely available than ever before. The Veronesi are undoubtedly a most resilient and resourceful people, as evidenced by the trials and tribulations their wine industry has faced and overcome over the last two thousand years. What remains to be proven is their ability to manage success.

2

THE GEOGRAPHICAL BACKGROUND

Verona's wine trade has always benefitted from the city's geographical location, and nowadays two motorways intersect just to the west of the city where the A22 connects the arterial hub of Modena with Trento and the Brenner pass, while the A4 links Milan with Venice. Easy road access is available in all directions. Just how privileged the position is becomes clearer when the unique growing conditions of the vineyards are taken into consideration. They occupy the lower slopes of the hills that extend downwards from the high karst table of Lessinia to meet the northern plain of the Adige river as it passes through and beyond the city, flowing eastwards. The hills mark the very western extension of the Venetian Pre Alps. The borders are quite clearly defined: to the west the glacial valley of the Adige, to the north the higher mountains of Lessinia, to the east the ridge that divides the Alpone and Chiampo valleys and, to the south, the suburbs of the city of Verona. The area has very particular geological origins. To understand them more fully, it is necessary to look back to the Mesozoic era which began approximately 250 million years ago.

GEOLOGICAL ORIGINS

Lessinia and the land below were formed when the western reaches of the ancient Tethys sea covered the area we now know as the Mediterranean. The Tethys itself (or Neo-Tethys, to be more precise) began to form during the Triassic period when the Cimmerian plate, consisting of parts of today's Turkey, Iran, Afghanistan, Tibet, the Shan-Thai terrane and the Malay peninsula, rifted away from Gondwana, the southern arc of the roughly C-shaped Pangaea supercontinent. (Pangaea was a continuous landmass made up of today's continents joined together.) The ocean formed in the wake of the Cimmerian plate as it moved northwards. The plate finally collided with Laurasia (the northern arc of Pangaea) during the Jurassic period and pushed the floor of the Paleo Tethys, the original ocean which lay between the two arcs of Pangaea, under Laurasia. Between the Paleogene and Neogene periods (also known as the Tertiary period), the carbonate sedimentary rocks which make up much of the terrain of the Lessinia table were laid down at the western tip of the Tethys. They were formed for the most part organically – from the build up of shell, coral, algal, skeletal and faecal debris – and evidence of this is visible today in the abundance of marine fossils found in the area. Continuing tectonic plate movement caused the sea to shrink and subsequently, when Gondwana began to break up, the northward movement of the African and Indian plates caused the orogeny of the Alps and the pre-Alpine territory of Northern Italy, where Lessina is located, in the late Cretaceous period of the Mesozoic era.

Tectonic-plate movement was accompanied by volcanic activity across the Lessinia table and extrusive, igneous rock such as basalt, tuff and hyaloclastite breccia were sandwiched between (intercalated, in geological terms) the earlier sedimentary formations. Evidence of significant volcanic activity in today's Valpolicella district dating back to the Paleocene and Oligocene epochs can be found along the spur which divides the upper Negrar and Valpantena valleys between Stellavena and the area just north of the town of Negrar itself, around the village of Marano, further to the east near Lavagno and also higher up the ridge that divides the Marcellise and Mezzane valleys. Later eruptions, mainly during the Eocene epoch, occurred at the very eastern border of Soave where the volcano complex of the Monti Calvarina, Crocetta and Duello forms the ridge that separates the Alpone from the Chiampo valley. Eruptions in this eastern sector were closely tied to the tectonic structure known as the Alpone-Chiampo Graben (a depressed block of land bordered by parallel faults and named after the German word for ditch or trench). The volcanic deposits, mainly layered or reshaped hyaloclastite basalt, are therefore found between layers of Tertiary sediment formations and together these form the classic structure of the Alpone valley. Even columnar basalt structures reminiscent of Northern

Ireland's Giant's Causeway can occasionally be seen, such as at the village of San Giovanni Ilarione which lies along the valley on the way up to the important fossil centre of Bolca. At the same time as these eruptions a complex system of faults was created in the central-western Lessini Mountains which was to have a marked effect on defining topographical structure. From a tectonic point of view, Lessinia has gone through extensional phases during the Mesozoic era and the Tertiary, a compressive phase in the Neogene period and a southward-tilting phase in the Pliocene–Quaternary.

During the later phases of this development, Quaternary glaciation was an important factor in creating today's classic Lessinia landscape. During the last glacial period (Würm) the pre-alps were only partially covered by glaciers. While just beyond the very western edge of the area, the Adige valley was carved out by a succession of giant ice tongues during the various glaciations of the Quaternary and a number of smaller-scale glaciers formed further to the east. These lay principally at the head of the Valon del Malera and the high Val (or Vajo) Squaranto, as identified by Ugo Sauro, retired Professor of Physical Geography at the University of Padua and a native of the municipality of Bosco Chiesanuova in Lessinia. Much of the erosion that continued to shape the area can therefore be attributed to the action of periglaciation. The climate at the time was probably that of the steppe-tundra: the Lessini mountains would have been covered with snow even in the summer, marked by an absence of vegetation in the prolonged low temperatures, and buffeted by high winds. When the glaciers finally began to retreat at the end of the Ice Age meltwater poured in torrents through gorges and valleys of the lower hills. As the climate warmed, further morainic debris, wind-blown detritus and rock dust were deposited as loess (typically an accumulation of clay, sand and silt loosely cemented by calcium carbonate) further down the slopes.

THE KARST ELEMENT

It is important to recognize the area's complex stratigraphy and how the differing rocks respond to the forces of their environment. Main Dolomite – the base layer of rock in the area – had been formed in shallow lagoons during the late Carnian and early Norian ages of the late Triassic period during the Mesozoic era. Though mostly degraded, it is considered to have a relatively stable structure. Grey limestones make up the next layer, formed in the early Jurassic and famous for bivalve fossils including lithiotis, followed by oolite or egg-stone limestone (early to middle Jurassic). Between the middle Jurassic and the middle of the early Cretaceous red Veronese ammonite was formed, the famous red marble of Verona which has traditionally been quarried in the Negrar valley above the villages of Prun, Fane and Torbe, up as far as Sant'Anna d'Alfaedo, beyond the heads of the Valpolicella Classico valleys and some 20 kilometres due north of Verona. This is a hard, compact and durable rock in contrast with the earlier oolite and grey limestones which are more susceptible to erosion. These rocks form the 'foundations' or bedrock over which the hills and valleys of the area have been shaped; they are rarely evident at surface level.

The marly limestones of Biancone and Scaglia Rossa (also known as Prun Stone) were formed through the mid-Cretaceous period; the former is widely visible as whitened rock mixed with pieces of flint, while the latter (pinkish red owing to its iron oxide content) is mainly found in the central and eastern part of the mountains and hills. Scaglia Rossa is still widely extracted and used for the manufacture of various stone-based products. Both rocks are prone to weathering. The final limestones are from the Eocene and Paleocene epochs; these are again quite loosely compacted and tend to be present in hilltop areas, as at Bolca. Over these layers of rock lies the composition of soils on which the area's hillside vineyards are planted.

The heterogeneous structure of Lessinia comes about as a result of the varying geomechanical properties of the different rock formations, resulting in a classic karst landscape. This is seen in the typical features of dolines (circular or oval sinkholes which vary in depth and diameter) and polje (large flat karst fields or plains) that characterize the higher areas as well as the spectacular formations of the Ponte di Veja (a natural arched stone bridge with a 40-metre span) at Sant'Anna d'Alfaedo or the 'rock city' in the Valle delle Sfinge (or Sphinx valley) near Camposilvano at Velo Veronese. The distinct absence of surface water is a very typical karst feature: many of the substrata rocks are prone to dissolution, creating underground channels and water courses which force water downwards to the underlying acquifers. These are the sources of the famous *progni*: *progno* is a local dialect word which refers to a stream, sometimes only visible after heavy rains further up in the hills, which percolates through the rock to resurface at lower levels. Examples of *progni* can be found across most of the area; those in the valleys of Fumane, Negrar and Val d'Illasi as well as the Montorio springs at the bottom of the Val Squaranto are the best-known. Clearly the karst effect plays a major part in ensuring excellent drainage throughout the length of the hills and in the higher vineyards in particular.

LOWER LESSINIA

Seen from above, the high table of Lessinia tilts down towards the banks of the Adige resembling either a palm-down outstretched left hand (with a few more digits added on for good measure) or a partially extended, prominently ribbed fan. The rounded dorsal ridges seem to lift the higher table up and away from the plains far below. The high peaks of Lessinia are covered in dense beech and fir forests, though the expansive summer pastures they overlook have few trees. Instead they are dotted with *malghe* or the Alpine farmsteads whose grazing land is the source of dairy products including the famous Monte Veronese cheese. This mid-mountain area is where most of the traditional villages are found. Many of these were colonized by people of Tyrolean and Bavarian descent invited into the area by the Veronesi from the tenth century onwards to practise their traditional professions of woodcutting and farming. Much of the terrain and the land below is criss-crossed by *vai*. A *vajo* (the singular form) is the local dialect name for a particular kind of valley – usually dry but typically steep-sided and very narrow, similar to a gorge or a ravine. The deep Val Squaranto, for example, is often referred to as the Vajo Squaranto. The *vai* are often covered with much thicker vegetation than otherwise seen throughout the area where both past and present anthropization has seen trees felled to create either pasture land in preparation for other agricultural crops or, historically, for use as firewood.

Immediately below here, the vineyards of the main valleys begin. The principal characteristics of the growing area's soil structure are therefore a composite of the factors described above in combination with the alluvial effect of both the valleys' watercourses and, at the lower levels nearer the plains, the Adige. The prime vineyard areas are found at altitudes of up to around 600 metres and cover the slopes of the valleys where they open out over the plains. The valleys generally run from north to south: there is a proliferation of suitable sites where both workable gradients and soils allow for vine cultivation where they broaden as they converge towards the Adige. Typically they face either from east through to south on the western slopes or from west through to south on the eastern sides, though both sides of the valleys are not always intensively planted. They mainly rest on Biancone formations and, like many of the *vai*, are set on tectonic discontinuities. Many examples remain of the classic terraces on which the vines were traditionally cultivated: these flat areas are often no more than just a few metres wide and were carved out of the hillsides to accommodate the preferred high-trellised pergola training system. They are frequently enclosed by dry-stone walls or *marogne* which gives a 'stepped' appearance to the hillsides when viewed from a distance.

OVERVIEW OF SOIL TYPES

Soil composition varies considerably, and sometimes even dramatically, throughout the Soave and Valpolicella vineyards as a result of the geophysical elements described above. As a consequence it is often difficult to identify particular traits and match up soil structures with the various communes or even, in some instances, individual vineyards. In general they are principally limestone-based, a mixture of marl, limestone, clay, sand, tufa and silt plus decomposed tuff and basalt of volcanic origin, the former more prevalent to the west and the latter in the eastern sector. (Geologists distinguish between tufa, a friable, calcareous bedrock and volcanic tuff, a porous, vent-based rock formed of fragments of volcanic cinders and other loose matter.) The workable topsoil is obviously more shallow in the higher vineyards where the poorer, stonier soils reflect closely their marine, volcanic and glacial origins (and where drainage is particularly effective because of the karst formation of much of the landscape). The picture changes markedly towards the extreme east of the region in the vineyards around Monteforte d'Alpone and on the other side of the valley above and below Ronca, where the soils have a more homogeneous structure owing to the effect of the localized volcanic eruptions. This feature has given the vineyards very distinct characteristics which in turn is reflected in the style of the wines. Around forty-five million years ago subaerial eruptions of basaltic lava were at their peak. The principal source of the eruptions, Monte Calvarina, had been formed of underwater molten rock and is a classic stratovolcano composed of lava and volcanic tuff in conical form (in a similar fashion to Mount Etna). Heading towards the summit from Ronca, the volcanic effect is readily visible in the form of grey and black lava-based soils, in parts quite compact and sometimes even column-shaped. Red-coloured clays are typical of the south-western reaches of the volcano around Terrossa (literally 'red earth') situated on the lower slopes of Monte Crocetta.

Moving down the hillsides towards the valley floors and beyond to the plains, the combined alluvial effect of the valleys' watercourses and of course the Adige is more evident, and it is again easier to generalize about localized growing conditions. During the Quaternary period and the early Pleistocene in particular, alluvial deposits affected the lower reaches of the major valleys creating richer, more fertile soils. Similarly, until early Christian times the Adige lay perhaps as much as several miles north of its current course and, in combination with its history of frequent flooding, the sedimentary deposits it left behind have again contributed much to the soil structure of the land closer to the foothills. Thus the lower-lying areas in general are composed of a mix of the alluvial fans of the Adige and from the various valleys, and the colluvial deposits of debris at the foot of the lower slopes.

The effect of the Adige is clearly more evident in the western parts of the area where the course of the river makes a significant change in direction, sweeping suddenly eastwards close to the bottom of Lake Garda. As well as pebbles and sand, the Adige has left behind traces of other rock formations – porphyry, mica schists and quartzite – which are not to be found in the Lessinia mountains. The main rock debris which collects at the feet of the hillsides and on the valley floors and which is consecutively degraded into soil by the action of time, environment and climate, is principally carbon/limestone based. The exception is the Illasi valley. Here the river, which starts high up in the Carega mountains, maintains its course more frequently throughout much of the valley as far as its lower extensions. The valley floor consequently has a greater presence of pebbles and stones than elsewhere.

CLIMATE

The forces of change continue to shape the region though very slowly. Tectonic plate movement continues unabated and other 'natural' phenomena – rotational landslips, downhill creep and sheet wash – are also considerations. Climate is a major factor in determining the rate of this particular kind of erosion. Many growers believe that one recent feature of weather patterns (a discernible change in climate over the last couple of decades) is already becoming apparent in the nature of the wines themselves. For now, the climate of the Bassa Lessinia can be described as generally mild and verging on continental – for example, trees such as cypress and olive are quite common amongst the vine-growing areas.

Winter

In winter, the higher mountains offer some protection by acting as a barrier against the more extreme weather of the Alps to the north. December, January and February in particular can be very cold if usually dry months; indeed February is frequently the month which sees the least rainfall during the entire year. It is during these winter months that fog is likely to occur though it is far more common on the plains (between twenty-five and thirty days a year) than in the hillier parts, where fifteen days a year is a more probable maximum.

Spring

Spring is usually one of the two rainiest periods of the year with spikes in April and May. Between the end of March and early to mid April, budbreak occurs in the Valpolicella though it will often happen slightly later in Soave (sometimes in mid to late April). As the temperatures begin to rise throughout late April and May, the full benefit of the mainly north to south orientation of the valleys comes into play, and flowering will usually have taken place by the end of May or early June.

Summer

The plains tend to be colder in the winter and warmer in the summer while fresher conditions are likely in the hills with cooling breezes during the warmer months. Temperatures in the early to mid thirties centigrade are not uncommon in June, which often sees a dip in rainfall as well. July and

August are the hottest months and a mid to high thirties range of daytime temperatures is quite likely with a span of perhaps ten to fifteen degrees lower at night. Rainfall can sometimes be high in these summer months; August, for example, is often the second wettest month in the valley of Illasi at the very centre of the area, but this example is atypical. The risk of hail is never far away as storms occur quite frequently – a serious worry for the ripening grapes which can be severely damaged. At the same time the presence of Lake Garda has a marked and mitigating effect on temperatures – there can be a difference of as much as 4°C between the cooler western (closest to the lake) and warmer eastern parts of the area during the summer.

Autumn

As harvest approaches and temperatures start to drop, rain becomes more frequent too. The grapes are generally picked in mid September in Soave and just a little later, from mid September and early to mid October, in Valpolicella where it can be a race to bring the fruit in by the middle of the month when heavier rains become more frequent. Average temperatures by this time have fallen to the low to mid twenties by day and are between 5 and 15°C at night. Occasionally some grapes will be left on the vine to achieve extra ripeness (*sovramaturazione* in Italian or *surmaturité* in French) but over the last decade the harvest has generally been fully underway by the middle of September throughout the area.

Rainfall and winds

In Valpolicella, rainfall averages out at around 850mm a year on the valley floors and plains, moving up to approximately 1,200mm at altitudes between 500 and 700 metres, and dropping back to about 1,000mm above 1,000 metres. In the viticultural Soave overall average rainfall figures are slightly lower at between 700 and 1,000mm. Both temperatures and rainfall are, of course, influenced by the various winds which visit the area regularly. These are the cool bora, which blows in gusts from the north west and can have a significant effect in maintaining meaningful diurnal temperature differences, and the scirocco which arrives from the south east. The scirocco originates in the Sahara, though its dry and scorching heat mixes with cooler air from the maritime cyclones over the Mediterranean creating storms at sea and cooler temperatures inland. The scirocco is most common in spring and autumn. Occasional föhn winds, which again blow in characteristically high gusts, are composed of warm moist air arriving from the Mediterranean on the lee side of the mountains.

Climate change

A marked difference in character of the vintages has become evident over the last couple of decades, though other considerations will also affect the nature and the timing of the crop. In particular, the way the *vignaiolo* looks after not only the vines (pruning, canopy management, treatments against pests, moulds and fungal ailments, etc.) but also the soil will create the desired conditions to achieve the ultimate goal of a successful harvest. Crucial stages of the growing season, budbreak, flowering, colour change and harvest time, are all affected by a combination of climate and environmental issues. It is difficult to quantify the former: weather patterns not only tend to occur in cycles but even then are most accurately viewed in retrospect when all the contributing factors are taken into account. A comprehensive study is long overdue but is constrained by the lack of data – for example, the dates at which the important stages of the growing season took place have only been readily available over the last decade or so. Nonetheless an overview conveyed by broad brushstrokes rather than scientific data is feasible.

Comparing the temperatures above with the period between the end of the 1940s and the end of the 1980s, a rather different picture emerges. In the hotter months (June, July and August) which are fundamental in ripening the fruit, average temperatures were slightly lower (22, 24, 23.5°C) with lower peaks at the very hottest times (32, 34, 33°C). Rainfall totals have also been marginally higher in recent years, but the distribution of rain over the course of the year has also changed; in the earlier period rainfall was more evenly distributed across the calendar year. In general terms, May and June experienced the highest rainfall; the two main summer months of July and August were appreciably wetter than they are now and the driest month was frequently September. The higher summer temperatures over the last twenty years have been accompanied by a drop in humidity levels.

Effects

With reference to the current period, beginning in the early 1990s, one of the drawbacks of warmer and drier summers is the issue of water stress on the vines. It is likely that the vine will have received sufficient water during its first two phenological phases, but if the supply is interrupted by a period of drought during the summer, the vine will respond at first by directing more of its resources to ripening fruit than to developing foliage. In prolonged dry periods, however, the vine can shut down which will have a knock-on effect on both photosynthesis and nutrient storage; irrigation will be required in these circumstances. The net effect of warmer and drier summers can be summarized as a trade off between the benefits of earlier ripening and those of longer 'hang time'. While higher temperatures tend to favour a reduction in bitterness, astringency and vegetal characters and an overall drop in acid levels, some winemakers prefer the flavour development from terpenoids and other aroma compounds and the comprehensive phenolic ripeness brought about by slower maturation and extra time on the vine. While the consistency and reliability favoured by the mainly warmer temperatures of recent years has, in some people's view, meant an overall improvement in quality towards a more elegant and balanced wine, for others the leaner and more aromatic wines that emerge in the cooler vintages of the same period give rise to a more classic and authentic style.

In some of the higher altitude vineyard sites, growers who have in the past spent the last few weeks leading up to harvest waiting anxiously for their fruit to ripen fully are now reaping the benefit of those hotter days. Others worry that the crop is starting to mature too early and the resulting sugar levels are becoming too high, too soon. For example, Antonio Fattori – whose family winery at Terrossa is on the eastern border of the Soave DOC area – foresees a promising future for vineyards planted in the cooler and rainier conditions that prevail higher up the Alpone valley or even on some of the upper slopes of nearby Monte Calvarina where once grapes wouldn't ripen properly; he believes frosts are no longer the danger they once were. Similarly the Franchetto family, his close neighbours, are grateful for the fact that some of their vineyards lie at around 600 metres above sea level at Vestenanova just below Bolca. Just a few kilometres away in the Soave Classico area, Damiano Fornaro's father Luciano, who has been farming the land all his life, welcomes the warmer temperatures that make his life so much less stressful around harvest time. He also agrees the climate is more extreme than it used to be: though rain is less frequent, it is more violent when it does arrive and while summers may be hotter, winters, he claims, have all but disappeared in recent years.

3

VITICULTURE AND GRAPE VARIETIES

TRAINING SYSTEMS

Two types of vine training are widely in evidence today: the traditional pergola, a modification of the high-training system which arrived via the Etruscans, and Guyot, the universal system of cane pruning with spurs popularized by Jules Guyot in the 1860s. The third of the three principal methods – freestanding, head or bush-trained vines (known in Italian as *alberello*) – is only very rarely in evidence. After some experimentation, Marinella Camerani at Corte Sant' Alda believes the system is not suitable for local varieties, while Maddalena Pasqua of Tenuta Musella has a vineyard of old *alberello*-trained Cabernet Sauvignon vines which she is however thinking of replacing before long, but these are isolated examples. Historically, pergola is far and away the most popular system: it has been used *da sempre* (forever), as the Italians like to say. Though Guyot has been around for a hundred years and more, and is still on the increase, it remains comprehensively outnumbered by pergola. The former system has really only become popular in the last thirty to forty years, thanks to a combination of the quality of the grapes it produces and the fact that its simple structure facilitates at least partial mechanization. Recent concerns over climate change have caused many to question how truly suitable Guyot is to the growing conditions of the Veronese. Prompted by this, the Soave Consorzio along with CRAVIT (the Viticultural Research Centre at Conegliano) undertook a research programme into examining the relative merits of the two systems in the area beginning in 2003. This is certainly further reaching than the usual 'traditional versus modern' debate, as there are many factors pertaining to the decision of which system to use. The study concludes that both options have their advantages and disadvantages. In Valpolicella growers have themselves come to similar conclusions.

Pergola

The pergola system developed out of the Etruscan practice of training vines high on trees, poles and other means of support, where a mixed cultivation system could be operated and other foodstuffs (including cereals) planted on the same patch of ground in and around the vines themselves. The practice of training vines on trees was still quite common in Valpolicella even after the Second World War, though the renowned Italian agronomist Professor Giovanni Dalmasso confirmed that the switch over to specialized vineyards was already well under way in Soave by the late 1930s. In other words, the pergola system, which was first recorded in the area in the sixth century, has evolved only recently in response to a burgeoning need for specialized planting: for example, as the silkworm industry fell into decline and mulberry trees – customarily used as a support system for the vine – began to disappear from the area. Currently there are three main variations: the traditional pergola, also known as *tendone*, the so-called Pergola or Pergoletta Veronese and the Pergola Trentina, each of which can be trained either simply forwards (single) or to both the front and the rear (double) by using twice the amount of shoots. All three use a supporting post with training wires spread out more or less horizontally in the case of the first two, and at more of an angle (20 to 30 degrees) in the case of the third. This forms a framework to support the fruiting canes and vine canopy and keep them suspended at up to 2 metres above the ground. The bunches therefore hang clear under the leaf canopy. The pruning system involves ridding the plant of the previous year's fruiting cane(s) and using one or more one-year-old canes that have been left to sprout from the top of the trunk. Planting density varies between 4 x 1.2 metres for the old-fashioned *tendone* system to an average of 3.5 x 0.8m for the often slightly lower Veronese form, and to around 2.5 x 0.8 metres with the Pergola Trentina. This translates to as little as 1,500 to 2,000 plants per hectare for the traditional method and moves up to at least 3,300 with the Pergola/Pergoletta Veronese. By and large a development of the older system, Pergola/Pergoletta Veronese must be used instead of the historical form for new plantings from either 1998 in Soave

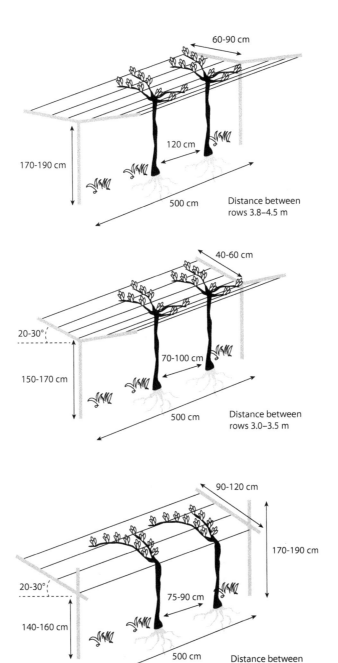

Pergola training systems: (from top) traditional 'double' pergola (or tendone); Pergoletta Veronese; single Pergola Trentina

or 2003 in the Valpolicella to allow for higher-density planting – another example of the method responding to the move over to more specialized or 'one crop' cultivation. The number of buds on the fruiting cane is a major source of concern, especially with the old *tendone* method with as few as 1,500 vines per hectare. In order to make viticulture more viable, as many as four fruiting canes may have been left to develop in order to increase fruit production per hectare. With Garganega, for example, where the first two buds are unproductive, as many as sixteen different buds may therefore have been present on the one plant thus reducing the amount of nutrients each bunch would receive: the risk of overproduction and poor-quality fruit is clearly manifest.

Pergoletta Trentina also makes use of foliage supports but which tilt upwards, in some cases almost diagonally. The single form is more common in hillside vineyards and the double version on flatter land where it occasionally operates as a 'closed' system, one completely covering the spaces between rows. Each year two or three shoots are left at the top of the trunk which are trained towards the middle of the row(s). Like the other pergola variations, it is not suitable for mechanization.

The conclusions drawn by the joint research project are confirmed by the word-of-mouth findings of growers who work the different systems on an everyday basis in both the Soave and Valpolicella areas. Basically, the advantages of the pergola system are manifold. It is seen as particularly suitable for those varieties that require a long pruning system and both Garganega and Corvina fall into this category. It offers a good balance between foliage and fruit in more fertile ground with a good water supply, hence its popularity on the plains and flatter, lower-lying ground, but it also performs well on hillsides as the canopy is super-efficient at blocking out the sun's rays. This latter feature is becoming increasingly important in the area with climate change and so is particularly relevant with varieties – such as Corvina – which are susceptible to scorching during the hottest periods. It also provides protection against frost damage, common in higher areas, and because the bunch is suspended free of surrounding foliage, permits all-round air circulation, a plus point in the fight against the development of fungal diseases and mould. The canopy system also provides an ideal microclimate around the bunches as they ripen. An open canopy will limit excessive leaf growth and allow some sunlight to penetrate through. Others argue that the pergola system is vital in conserving good levels of acidity in the ripening grapes, a fundamental factor for fruit destined for the *appassimento* process. Because the bunches hang at around head height, harvesting them is much less backbreaking work. This again is a major consideration for grapes selected for *appassimento* which, by definition, are individually chosen ahead of the main harvest and thus can only be picked manually.

There are clearly disadvantages too. Firstly there is the high set-up cost of establishing a new pergola-trained vineyard. Renewing the system is extremely labour intensive and mechanization is not possible. The system is also prone to the danger of the fungal disease esca which generally affects, and can easily kill off, older vines. Overproduction from careless pruning can lead to grapes being unable to accumulate sufficient sugar levels, so creating optimal conditions through meticulous pruning is vital. Shading can also have a down side: when excessive there are negative implications for the development of anthocyanins, tartaric acid and sugar levels. Above all, because of the large amount of space it takes up, the system is suitable only for lower-density planting which, in conditions where monoculture is in danger of becoming the norm, is seen as extremely inefficient.

Guyot

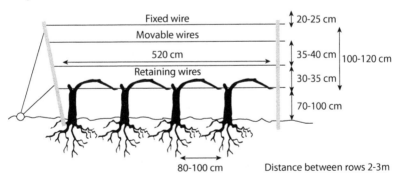

Guyot training system

Similarly, Guyot has its pros and cons. This method works off a shorter trunk than pergola and, in the case of single Guyot, utilizes a fruiting cane from the previous year's new wood tied along a training wire plus a spur with two further canes. The one closest to the permanent cordon (or branch), is pruned to leave a replacement two-node spur and the one further away becomes the fruiting cane the following year. Double Guyot again 'doubles up' and uses two fruiting canes, one trained to either side of the trunk. In its favour, Guyot allows for easy pruning, high-density planting (between 5,000 and 10,000 plants is typical in European vineyards) and ease of mechanization, the lie of the land permitting. In poorer soils, such as the higher limestone-based vineyards of some areas of both Soave and Valpolicella, higher-density planting increases the effective leaf surface and compensates for the fact that the vine will be less vigorous. Increased density also stimulates competition between the plants' roots to penetrate deeper into the ground in search of water, thus helping to ensure healthier plants. However, on the richer soils of the lower-lying land, canopy management is a much more demanding task and lower-density planting is desirable. There are further concerns that higher temperatures can cause a rapid drop in acids and a subsequent loss of aroma in the fruit with the system. Those who defend Guyot claim the quality of grapes it delivers is consistently high and that it is easier and both more cost and labour efficient to work, whether mechanization is practised or not. Though with Guyot there may be the constant worry over the danger of the grapes scorching and burning in the hot temperatures of July and August, in particular, the simple expedient of not removing any of the leaves surrounding the fruit partly gets round the problem. Local agronomist turned oenologist for the historical house of Bertani, Andrea Lonardi – a native of San Pietro in Cariano – believes there is another solution. By adapting the Vertical Shoot Position (VSP) that Guyot uses, the foliage can be trained upwards and outwards over parallel horizontal wires to form a 'Y' shape, keeping the grapes in partial shade at the hottest time of the day when the sun is more or less overhead.

Regarding the question of altitude, both methods appear to be suitable for planting on hillsides, though in the very highest vineyards where cooler temperatures are the norm and the power of the sun's rays is less, the tendency for Guyot to ripen fruit earlier and more efficiently can be a crucial factor. Pergola, for the opposite reason, can work better at lower altitudes where protection of the ripening fruit is usually a greater concern. In the Valpolicella today approximately 80 per cent of vineyards are trained using the pergola system, dropping to 78 per cent in Soave. But according to local beliefs (and the findings of the joint research commission), different varieties are suited to different systems. In the following section on grape varieties, both local and 'foreign', common in the area, this issue will be explored further. The key element – as ever with wine – is one of balance: a carefully tended vine with the correct distribution of foliage and fruit will always give the best results.

GRAPE VARIETIES IN THE VERONESE

The Veronesi have an uncommonly broad range of different grape varieties at their disposal for the production of both red and white wines. The first great chronicler of these was undoubtedly Ciro Pollini who, though born in Alagna in Piedmont, was to become a teacher of botany and agriculture in Verona where he lived in his later life. In his *Memorie Accademmia Agricultura Scienze e Lettere di Verona* of 1824 Pollini compiled the first comprehensive list of grapes planted in the Veronese. He catalogued fifty-five red and twenty-five white varieties, many – though not all – of which had already been recorded though never before as part of a dedicated and subsequently published study. The list contains many of the varieties still present in the area and others which have since disappeared. Subsequently, in 1904, Luigi Sormani Moretti recorded over two hundred different grapes in his study, *La Provincia di Verona*.

The reasons for such an abundance of choice have again to do with Verona's lengthy history at the crossroads of various civilizations and the arrival of, firstly, the Etruscans, followed by the Romans and then the Venetians. All were strong traders, and the first two in particular were great proselytizers for the culture of wine. The sale or exchange of vine cuttings would in all probability have been commonplace. Both Andrea Lonardi of Bertani and Paolo Speri, of the eponymous Pedemonte based winery, propound the similar theory that it was customary for the landed gentry and nobility, who for many centuries were the main vineyard owners in the area, to offer cuttings of their local vines almost as a calling card when paying visits elsewhere to those with similar interests in wine production.

Since phylloxera, and following the economic hardships of the first half of the twentieth century, different priorities have emerged which have brought about a rationalization of this rich heritage. Today's list of varieties authorized for cultivation within the province of Verona consists of thirty-six red grapes, twenty-five white grapes, one 'grey' (Pinot Grigio) and one 'pink' (Traminer Aromatico). Approximately 75 per cent of these are considered to be 'native' Italian and of that percentage just under 40 per cent is thought to have originated in the Veneto, an impressively healthy proportion which reflects the growing interest that Italians have in championing specifically local values. The varieties discussed below are those most frequently encountered in the production of the various DOC wines. Not surprisingly the vast majority of them are typically Veronese.

White grape varieties

One white grape variety dominates the viticultural Veronese and accounts for some 88 per cent of the vineyards planted. Two others seem to have promising futures while other minor local and international varieties seem – for now – to be slowly disappearing.

Garganega

Of all the grape varieties, both red and white, found in Verona's vineyards, Garganega has the longest documented history though the precise origins of the variety are unknown. It was first recorded as 'Garganica' at the start of the fourteenth century by Pietro de' Crescenzi as the most widely planted variety of the era, so it has been around for seven hundred years and more. A further reference to the variety at the end of the sixteenth century registers its presence in the vineyards of Brognoligo. As Garganego, the variety was referred to repeatedly by Alessandro Peccana in 1627. Garganega Comune, to give the grape its official title, has been shown to be closely related to Sicily's Grecanico and have links with both Trebbiano Toscano and Malvasia di Candia, though the similarly-named Garganega Grossa (Garganegona) is now officially a distinct variety identified as Dorona. Ian D'Agata, in *Native Wine Grapes of Italy*, goes on to list several biotypes of the grape common in Soave: Garganega Tipica is the grape we usually think of as Garganega and is widely used; Garganega di Dario is mostly found around the Brognoligo *frazione* of Monteforte d'Alpone and is a larger-berried, earlier-ripening strain; Garganega Verde (smaller berried, looser bunches) is seen in the western parts of the Soave Classico area around Costeggiola; and the poorer quality, low-acid Garganega Agostega, which is being phased out owing to its propensity to rot, can still be seen in a few older vineyards in the area between Soave and Monteforte d'Alpone. Outside the Soave area, the variety is also present in neighbouring Vicenza and to a much lesser degree in Padua, though plantings in those two areas do not seem to be increasing.

Garganega really began to dominate the vineyards of Soave once more just over a century ago in the wake of the double blight of oidium and peronospera during the second half of the nineteenth century. It gradually began to replace Trebbiano di Soave, a variety whose more compact bunches of grapes render it susceptible to humidity-related problems, and by the close of the last century Garganega was becoming dominant. Garganega has a protracted vegetative cycle, at 160 days a longer one than most white grapes and, if allowed extra hang time as a result, it can develop surprisingly expansive aromas as well as maintaining decent levels of both sugar and acid. It is vigorous and also tends to be highly productive – a determining factor for its rise in popularity at a time when quantity rather than quality was the aim of the *vignaiolo*. In more recent times, its ability to cope with water stress has stood Garganega in good stead: recovering quickly from a lack of water during hot summer months is a distinct advantage in the face of changing weather patterns. The variety's positive characteristics have been highlighted by extensive research into clonal selection to identify and maintain such advantages and, as a result, a number of clones – R4 and ISV CV 24 in particular – are now in widespread use. It is a fairly similar story with the choice of rootstock where SO4, thanks to a ready adaptability to either plains or hillside sites, has gained popularity over the previously more widespread 420A, being better suited to both the planting of new vineyards and the continuing need to replace individual plants which are no longer productive. In some of the older vineyards, it is still possible to find Garganega vines that are over a hundred years old and thriving on their original pre-phylloxera rootstocks.

The variety has big, sharply indented, five-lobed leaves and bears large, long, loosely-clustered bunches of fruit which frequently exceed 25 centimetres in length and on average weigh around 185 grams. The skins are fairly thin and their classic golden yellow colour turns an amber pink colour when fully ripe. Garganega is fairly sensitive to cold temperatures and common vine diseases such as rot and mould, to the attack of insects and other parasites, and is particularly susceptible to *diseccamento del rachide* or bunch stem necrosis. The plant's extreme vigour and the failure of the first basal nodes of the fruiting cane to produce make pergola training an almost automatic choice.

The pursuit of quality over the last few decades has clearly had a major role to play in the variety's comeback. Selected clones and rootstocks backed up by attentive vineyard management and the curbing of the vine's natural vigour, plus of course careful handling in the cellar, have taken Garganega-based wines to heights that would not even have been dreamed of some fifty years or so ago. The distinctive characteristics of a classic Garganega wine are its subtle yet expansive aroma, a remarkable overall balance between its component parts and its rather surprising capacity to age well in bottle, whether oaked or not.

Trebbiano di Soave

References to varieties called Trebiano, Turbina, Turbiana and Torbiana abound in texts relating to the history of wine production in the Veneto. It is more than likely that they relate to the variety known today as Trebbiano di Soave. At the beginning of the 1990s the variety was first shown to be genetically identical to the Marche's Verdicchio and subsequent studies have corroborated the original findings. Indeed some now believe that Verdicchio arrived in the Marche from the Veneto via cuttings taken there by traders, given as gifts or because, as D'Agata says, 'plague-affected areas of the Marche were repopulated (at the end of the fifteenth century) by farmers from Veneto who brought animals and plants with them'.

By 2014 the amount of land planted to Trebbiano di Soave within the overall boundary of the DOC territory (surrounding and including Classico and the Colli Scaligeri) had grown slightly from a mere 78 hectares in 2003 (or approximately 1 per cent of the vineyard surface) to 95 hectares (1.35 per cent). This is still appreciably less than Pinot Grigio (3.52 per cent), Chardonnay (3.22 per cent) and Durella (2.65 per cent), though the almost total dominance of Garganega shows no sign of abatement, covering almost 90 per cent of the designated area. It is perhaps the very fact that the Soavesi have only rediscovered the true value of their beloved Garganega over the last century or so which means that Trebbiano di Soave has been so largely overlooked, as there is no doubting its intrinsic value as a wine-producing grape. Indeed a number of producers – for instance, Suavia and Filippi –

make excellent varietal wines from Trebbiano di Soave which cede little if anything in terms of quality to premium examples of Soave itself. Moreover the wine that many consider to represent the absolute pinnacle of excellence for the denomination, Pieropan's Soave Classico Calvarino, is one that takes advantage of the maximum percentage the law allows of Trebbiano di Soave (30 per cent) in the blend. Other top examples including the variety are Monte Tondo's Soave Classico Casette Foscarin, Nardello's Soave Classico Vigna Turbian, Coffele's Soave Classico Ca' Visco and Filippi's Soave Colli Scaligeri 'Vigne della Bra'. Agostino Vicentini, current owner of the family winery at Colognola ai Colli, who uses some 25 per cent of Trebbiano in his Soave Terre Lunghe blend, recalls a time when the two varieties were planted three to one: one *campo veronese* (equivalent to approximately 3,000 square metres) of Trebbiano to three of Garganega. Meri Tessari of the Suavia winery, based at Fitta in the Classico area and whose Massafitti Trebbiano di Soave is perhaps the most heralded example of the variety, points out that prior to the Second World War Trebbiano di Soave was still much more common (perhaps covering even as much as 60 per cent of the vineyard area in some places) than it is today and recalls how local growers have always spoken of the variety with great fondness. Perhaps when the current love affair with Garganega has matured, more growers will begin to re-evaluate the other 'staple' of the Soave blend. As Lamberto Paronetto declared over twenty-five years ago in *Viti e Vini di Verona*, Trebbiano di Soave has been neglected in favour of Garganega when 'this autochthonous Veronese variety merits greater attention for its capacity to improve the quality of Soave'.

Like Garganega, Trebbiano buds in the second half of April but matures a couple of weeks earlier. It has medium to large leaves which are shaped rather like a pentagram (though in reality it has three lobes). The bunches are medium-compact and in the form of an extended pyramid while the berries themselves are fairly round with a yellowish green colour. Another highly vigorous variety, Trebbiano di Soave also seems to work especially well when trained on pergola and is consistent and constant in terms of fruit set and productivity. Though, like Garganega, it is prone to bunch stem necrosis, it is nonetheless more resistant to colder temperatures. Though the drawback of its sensitivity to humidity (as above) may have played a significant part in its decline, the warmer and drier conditions that climate change seem to bring may yet see the variety return to favour. Trebbiano di Soave typically makes a linear style of wine with interesting grassy and flinty notes and is characterized by an excellent, nervy, even tingling, acidity that also brings impressive length and structure.

Chardonnay

The other recognized or named variety in the Soave blend is the well-known Chardonnay grape. While it has been around in the Veronese for over a century, it was in the past often confused with Pinot Bianco and indeed thought to belong to the Pinot family. As such, it was very much a bit-part player on the Veronese wine stage until the whole world fell in love with the variety in the 1980s and 1990s and all of a sudden any white wine containing even a proportion of Chardonnay seemed to be guaranteed fifteen minutes of fame. Consequently, when considering new plantings throughout this period, the choice of Chardonnay was made even easier thanks to the fact that it buds and matures much earlier than the other two main varieties – indeed, as it generally ripens by mid to late August, the fruit will be harvested as much as a month ahead of the main crop. However, like the ensuing success of Pinot Grigio, the boom had a limited lifespan, though notable wineries such as Guerrieri Rizzardi remain convinced that a healthy injection of Chardonnay can work wonders alongside Garganega by adding richness and complexity to the blend. They are one of the few producers to admit to an admiration for international varieties when it is becoming increasingly unfashionable to do so. Others, like Filippi, who planted the variety when it was at the height of its popularity, continue to produce the wine but as a pure varietal or to sell off in bulk. There is little doubt that the variety can produce extremely good wines in the Soave area but the fact that it works at least equally as well in the rest of the world seems to suggest that it will play even more of a supporting role in the not too distant future.

Durella

While plantings of this highly distinctive and ancient indigenous grape are largely restricted to the very eastern part of the area (it has occasionally popped up in Valpolicella), the wine it produces is certainly on the march. The history of the variety dates back to the thirteenth century when as

Duracina or *Durasena* it was referred to in both the Statutes of Vicenza (1264) and Costozza (1292). Both names support the view that Durella is so-called because of its rather tough, thick skins, and the origins of the word are from the Latin *durus acinus*. The variety has many other synonyms including Cagnina, Dorasiga, Durola, Rabbiosa and even Nosiola. Theories that this last variety and Durella are closely related have been shown to be without foundation, as Italo Cosmo first suspected back in the 1930s. As a wine grape grown in the area, it can be traced back to the middle of the sixteenth century and the writings of Ortensio Lando, a Milanese humanist who described Durella as the source of 'a tart white wine produced in the three castles area [around Montecchio and Arzignano] which is appreciated for its ability to subdue the wild flavours of kid [goat]'. References to Durella and its synonyms continue throughout the eighteenth, nineteenth and twentieth centuries: in 1862, Zantedeschi referred to 'Durasana' and in 1925 Giuseppe Acerbi in *Delle Viti Italiane* noted that 'Duron' was found in the Val d'Illasi and other places. The bunches are cylindrical, medium-sized and very loosely clustered so the variety has customarily been favoured for use in the *appassimento* process; the berries have a pale, apple-green colour and the leaves are tri-lobed. The grape seems to have found its true vocation as the base for sparkling wine much more recently, probably not before the end of the 1960s by which time it was gaining some notoriety as good 'cutting' wine owing to its salient characteristics of high acidity, low alcohol and lack of strong, defining aromas or flavours. Its main attribute remains, of course, that sometimes searing acidity: Gianni Tessari of Marcato recalls that in the notoriously difficult vintage of 2014 the variety had almost 16.0 g/l when harvested. A Durella-based wine will have delicate aromas of, above all, hawthorn blossom with notes of green apple and citrus fruits, and an alcohol content that rarely exceeds 12.5% abv.

Other white varieties

Other grapes authorized for growing in the province of Verona can also be included at up to a maximum of 5 per cent. In real terms they have little relevance: only 1 per cent of the area's vineyards are planted to varieties other than those already referred to above – Garganega, Trebbiano di Soave, Chardonnay, Durella and Pinot Grigio.

Mention should be made here, though, of Sauvignon as a number of commentators and pundits in recent years have noted how Soave can sometimes smell surprisingly similar to Sauvignon Blanc. While the amount of land planted to the variety in the area works against the connection (less than 1 per cent), other factors, most notably the influence of certain winemaking techniques, need to be taken into account. These include early harvesting, prolonged skin contact (aroma precursors are mainly present in the skins of grapes), individual yeast strains (some are much more effective than others in transforming aroma precursors into thiol compounds), reductive winemaking and low fermentation temperatures, all of which can favour the production of thiols. Polyfunctional volatile thiols are sulphur-containing compounds formed during fermentation from aroma precursors that have developed while the fruit ripens on the vine. Certain individual thiols impart not only tropical or citrus aromas to a wine but also the cat's pee and elderflower notes that are typical of the Sauvignon Blanc variety. When present to an unacceptably high level (through sloppy winemaking) they can also give rise to the undesirable smells of onions or sweat, features which are unfortunately all too common with many examples of Sauvignon produced in Northern Italy. While thiols are a very typical feature of Sauvignon Blanc they are clearly present in other grapes too and it is probable that, in many instances, those telltale 'green' or 'grassy' fruit aromas that can be detected in Soave have come about as a direct result of the fermentation policies chosen by individual wineries.

Red grape varieties

The red wines of the Valpolicella area are based on a classic *uvaggio* or blend of grape varieties. Traditionally this mix was present in the vineyards but is now more likely to be brought together in the cellar, though the term can be applied in either instance. The main components listed in order of their typical percentage in the final blend are Corvina, Corvinone and Rondinella, to which can be added much smaller amounts of other permitted grapes. It follows then that their presence in the vineyards shows similar weighting.

Corvina

When it comes to red grapes, first and foremost in the hearts and minds of the Veronesi is Corvina, the variety that gives the characteristics which distinguish their wines from all others. Its origins remain unknown, though if we accept that Alessandro Peccana's mention of 'Corvino' in *On the Problems of Cold Drinks* refers to Corvina, the first citation of the variety would be in 1627. Other references to what could well be the same grape abound from the following century onwards but it is widely accepted that the first 'official' record of Corvina Veronese being planted in the Valpolicella came from Ciro Pollini in 1824. There are many similarly named grapes – for example, Corvina Gentile, Corvina Rizza and Corvinone as well as Corbina and Corbinella – which only adds to the confusion, but the grape known locally as Cruina has since at least the second half of the nineteenth century gradually become the mainstay of Valpolicella.

The variety is characterized by a five-lobed leaf with an open 'U' shape where it is joined to the stalk (the beginning of the petiole). It bears medium-sized bunches (usually weighing between 200 and 250 grams) which are pyramid-shaped and winged while the grapes themselves are ellipsoid in shape and dark blue in colour; they are thickly covered with bloom by harvest time. It buds relatively late and is typically ripe between the middle of September and early October. Up until a couple of generations ago, at least, it would regularly mature rather later. Paolo Speri recalls how his grandfather Sante had very clear ideas about when to harvest. His birthday was 2 October and no one was allowed to touch a single grape until after that date, not even to make *pissota con l'ua,* the traditional local cake similar to a sponge filled with grapes which is popular at harvest. Corvina's reasonably durable skins make it a suitable grape for the *appassimento* process. It is a vigorous and productive variety but is reasonably sensitive to both fungal diseases and water stress. As the buds at the base of the fruiting cane are not productive, the variety requires lengthy pruning and therefore needs a lot of space. This, in common with the tendency for the grapes to scorch in hot weather, makes pergola the training system most growers prefer.

Clonal selection for Corvina is quite advanced and the grower has a wide range (around eighty or so) of options though the most popular if also rather controversial choice over recent years has been ISC CV 48. Some claim that its small, loosely-clustered bunches and capacity for generating good levels of sugar make it an ideal candidate for, above all, the *appassimento* process, while others maintain that apart from its deeper than average colour it has few other positive attributes. Meanwhile others, such as ISV 7 and ISV CV 13, are favoured for the *tipicita* they confer to the wines. The selection process continues and current research points towards identifying biotypes which either produce richer and more structured wines or adapt well to *appassimento*. Regarding rootstocks, the preferred options are Kober 5BB, 420A and SO4 though 41B, 140Ru and 1103P are also quite common.

In terms of the style of wine it produces, it should be remembered that Corvina's traditional use is as a part of a blend, even though a pretty dominant one at that. While a good young Valpolicella will give the taster a pretty clear view of what the grape smells and tastes like, examples of 100 per cent Corvina are also quite readily available, if usually produced as a Rosso Veronese IGT/P. Perhaps the most famous of these is Allegrini's La Poja, recent vintages of which have been a great showcase for the perfume, elegance and finesse which are the wines' most striking characteristics. Thankfully, in the wake of the Brunellopoli scandal towards the end of the new millennium's first decade, lovers of Italian wine have learnt to accept that many of their favourite red wines – those made from Nebbiolo and Sangiovese, for example – do not have an especially dark colour. The same applies to Corvina which typically produces a wine that is more of a deep cherry/ruby red. Aromas show remarkable clarity and purity, acidity is balanced but brisk and tannins, though not abundant, are elegant and fine. The best examples can age remarkably well.

Corvinone

If there is one grape variety that divides opinion in Valpolicella then it is most certainly Corvinone. It was until quite recently generally regarded as a biotype of Corvina (and frequently referred to as Corvina Grossa) and was only officially recognized as a separate variety in the *Catalogo Nazionale delle Varieta di Uve* in 1993. Some of the confusion at least may have to do with the name: 'Big Corvina' lives up to its name in that the grape berries and indeed bunches are very large – at between 350 and 450 grams, as much as twice the size of those of Corvina. The uncertainty was finally put to rest in 2003 when Vantini, Tacconi, Gastaldelli, Govoni, Tosi, Malacrino, Bassi and Cavitelli identified Corvinone as a variety in its own right and not related to any other Veronese grape including Corvina in their *Biodiversity* *of grapevines (*Vitis vinifera L*) grown in the province of Verona.* There are other similarities: like Corvina, Corvinone buds and matures quite late (traditionally mid/late April and late September/early October respectively), is a vigorous and productive vine and has unproductive nodes at the base of the fruiting cane. Corvinone is quite resistant to cold temperatures but is particularly sensitive to a lack of water. It seems to perform best in hillside sites with good ventilation (it is also sensitive to peronospera) and likes less fertile, pebbly terrain. It performs much less well in richer soils and on the plains where it tends to produce poorer-quality fruit. One particular characteristic of Corvinone that can sometimes cause concern is that the berries do not always ripen homogeneously: some remain green even when the rest of the bunch is approaching full ripeness if production is not carefully limited. Unless winkled out, these can be a source of unwelcome harsh and bitter notes. On the plus side, Corvinone is a more tannic variety than Corvina and therefore is considered to add to the potential longevity of the blend.

There is more to the controversy than a few under-ripe grapes, though managing the fruit through to full maturity can be an issue. Marco Speri (see Secondo Marco, below) is a fan of the peppery and spicy notes that ripe Corvinone can bring while Claudio Viviani, who works vineyards high in the Negrar valley around Mazzano and Panego, finds that it can often be his most successful variety. Claudio is a great believer in the virtues of the Guyot training system when it comes to getting the best out of Corvinone: 'It surprised me in both 2014 and 2015 with the quality I managed to get, particularly in 2015.' The reason, he believes, is that higher up in the poorer soils of hills around Mazzano, the greater density of plants per hectare that Guyot offers creates competition between the root systems of the individual vines, forcing them to penetrate deeper into the soil to find water. 'That was a really dry summer up here but my Corvinone hardly seemed to suffer,' he says. Claudio's description of the variety as our 'Pinot Nero', however, may be a little far-fetched for some. But where some growers prize the variety for the structure it brings to support the elegance and perfume of Corvina, others feel its wines are a little too rustic and can actually compromise the quality of its partner.

It follows from the confusion over its origins that the process of clonal selection with Corvinone is less advanced than with Corvina, for example. But, given its high genetic variability, a number have already been developed of which ISV CV3 and VRC18 are the most popular: they produce less enormous bunches of fruit which are loosely compacted and therefore well suited to *appassimento*. Regarding rootstocks, the most common in use are Kober 5BB, 420A and SO4.

Rondinella

There are surprisingly few historical references to this variety and it seems to have been first recorded in a study of Veronese agriculture in 1882. While the debate continues over Corvinone, pretty much everyone is agreed about the worth of Rondinella: 'It's a donkey,' suggests Claudio Viviani dismissively, though not without affection. And it does seem that the variety's virtues are simple and straightforward: a reliable vine that produces a good-sized crop year in year out. It is hardy, resistant to most diseases and copes well with both cold snaps and dry spells. Furthermore, it ripens slightly ahead of the other two grapes, allowing growers the luxury of a slightly staggered harvest. Because, unlike Corvina and Corvinone, the first buds on the fruiting cane can be productive and the bunches of grapes on the large side without being too big (some 20 centimetres or so long and weighing 200 to 230 grams on average), it works well with both of the main training systems. Put these factors together and its rise in popularity is hardly surprising; even the timing is perfect. It is an instantly recognizable grape leading up to harvest time, easily distinguished by its almost perfectly spherical, dark purple-blue grapes (reminiscent of the colour of a bird's plumage) which are usually heavily pruinose by that time.

The downside to Rondinella is that, apart from a certain degree of colour and body though little tannin, its contribution to the blend is minimal as it tends to produce a rather neutral and even slightly bitter wine. Growers do seem (if a little grudgingly) to acknowledge that it plays a useful role in the production of Recioto, however, as Rondinella accumulates high levels of sugar easily. While Corvina is often considered to produce a wine that can be too highly nuanced for Recioto, so the 'neutrality' of Rondinella becomes, for once, a virtue.

Rondinella works well with the various standard rootstocks in the area (Kober 5BB, 420A and SO4) and plenty of different clones are available to the grower none of which – for now – stand out. But its fortunes may be about to turn. 'You know that crisp and juicy sensation when you first bite into a cherry? That's Rondinella at its best,' claims Paolo Speri. 'And after years of looking we think we may finally have found the right one.' Paolo admits that the problem is one of time: 'It takes forever to carry out research into anything agricultural,' he says, ruefully. It will indeed take several more years of development before they can be sure of what they have and even then they would need to wait several more before any vines become productive. But at least there is a glimmer of hope for the 'little swallow'.

Other red varieties

As with Soave, the list of other grapes which can in theory be part of the make up of Valpolicella is a lengthy one. Some of the other sanctioned varieties are rarely found in the vineyards of the Valpolicella and have greater relevance elsewhere in the province. Those listed below are therefore the mainly local, secondary grapes. Excluded are the various French grapes but included are also a few very minor varieties believed to be Veronese in origin and which may have a future role to play. While French varieties (and especially Merlot) have some popularity, they are falling out of fashion.

Molinara

Up until 2003, Molinara was a mandatory part of the Valpolicella grape mix. It was first recorded by Pollini in 1824 and Acerbi the following year and, though associated with the wine since it came of age, it has recently fallen out of favour. The main reason is that it produces wines which are light in body and very pale in colour, in fact more of a rosé than a red. At one time, according to Alessandro Castellani of Ca' La Bionda, plenty of white grapes were also to be found in the Valpolicella vineyards and often made up a part of the final blend. Over the years they have slowly disappeared and Alessandro is rightly concerned: 'By uprooting these old vines, we're losing track of our heritage,' he observes. Molinara is clearly a significant part of that patrimony. While the colour of a wine doubtless makes a strong initial impact, it represents the opening chapter rather than the full story and there are enough admirers of Molinara around to ensure that the variety does not suffer the same fate as those white grapes Alessandro is concerned about.

The name of the variety is believed to come from the Italian word for miller, *mulinaro*, because as harvest time approaches the berries become covered in a white bloom which makes them look as if they have been dusted in flour; anyone who has ever visited a working flour mill will be familiar with the idea. Molinara is another vigorous and productive variety which, like Corvina and Corvinone, has unproductive buds at the base of the fruiting cane, and is clearly then a vine best suited to the pergola. The tri-lobed leaves are coincidentally like the berries themselves, quite pale-coloured and almost translucent, while another singular characteristic is the variety's relatively high resistance to esca, the disease that affects the trunks of grapevines. As it is quite sensitive to humid conditions, it is generally best suited to the well-ventilated and drier growing conditions found in hillside vineyards.

Sapidity is the main feature that the grape's admirers single out. It is worth recalling the thoughts of Emile Peynaud and Jacques Blouin on sapidity, and in particular succinic acid, as described in *The Taste of Wine: The Art and Science of Wine Appreciation*:

'Wine is known to contain six principal organic acids which play a part in the acid taste. Three come from the grape and have a pure acid taste; these are tartaric, malic and citric acid. Tartaric acid is hard, malic acid green and citric acid fresh in taste. The three others – succinic, lactic and acetic – are formed by alcoholic fermentation and bacterial activity. Their taste is more complex. Lactic acid has a lightly acid taste, rather tart and sour; acetic acid has a vinegary taste; succinic acid has an intense taste, bitter and salty at once, which also makes one salivate. It is the acid in wine which has the most taste; it gives fermented drinks the "winy" savour they have in common. In wine succinic acid gives sapidity, vinosity and sometimes bitterness. In this connection it is worth remembering the common chemical origin of succinic acid, a sapid substance in fermented drinks and of glutamic acid, a substance with a meaty flavour, used in cooking in the form of monosodium glutamate.'

The authors could almost be describing Molinara! It is this very salinity that makes Molinara such a tasty wine and able to go with a surprisingly wide range of foods. Although the part that Molinara traditionally had to play in the make up of Valpolicella was potentially a substantial one (up to 25 per cent of the total), its presence has been reduced to a maximum of 10 per cent under current legislation and therefore its contribution to the overall aroma and flavour is likely to be minimal. Some producers do continue to keep the faith and it is occasionally possible to come across an example of Molinara *in purezza*, that is as a mono-varietal. Carlo Boscaini produces a convincing rosé version as a Molinara Veronese IGT which drives home the point about Molinara's ability to work well with food. Le Salette of Fumane also make delicious Molinara Rosato. The most talked-about version was the almost mythical Molinara IGT produced by Bepi Quintarelli which is sadly no longer in production. Sandro Boscaini of Masi, who have identified and cloned a particular biotype on the Serego Alighieri estate, and a few other important names also foresee a positive future for the variety. Perhaps a new twist in the plot of The Miller's Tale will highlight the virtues of lightening up both the colour and the flavour of Veronese red wine.

Oseleta

Concurrent with the demise of Molinara, there has been an upsurge of interest in neglected local varieties which are capable of adding both colour and structure to the Valpolicella blend. Prominent among these is Oseleta. Where D'Agata ascribes the first reference to Oseleta or Oselina (as the variety seems to have been traditionally known in the Veronese) to the sixteenth century Veronese historian and antiquarian Onofrio Panvinio, this appears to be an isolated incidence as the variety only really surfaces from the late nineteenth century onwards in various lists and studies of the time. Even then it remained of largely academic interest until Masi spotted the grape's potential in the 1980s. Oseleta has various attributes which the main local varieties lack: a deep, dark colour, full body and abundant tannins. In addition to these advantages, the timing of its rediscovery was perfect, coming in an era when producers were looking beyond the classic style of fresh, young Valpolicella and trying to develop what Italian winemakers like to refer to as more 'important' – more structured and longer lasting (and frequently less drinkable) – wines. Over the last twenty years the variety has gone from strength to strength and nowadays plays a supporting role in a number of the area's 'aspirational' wines.

Though grown quite widely throughout the area these days, its uses are relatively restricted apart from this auxiliary role: vinified as a varietal as by Masi (Osar) or Celestini Gaspari at Zyme, for instance, it shows itself as a dark, muscular and brooding spicy red with plenty of ageing potential. However, Oseleta-based wines can at the same time lack the effortless charm normally associated with the area's red wines. Berry size is Oseleta's big drawback: with thick skins and large pips, the individual grapes are really quite small with a very low skin to pulp ratio, thus rendering the variety unsuitable for the lengthy period of *appassimento* required by law for Amarone grapes. Otherwise it has the added benefit of being a particularly hardy vine which is resistant to most diseases. Late to flower, Oseleta is quite a vigorous plant though it produces a high number of unwelcome lateral shoots. Theories – as yet unproven – date back to the late nineteenth century which suggest that Oseleta may in fact have descended from wild grape vines.

It is worth drawing attention to a few other varieties sometimes found in the local vineyards. Corbina fell out of favour following phylloxera owing to the wine's deep, dark colour (thought of as actually excessive and therefore untypical at the time) and apparent coarseness or rusticity. There has been a change of heart more recently and, following its inclusion in the National Register of Grape Vines in 2007, people are once more talking up Corbina's good points: fresh, red and black fruit aromas, full body, positive acidity and assertive tannins. Corbina is a resistant vine of good vigour and is reasonably productive; the medium-sized bunches of blue-black grapes are fairly loosely clustered, suggesting it could adapt well to *appassimento*. Thanks to its plentiful but soft tannins, deep colour and moderate acidity levels, Croatina is sometimes seen as a secondary component of Amarone – the variety's large bunches are also quite loosely packed and the skins robust.

Dindarella has been documented since the early 1800s by authors such as Pollini and Acerbi but, rather like Molinara, it has fallen from favour in recent years: its violet red grapes are low in anthocyanins and produce an unfashionably lighter style of red wine which has a pale ruby colour. Though there are fewer producers that champion Dindarella's cause, those who do – Aldegheri and La Brigaldara in particular – admire its spicy and slightly aromatic style. Indeed, La Brigaldara find the variety works well as a rosé thanks to its highish acidity while the Aldegheri version is darker and more tannic than might otherwise be expected from the variety. Dindarella is a fairly vigorous and productive vine whose large, loosely clustered bunches of thick-skinned grapes are regarded as eminently suitable for the *appassimento* process. Though once considered as a separate variety, Pelara is nowadays seen as a biotype of Dindarella – by Angelini et al. in 1980 and Vantini et al. in 2003 – although G. B. Perez had originally put forward the idea that the two were closely related at the start of the twentieth century. Pelara is a much less productive vine and suffers from flower abortion causing poor fruit set and fewer berries per bunch. It is even rarer these days than Dindarella.

Forsellina, a vigorous variety with balanced foliage, is fairly disease-resistant; it seems to perform best in poorer soils where it also benefits from longer pruning. The fruit comes in medium to large bunches of oval blue-black grapes; however, the bunches are quite compact and therefore sensitive to botrytis. The wine is a pale-coloured red with lightly aromatic red fruit aromas and balanced flavours that show a positive sapid character. Though well-regarded by pundits for its typically Veronese character, Forsellina is unpopular as it does not work in *appassimento*, a sad reflection of where priorities lie these days. If and when wines produced from freshly gathered fruit return to favour, then promising varieties like Forsellina may have more of a future.

Even less widely seen, though occasionally to be found, is Rossignola whose lack of evident colour and delicate aromas suggest that the variety may become another victim of the fashion for darker-coloured red wine. Spigamonte, only discovered by the Cantina Valpolicella Negrar in 2000, can work well as a blending component particularly where longevity is a consideration according to the cooperative's oenologist and general manager Daniele Accordini. Turchetta may also be a useful part of the Valpolicella blend. Italo Cosmo felt that it merited greater attention and plantings should be encouraged. Turchetta shows medium vigour and constant if not abundant productivity; atypically for a Veronese grape the basal node of the fruiting cane is productive and so a short pruning system can be recommended.

Two other grapes more commonly associated with the Trentino – Marzemino and Teroldego – have some historical presence in the Veronese and are still occasionally seen there (Marion produce a varietal Teroldego from their vineyards at Marcellise, for example). Finally Sangiovese – better known as Sangio'eto in the Valpolicella – is seldom seen these days and only then as a minor part of any blend.

THE CHOICE OF ROOTSTOCK

While usually seen as being of secondary importance, the choice of rootstock nonetheless has a significant role to play. It is not, however, just a question of identifying the most compatible rootstock on which to graft the selected cultivar: the grower must take a number of other features into account. The choice of training system (and therefore planting density), sensitivity during the flowering period and susceptibility to various diseases must all be factored in. In particular, soil type is a major consideration, and whether conditions are especially acidic, sandy, saline, etc. A rootstock's tolerance to the active limestone content in the soil can often be critical as many of the area's vineyard sites show relatively high levels. The rootstocks that encourage strong growth suit the high-vigour varieties typical of the Veronese as an active root system locates water and nutrients in the soil more effectively and is thus better able to sustain canopy growth. Tolerance to drought conditions or to poorly draining soils must not be forgotten either. The choice is rarely a straightforward one.

Over the years patterns have developed which reflect the popularity of the various rootstocks most frequently seen today. For red grapes, Kober 5BB (a vigorous rootstock which is limestone tolerant) is widely used for all three main varieties, as are the slightly less vigorous SO4 and 420A (weaker again and though historically important, starting to fall out of favour). Corvina works less well on 1103 Paulsen (which is not quite so limestone resistant) than Corvinone, though both perform reasonably with 140 Ruggeri and 41B; 140 Ruggeri, for example, is resistant to drought and prefers limestone and poorer soils while 41B is also drought resistant and prefers limestone soils to those which are heavy or 'cold' (poorly draining). Although less compatible with the final two, Rondinella otherwise follows a similar pattern to Corvina.

It is a wholly different story with the white grapes: Garganega does not work on Kober 5BB, probably the most common choice in Valpolicella, and much prefers SO4 (in fact 60 per cent of Garganega vines are planted with this rootstock). Though, as in the Valpolicella, 420A was once considered a safe option, its popularity is in decline and the more adaptable and drought-resistant 1103 Paulsen is now more evident. The other alternatives (140 Ruggeri and 41B) are also of minor relevance in the Soave area.

BIODIVERSITY

The final piece of the jigsaw in the discussion of the vine and its environment is precisely that: the environment itself. There is a healthy and growing concern in the Veronese over 'green' issues and biodiversity is the word on many people's lips. The question of biodiversity has, of course, great relevance for major viticultural areas given the benefits it brings to growing conditions and the environment in general. The term itself is a portmanteau word combining 'biological' and 'diversity', and is generally defined along the lines of 'the variation and interaction between and across species and ecosystems'. Biodiversity is the starting point for a healthy ecosystem which serves to purify the natural resources of air and water, mitigate against drought and erosion and regulate the chemical composition of the soil and the atmosphere. These factors will in turn influence the growth cycle of the vine.

In the mid-nineteenth century, before the arrival of the triple whammy from America of oidium, peronospera and phylloxera, the growing of different crops (including the vine) and the rearing of animals on the same plot of land was pretty much standard practice and viticulture, thanks to the viable balance between the production and consumption of wine, was just one of many features of the local economy. Then disaster struck the vineyards and they were not to recover fully until after the ensuing economic and social hardships of two world wars a century later. During the boom years of the 1950s and 1960s, with the scramble to plant new vineyards, the ability to maintain a healthy balance in the environment had little relevance and by then the use of pesticides, herbicides and synthetic fertilizers in agriculture had become endemic as growers sought to maximize production. In addition to the damage such treatments cause, the dangers of the drift towards monoculture were slowly becoming apparent. Resources were being consumed at an unsustainable rate and poor soil conservation was beginning to cause its own problems. Harsh lessons were to be learnt during the late 1970s and throughout the 1980s as markets began to falter. The impact of poor soil conservation, impure water and air and a potential loss of biodiversity was becoming an economic as well as an environmental issue.

There is nowadays a surprisingly broad and generally realistic approach to the issue of biodiversity. This operates on a number of different levels as the idea of at least 'sustainable' farming has certainly taken root. It is particularly encouraging to note that many of the local cooperatives are buying into the idea: while the decision to aim for organic or even biodynamic farming might be feasible for the small- to medium-sized operation, to apply at least some of the underlying principles on a larger scale is far more difficult a proposition. Even so the Cantina di Negrar have in recent years made available bottlings of organic wines. Although they do not offer certified organic wines yet, the Cantina Valpantena have introduced alternative green programmes to encourage members to move way from the use of herbicides and insecticides in the vineyards, as has the Cantina di Monteforte in Soave. The use of leguminous green manure, a practice known as *sovescio* in Italian, is becoming increasingly common: cover crops and other plants serve as mulch and are ploughed under to enrich and protect the soil in a multitude of different ways, such as the release of nitrogen and the decrease of alkalinity. Meanwhile, some of the important historical houses like Gini in Soave and Speri in Valpolicella have converted to organic production and a handful of medium-sized estates like Musella, owned and run by members of the Pasqua family, have achieved Demeter biodynamic certification. So far, it seems, these wineries could not be happier with the choices they have made and, encouraged by their success, numbers are growing. At the extreme end of the spectrum, Zeno Zignoli operates an entirely individual approach to wine production at his Monte dei Ragni estate at Marega in the Fumane valley. Zeno ploughs his land with a horse and plants wild vines (for use as future rootstocks for grafts) according to the old Roman quincunx system where alternate rows are staggered to appear in diagonal lines from whichever side of the vineyard you look (imagine a free-standing vine planted at each intersection of an extended rectilinear lattice pattern). As well as growing many other crops including rare and neglected species, he jealously protects the woodland on his property which he considers to be a vital part of any balanced environment.

While the subject may be a hot topic these days, the extent to which biodiversity is being fostered is difficult to quantify. In classic Italian fashion, there are plenty of producers who claim to practise what amounts to an organic system but choose not to follow someone else's guidelines or indeed seek the approval of certification. Leaving aside the issue of official approbation (and any suggestion of commercial cynicism), the overall tendency to recognize the importance of biodiversity and its implications for the wine industry is timely to say the least. Over the last few decades, the land under vine in the Valpolicella has increased by over 50 per cent (4,902 hectares in 1997 to 7,596 in 2015) thanks to the stellar rise in popularity of Amarone and Ripasso. There has been a particular surge of interest in the eastern part of the area, beyond Classico, where land was both much cheaper and more easily available. Important growers like Allegrini and Tedeschi based in the Classico area have expanded into the so-called extended zone, as have many of the big names in Soave such as Ca Rugate, Gini and Pieropan. In order to put a brake on this expansion, there has been an embargo on the planting of new vineyards by the Veneto region in the area for the last couple of years. So what land does become available is necessarily more expensive, thereby discouraging some of the speculation which was threatening to send things spiralling out of control; even so, the price of a hectare of land over the last three decades has increased by over 1,350 per cent! Similarly in Soave: the current amount of land under vine within the DOC/G territory is frozen at just short of 7,000 hectares.

For now of the 30,000 hectares of land which comprise the entire area of Valpolicella, a quarter is under vine while in Soave it is over half the total of 12,000 hectares. In Valpolicella approximately 60 per cent of the surface area is devoted to different forms of agriculture (including vineyards), 30 per cent is 'natural' or uncultivated land such as woods or heathland, with the remaining 10 per cent given over to human habitation and development. In the Soave area other forms of agriculture are much less apparent and vineyards themselves cover almost 60 per cent of the land surface. The area not under vine is mainly either woodland or habitation and what little industrial development exists is present on a very small scale, covering just over 3 per cent of the surface area. Both *consorzi* are concerned with driving home the message to their members that respect for the land must include the need to preserve the area's natural beauty and make it a more attractive place to visit, thereby encouraging growing numbers of wine tourists. Around the pretty stone villages, magnificent villas with their formal gardens, medieval towers and ancient churches which already decorate the landscape, the terraced vineyards with their pergola trellising and dry-stone walls help to create an atmosphere of abundance and timeless serenity. A future for Soave as a 'Wine Park' is being talked up and already the more energetic wine lover can enjoy the 'Percorso dei 10 Capitelli' or the 'Ten Shrines Way', a 10-kilometre circular walk taking in ten picturesque wayside religious shrines (or *capitelli*) which meanders through some of the most famous vineyards of the Classico area.

Capitello Foscarino, Monteforte d'Alpone

Crops once critically important to the local economy have had to make way as a result of the expansion of the vineyards. The local silk industry was the first to disappear, and now other traditional crops are in severe decline too; cherry farmers in particular complain that their business no longer pays. Verona was once one of the leading centres in Europe for the production of cherries but many are sadly beginning to move away from cultivating the trees which once seemed to be everywhere in the Veronese and which, in springtime, would drape the hillsides in their white blossom. A sense of growing responsibility to protecting the health of the environment may however ensure that some sense of order is maintained. The wine business, it seems, is one of the few agricultural industries where it is still possible to turn a healthy profit; clearly it would be an extremely wise move to invest a substantial proportion of those profits back into preserving the health of the environment.

4

AT THE CELLARS

THE HARVEST

The months of September and October are, in the cellars of both Soave and Valpolicella, the busiest time of the year. Despite the differing ripening times of the varieties, all nonetheless come to full maturity over the same two-month period. Maturity depends on the fruit achieving the right levels and balance of both sugars and acids and, with red grapes in particular, full phenolic ripeness. Phenols are a large group of complex chemical compounds – made up mainly of flavanoids (anthocyanins and tannins, etc.) and different non-flavanoids such as stilbenoids and phenolic acids – which are present in grapes and which affect the colour, taste and 'mouthfeel' of a wine. They arrive at ripeness when the bitter flavours of their unripe state gradually soften and sweeten; when fully ripe they will eventually confer a supple sensation on the palate in the finished wine. The best way of gauging when full ripeness has been reached is, of course, by tasting the fruit. A wine produced from grapes which have not reached full phenolic ripeness will taste green, bitter and astringent. As harvest time approaches, the Veronese winemaker is faced with a number of choices which will in turn determine how the new crop is managed. 'Vintage variables', or weather conditions leading up to and throughout the growing season, play a major part and will guide these decisions appropriately.

The first major issue will be which grapes to set aside for the *appassimento* process. The answer may perhaps seem rather counterintuitive: those selected are not necessarily merely the 'ripest' ones, those with the highest sugar content. The origins of this frequent misunderstanding lie in the production history of Recioto. The term is thought to derive from the Italian word *orecchie* or ears: traditionally only parts of the bunches were selected for drying, the lateral 'wings' or mini clusters located at the top of the main bunch. These, it has been widely assumed, received the most sun and would therefore be riper than the rest. While ripeness is clearly an important factor, it is by no means the sole concern: rather these 'wings' are those that form the most loosely clustered part of the bunch with the maximum amount of space surrounding the individual grapes to allow for as much air circulation around them as possible. When the fruit is more tightly packed, as at the centre of the bunch, the risk of infection by fungal diseases during the lengthy drying period becomes much greater. Those selected for *appassimento* nowadays are usually picked up to as much as two weeks in advance of the main harvest and are chosen on the basis of their healthy appearance and how tightly together the individual berries are packed – clearly the more loosely, the better. They must be free of any sign of rot or damage so as to avoid any precocious fermentation or the development of acetic acid. While the overall shape and compactness of the bunch is one of the main determining factors of the selection procedure, the earlier harvest also means that these grapes will contain high enough acidity levels to ensure a wine of good potential longevity. As this selection happens ahead of the main harvest, the only way to collect the fruit is picking by hand.

The slightly later harvest will be – conditions permitting – of fully ripe fruit, and a certain proportion may also be left on the vine to take on some *sovramaturazione* or 'over-ripening'. In this instance, as the grapes start to shrivel on the vine the must is concentrated naturally through evaporation; the skin cell walls begin to deteriorate and a more intense, richer and softer style of wine is made possible, although a sudden change in the weather can ruin everything. Given the overall quality of the raw materials, winemakers will have a clear idea of how to divide up the fruit at their disposal. As the grapes selected for *appassimento* will already have been set aside, the focus is now on the rest of the crop. The 'freshly picked' grapes will be used to make wines which are either fruit forward, approachable as soon as they are in bottle and so designed for consumption young, or for further maturation in bottle or barrel and are suitable for medium- or long-term ageing. The fermentation policy will then be decided: whether to ferment in stainless steel, cement or wood; whether to age in barrel and if so what size and which type of wood should be used, etc. Inevitably there are points of crossover between the various production methodologies and where basic styles are bridged, including the use of the idiosyncratic *ripasso* technique which has its roots in the ancient feudal system and which will be examined in depth later in this chapter.

WINES FROM FRESHLY GATHERED GRAPES

Producers who bottle their own wine invariably earmark individual batches of fruit for different treatments. For example, most cooperatives will produce a number of different wines under the same denomination, whether from specific vineyard sites or a selection of the finest fruit from a number of different vineyards where particular viticultural practices may have been introduced. The 'range division' will usually take the form of one or more 'premium cuvées' and a 'basic' or entry-level wine. Where the aim is to come up with a wine that is enjoyable from an early stage in its development, a relatively simple and straightforward system of vinification can be applied. When producing a wine that has the capacity to last and even improve in bottle, winemakers have the opportunity to show the full scope of their talents. Fortunately the enterprising Veronesi are great individualists and experimenters, and although the denominations they work within can sometimes lack clarity for the consumer, there is a wealth of *vini d'autore* (individual wines made by quality-conscious producers) waiting to be discovered.

WHITE WINES

Pre-fermentation

In most cases, on arrival at the winery the fruit will be loaded into large V-shaped stainless steel containers from where it is transported by conveyor belt to a de-stemmer/crusher which separates the fruit from the stalks and stems, and lightly crushes the grapes to a semi-liquid pulp by splitting their skins as they pass between rollers. The mass is then pumped through to holding tanks. The must and skins may at this stage be subjected to a 'cold soak' or pre-fermentation maceration for a period of anything up to twenty-four hours, with the addition of sulphites and/or in the presence of an inert gas such as nitrogen, to prevent any undesirable activity from micro-organisms which could cause spoilage. Pectolytic enzymes may be added which, as well as helping to leach out the aroma precursors located in both pulp and skins, will also favour juice extraction. When used, this pre-fermentation maceration will normally take place at cool temperatures of between 5 and 10°C. However, the process is gradually falling out of favour as many producers prefer to extend the period of post-fermentation contact with the lees instead (see below). Some producers will use a combination of the two. The next step is for the must to be left to settle and separate from the solids, a practice known as static decantation. If pectolytic enzymes have been added, they will have helped to accelerate the process through the degradation of the pectic substances present, thus lowering the viscosity of the must. The juice drawn off the solids is known as free-run must (not extracted as a result of pressing) and is ready to be fermented. In some cases the 'cap' of skins and other solids left over may be transferred to the press to extract further juice. However as this part of the mass will inevitably have a higher pH and greater phenolic content, it is usually excluded from so-called quality wine because of the increased risk of bitter and astringent flavours.

Exceptions to the above come with the use of 'whole bunch pressing' where the fruit is loaded straight into the press before being submitted to gentle-enough pressure to allow for extraction of the must with minimal damage to the skins. The presence of stalks in this instance helps to create drainage channels for the juice which in turn improves clarity. The delicate handling of whole bunch pressing for white wines can bring about impressive results without the need for too many technical aids, but is clearly a much more practical solution for smaller batches of fruit. The spontaneous fermentation of must and skins together as championed by the 'Natural Wine' movement is only infrequently encountered at present in the Soave area, though oral tradition maintains that the wine was often made this way in the past. The man to talk to on the subject is Gianni Tessari, owner of Marcato Vini in Ronca. During his time as oenologist at the Tessari family's Ca Rugate estate, Gianni made several vintages of a wine called Bucciato because it was partially fermented on the skins (*bucce*) of Garganega grapes. The wine was intended as a testament to the particular local practice (in smaller wineries) of making wine in this way which had virtually died out with the introduction of improved technology in the 1960s. For now Bertani are one of the very few to maintain the tradition: their Vintage Edition Soave is in part made this way. Meanwhile Filippo Filippi at Castelcerino, for example, is certainly prepared to produce wines that rely only to a very limited extent on the use of technology but, at the same time, remains a true individualist. Though Marinella Camerano in the Mezzane valley produces a so-called 'orange wine' by fermenting Chardonnay grapes in cement tanks, her Soave DOC wine follows a more conventional vinification regime. Andrea Fiorini Carbognin, who works a small parcel of Garganega vines at Montecchia di Crosara, produces a DOC Soave called 'Garganuda' which some claim to be the first 'Natural' Soave and which shows some promise. His first vintage was 2014 and so far production is limited to a few thousand bottles only. On a broader footing, the use of indigenous yeasts and minimal temperature control is slowly becoming more popular as more and more winemakers are prepared to take the leap of faith required in pursuit of a more 'natural' product. Some question the authenticity of these methods, particularly the use of so-called 'indigenous' yeasts, just as others claim that the use of added tartaric acid to achieve the desired overall balance is far more common than might at first appear. Some secrets are best left in the cellar.

Fermentation

Stainless steel and cement

Most wineries in Soave embrace the principle of close control over the vinification process when the objective is to capture and preserve the primary aromas and flavours of the various varieties in a wine to be enjoyed young. Stainless steel fermentors are by and large standard throughout the area as they allow the winemaker to have a quick and efficient means of control over the temperature of the fermenting must. They help avoid oxidation, make monitoring fermentation simple and straightforward, and are also much easier to keep sterile. However, a growing number of wineries – such as Pieropan, Bertani and Roccolo Grassi – declare a preference for cement. Not only is the lack of temperature fluctuation that cement guarantees seen as a major benefit but also, as Nino Pieropan explains, wine needs a tranquil environment in which to develop away from the turbulence caused by the electrostatic charges that stainless steel tanks are sensitive to. Some wineries prefer to work with epoxy resin-lined cement though others argue that unvarnished cement combines the flavour neutrality of stainless steel with the porosity of wood and therefore represents the best of both worlds. Cement tanks first appeared in the area shortly before the Second World War while stainless steel was introduced in the 1970s.

Yeasts for larger batches of fruit to be fermented in inert materials are generally cultured to ensure a clean, smooth and linear fermentation, though the cachet of using indigenous yeasts – a technique known as 'wild ferment' – is sometimes preferred for premium wines. As white wines inherently lack the natural preservatives that are found in the skins of red grapes, fermentations tend to be carried out anaerobically in closed-top fermentors where the carbon dioxide released by the fermenting juice will protect the contents from spoilage by oxygen or harmful bacteria. Temperatures are generally maintained between approximately 14 and 16°C, at which level the integrity of fruit aromas and flavours remains as far as possible intact and the extraction of less desirable elements is avoided. As the activity of the yeasts is slowed by the relatively low temperatures the process can take up to ten days or so. A few producers such as Nardello will allow temperatures to climb slightly higher after the fermentation process is complete in order to disperse any remaining carbon dioxide more effectively.

Either at the beginning or, more likely, towards the end of the fermentation, the winemaker will check and modify the wine's composition if necessary. The addition of tartaric acid to improve the overall balance of the wine may be required, particularly in warmer vintages when the levels of acid in the grapes turn out to be lower than desired. This adjustment will help to maintain a low pH which allows, amongst other benefits, for the more effective use of sulphur dioxide, and lower dosage levels will be necessary. De-acidification of the must is rarely practised though may be deemed necessary in the occasional particularly unripe vintage such as 2014. At the end of fermentation in stainless steel or cement the wine is often left to rest for a couple of days under the protection of the blanket of the carbon dioxide produced during the fermentation. The addition of sulphur (in many cases for the first time during vinification) will usually take place immediately prior to the first racking of the wine.

Wood

It is easy to forget that the most traditional vessel for fermenting wine, of whatever colour, is of course wood (the use of earthenware amphorae has a far more episodic track record down the ages). When choosing to ferment a white wine in barrel, the modern winemaker's intention is primarily to boost breadth of aroma and flavour as well as texture, and produce a wine which will in time fully integrate the characteristic features of wood fermentation to become a harmonious whole. Fermentation barrels are with very occasional exceptions made of oak, typically either French or Slavonian. Both types are quite tightly grained and there is thus a relatively delicate extraction of aromatic and flavouring elements. There are many advantages of wood for fermentation, especially when followed by an extended ageing period in the same barrel. In addition to conferring aromas and flavours on the toasted bread, vanilla and nut spectrum, these include the protection from both oxidation and 'reduced' characters provided by the wood tannins, the fuller and richer texture or 'creamy mouthfeel' that wood imparts, and – of course – the effect on the structure of the wine and its consequent potential longevity. The main drawbacks are the initial cost of the barrels which need to be renewed on a fairly regular basis, the high level of maintenance involved and the fact that oak may mask the aromatic expression of a younger wine (depending of course on the age and size of vessel). Regarding the size of barrel, there are many options from the familiar 225-litre barrique, the increasingly common 500-litre tonneau through to classic Italian *botti* of varying capacities. The old-fashioned *tini* – upright, conically shaped wooden tanks of different sizes – are making a comeback too and can be found in a number of wineries nowadays. Many of the larger oak fermentors will even have some means of controlling temperature built in: the presence of a central coil or pillar containing glycol or similar coolant, for example. With smaller barrels, ambient conditions remain the principal means of control over fermentation as temperatures climb owing to the action of the yeasts which generate heat as they work.

Post-fermentation

Most examples of Soave do not undergo the secondary or malolactic fermentation that is pretty much indispensable for red wines in order to maintain freshness and crisp acidity in the final product. The malolactic, or MLF, can be avoided by taking a number of simple steps. Early racking and the addition of sulphur dioxide following fermentation will reduce the presence of nutrients left in the newly made wine and inhibit the growth of the bacteria responsible for provoking the transformation of malic into the softer and more gentle lactic acid. Cool cellar and fermentation temperatures are a further means of 'blocking the malo', as the process generally requires a relatively high range from around 16°C upwards. In any case, the Garganega grape typically has a relatively low malic acid content compared to other white varieties. Generally speaking, where less technology is employed, the greater is the likelihood of the malolactic being completed.

White wines vinified in stainless steel or cement are left for varying lengths of time on their fine lees after racking off the more solid deposits left over from fermentation. These lees are primarily composed of dead yeast cells but can still add much to the aroma and flavour of the wine. If the wine is destined for youthful consumption it will spend just a short time on the lees before bottling in the spring following the harvest. A wine with some ageing potential will generally remain in contact longer. The aromas and flavours produced through yeast autolysis have certain aspects in common with those of wood fermentation/maturation, and in particular the notes of bread crusts and toast that are directly associated with yeast. These are created from the interaction between the wine and the various compounds (such as mannoproteins and polysaccharides like glucose) released as the yeast cells break down. The lees also absorb oxygen thus boosting the wine's stability by helping to prevent oxidation. Contact with the lees can continue to enrich a wine over a long period (as seen with the *méthode champenoise* process, to state the most obvious example). On the whole up to twelve months on the lees is not uncommon for 'premium' Soave, but an intrepid few will go even further, up to some eighteen months in total – for example, the Sandro de Bruno winery at Montecchia di Crosara or Filippo Fillipi at Castelcerino.

When the wine has been fermented in wood it may remain on what are known as the 'total' rather than 'fine' lees. Surprisingly perhaps, this approach can – owing to the number of complex chemical interactions between yeasts, wine and wood – produce a wine with a less yellow colour and a lower tannin content than the same wine aged on fine lees in tank (see Ribereau-Gayon et al.'s *The Handbook of Enology*). In simple terms, the total lees act as a natural fining agent and bind with the slightly bitter-tasting ellagic tannins to reduce the perceived tannin content. While the wood characters arising from barrel fermentation will thus be less pronounced if the wine is left in contact with its total lees, it can quickly lose fruit characters and develop oxidative aromas owing to a relative lack of structure if racked off too soon.

When aged *sur lie* in either inert containers (cement or stainless steel) or in wood, the key element is lees stirring (the French term *battonage* is widely used in the Veronese). Periodic *battonage* helps keep the lees in suspension, thereby maximizing their contact with the wine to enhance both texture and complexity of flavour. There are additional benefits: in stainless steel the potential pitfalls of reductive winemaking can be kept at bay as lees stirring potentially exposes the wine to a limited amount of aeration. (Those pitfalls are the formation of volatile sulphur compounds including hydrogen sulphide – the foul 'rotten eggs' smell – and various mercaptans and other sulphides/disulphides.) The passage of some air though the porosity of the wood (or unlined cement) carries out a similar function, so the risk of 'reduced' aromas is diminished with barrel or cement storage. *Battonage* thus performs a remarkable double role: helping to protect the wine against oxidation through the absorption of oxygen by the yeasts while at the same time buffering the formation of undesirable volatile sulphur compounds. Performed on a regular basis, *battonage* is an essential part of the production regime in maintaining young wine in a healthy state. Regular topping up will be required throughout barrel ageing as there is loss of liquid through evaporation: like the effect of lees stirring, this exercise also allows the wine a controlled amount of exposure to oxygen. At the end of the lees-ageing process, the wine is ready for any final pre-bottling treatment, including cold stabilization, fining and microfiltration.

RED WINES

While many of the principles outlined above relating to white wine production can be applied equally to red wines, there are also a number of fundamental differences in approach. On arrival at the winery the red grapes will usually undergo a light crushing: the juice will not at this stage be separated from the grape solids (skins, stalks, pulp and pips) from which colouring materials, tannins and aromatic substances will be extracted during fermentation. If the must and solids are not to undergo cold soak treatment, and this is usually the case in the Veronese, they will be transferred directly to the fermentation tanks. As with whites, the type of vessel will be determined by the style of wine the winemaker has decided to produce. The three options are almost invariably either cement, stainless steel or wood. Given the lighter, fresher, fruit forward style of the simplest Veronese reds (i.e., youthful Valpolicella), it might be assumed that the use of the *maceration carbonique* technique best known for producing Beaujolais would be in quite widespread use. However, this method, which involves the fermentation of whole berries in an atmosphere saturated with carbon dioxide prior to crushing, is rarely encountered although Cantina di Negrar have experimented with the production of a 'Novello' style wine released just a couple of months after the vintage.

Fermentation

Fermentation revolves around the transformation into ethanol (ethyl alcohol) of the fructose and glucose sugars present in grape juice through the action of yeasts. Optimum conditions involve a combination of the right temperatures, an adequate presence of the nitrogenous substances upon which the yeasts depend for sustenance and reproduction and, in the case of red wines, various tannins which will help stabilize colour in the early stages. While the yeasts present on the grape skins and within the atmosphere of the winery may be sufficient to provoke the start of a 'spontaneous' ferment, most winemakers will decide to exercise stricter control by adding alcohol-tolerant cultured yeasts to help steer the process in the direction of pre-determined stylistic traits. This is frequently the case with simpler styles of wine though with certain batches of fruit or in some of the area's smaller wineries, the idea of relying on the unique characters of the microflora of a particular vineyard – or the cellar itself – is an attractive proposition. However, such yeasts are less resistant to alcohol and more likely to promote the development of volatile acids which will in turn cause off flavours, so even greater care and attention is required. An increasingly popular solution to the dilemma is for a winery to replicate and propagate versions of 'personalized' yeasts in their own laboratory.

Fermentation temperatures for red wines are generally speaking at least a couple of degrees higher than those used for whites. Lower temperatures up to around 22°C help to maintain primary aromas (those directly related to the aromas of the fresh grapes themselves) while higher temperatures around 30°C favour the extraction of colouring materials, phenolic compounds and tannins. The role of temperature is thus primarily to control the speed of fermentation as the chemical reactions of the process itself force temperatures to rise. Higher alcohol levels will also help to put a brake on the activity of the yeasts, so the two features function in tandem especially towards the end of fermentation. Young Valpolicella wines, for example, benefit from a lower temperature range in that their typical perfumes depend on a high concentration of volatile esters which are more easily lost through evaporation in warmer conditions.

Another key factor in red wine is the maceration period when the fermenting must remains in contact with grape solids and, in particular, the skins which contain both colouring and aromatic elements. Maceration may partly take place pre-fermentation (the 'cold soak' option) but becomes of critical importance during the first or alcoholic fermentation. There are several variations all of which have the same objective: to maximize the extraction of colouring, flavouring, textural and structural elements. All involve mixing up the cap of floating solids forced up to the top of the fermentation vessel by the carbon dioxide produced during fermentation with the fermenting liquid. The most common is known as remontage (*rimontaggio* in Italian) or 'pumping over', where the liquid drawn off from under the cap is pumped back over the solids. The process, sometimes continuous, is repeated on a regular basis, with frequency determined by the required style of wine – for instance, more often when the aim is to extract the maximum amount of colouring as quickly as possible in the case of wines for early consumption. Another common practice is *follatura* or 'punching down' where the cap is broken up with poles and then held down under the surface. This operation is frequently encountered in smaller wineries with limited resources but can be carried out automatically as well. A third variation, known as *capello sommerso* or the 'submerged cap' system, involves the installation of a metal grille part way down the tank to prevent the cap from rising above the surface of the fermenting juice. As the contact is therefore prolonged and a greater extraction of phenolic substances brought about, this method is more suitable for the production of wines which will require further ageing. A fourth alternative, always referred to under its French name, is *délestage* where the juice is drawn off the solids and transferred to another tank leaving the cap to settle and drain. This provides an opportunity for the winemaker to get rid of grape seeds left in the mix of solids through coarse filtration as they contain various bitter tasting tannins and phenols. The wine is then pumped into the original container back over the cap. This technique is especially useful with old-style concrete tanks, for example, where other options such as *follatura* may be less practicable. Maceration can last from seven days for young reds up to around three weeks for ones destined for ageing. A further technique, the use of roto-fermentors, offers winemakers the option of a shorter maceration time where the extraction of colour, etc. comes about through the 'spinning' effect of the horizontal stainless steel cylinder which maximizes contact between liquid and solids. This produces a full, ripe, deeply-coloured wine which more traditionally-minded producers argue lacks the *tipicita* and some of the delicacy associated with Valpolicella.

Unlike Soave, Valpolicella wines undergo the malolactic fermentation as a matter of course. In a red wine which already has a high acid content and will often make a certain degree of astringency a virtue, any residue of harsh-tasting malic acid (think of sour green apples) is considered wholly inappropriate. The way in which the MLF is managed will again depend on the style of wine to be produced. In a wine due for early release, it is important that the malo is performed as quickly as possible, ideally immediately after the alcoholic fermentation. The safest way to bring this about is through the addition of lactic acid bacteria but, if before the first racking is carried out, temperatures are maintained above 16°C and levels of sulphur dioxide are kept low, the conditions are ideal for the process to be completed without further intervention, as these bacteria will in any case be present naturally in the wine. As well as reducing the acidity levels, the completed malolactic also gives the wine a softer and rounder mouthfeel. In wines which will spend further time at the winery, it is less critical that the malo be carried out so quickly and some winemakers are content to wait for the rise in ambient temperatures in the spring. Indeed the idea of having the MLF happen in the same barrel in which the wine will subsequently age is often preferred by those who claim this offers a more complete integration of oak and fruit characters.

Wood ageing

A spell in barrel will affect the colour, aroma, flavour and structure of a red wine. The mechanics of the process are brought about through an alternation between oxidative and reductive ageing conditions. Oxygen will be present in the wine either as a result of racking or through the porosity of the wood, but conditions become reductive when the remaining yeasts and lees consume the oxygen within an anaerobic environment. The ability to manage this balance is the key to achieving a successful period of wood (or alternatively cement) ageing. Between the two extremes lie the dangers of, on the one hand, the formation of the unpleasant smelling, sulphur-based compounds which characterize reduced aromas and, on the other, oxidation where the wine will gradually lose colour, freshness and fruit. The former can happen where sulphur – added as a prophylactic or present in low levels naturally in the wine – has combined with other molecules such as thiols. Once more, phenols have a fundamental role to play as they also consume oxygen so that a wine rich in anthocyanins and tannins will age (or resist the oxidative process) better. Wood releases substances which interact with wine and these have a significant role to play in the development of flavour and aroma, though a loss of both colour and aroma will inevitably occur if the wine remains too long in barrel.

Wood type and size are both major considerations. To begin with capacity, it is logical that the smaller the barrel, the greater the influence of the wood given the proportional increase of contact between the two surface areas. In contrast, with a large barrel (in certain cases up to a capacity of close to 300 hectolitres with almost every conceivable volume in between), where the proportion of wine to wood is much smaller, the effect of the exchange is less pronounced. The age of the wood will also have a marked effect: smaller barrels 'have currency' or remain valid for up to five to seven years, though they are at their most active in the first two to three years of use. Larger barrels often remain in use for decades and become, as the years pass, almost neutral ageing containers as their contribution to the development of smell and taste diminishes over time. Regarding the type of wood, French and Slavonian oak are the most popular for reds although a number of others once far more common in the area are creeping back into the frame. These include chestnut, cherry, acacia and even, very occasionally, mulberry. The first two were once relatively popular though the decline of chestnut is largely unchecked owing to its dangerously high porosity and the rather harsh and hard tannins it confers. Cherry wood is less widely available than it used to be in the area given the gradual disappearance of cherry orchards over the last few decades though several wineries, including notably Antolini, Bertani, Corte Sant'Alda, Santi and Masi (Serego Alighieri), continue to use cherrywood barrels on a regular basis. Indeed the Antolini brothers use all the woods mentioned above and Pier Paolo has characteristically clear thoughts on the advantages and disadvantages of each (see below). Mention must also be made of American oak among the various types of barrel seen in the Veronese. Like the common European oaks *Quercus robur* and *Quercus petraea*, *Quercus alba* is a white oak and is widely manufactured into barrels for use in the drinks Industry. American oak barrels are generally less favoured in European cellars because of their highly aromatic nature: much of this character comes from a chemical compound called methyl octalactone (also known as the whiskey lactone), and which introduces strong notes of caramel, cocoa, coconut and, in particular, maple syrup, often deemed excessive for use with wine in anything but the smallest measures.

The oak staves from which barrels are constructed are not usually left in their raw state before the container is filled with wine and are normally steamed and/or toasted during production. Steaming makes the wood more pliable and is essential in order to bend each stave to the required curve. Toasting will usually be done over an open flame: this operation will help to soften the tannins in the wood as well as giving the basic flavours of the raw wood, spicy notes and the well-known vanilla tones that are so closely associated with new oak barrels and in particular 225-litre French barriques. In this case the action of toasting facilitates the release of vanillin from the cellulose in the wood. Toasting is carried out to different levels or strengths: a high toast will bring out these aromas and flavours in quite an aggressive way while medium through to light toasts will have a lesser impact. Barrels can also be charred but in this state they are rarely if ever used for wine and, like barrels made from *Quercus alba*, are perhaps of greater importance in the ageing of whisk(e)y.

Regarding the aromas and flavours that oak barrels in particular bring, this happens over a course of time through the interaction between the wine and some of the complex chemical compounds the wood is composed of. As well as the volatile phenols responsible for vanillin notes, the process of carbohydrate degradation leads to the development of sweet and toasty aromas while oak lactones introduce woody notes and various terpenes confer aromas of tea and tobacco, etc. But it is the mixture of wood and grape tannins which are fundamental to creating the structural nuances of velvety, textural notes prized by all lovers of red wines and which are brought about through the chemical process known as polymerization (or the gradual formation of longer molecular chains of condensed tannins which repeatedly break up and re-form during the ageing process). The degree to which these influences are more or less noticeable in the finished product is governed by the wine's length of stay in wood, which can be anything from a matter of months to several years.

WINES FROM SEMI-DRIED GRAPES

The *appassimento* process

While some form of dessert wine is made in most wine-producing areas, the method of production will differ radically from region to region as well as from country to country. Where a reliably warm and dry climate extends though into the early autumn (typical of southern Mediterranean countries), the harvested fruit is left on straw mats to dry in the sun – for example, the French *vin de paille* or, closer to home, the Passito wines from the island of Pantelleria, to name but two. Towards the northern edges of the European vine-growing belt, for instance in parts of the Mosel and Rhine valleys, selected grapes will even be exposed to mid autumn's sub-zero temperatures and left to partially freeze on the plant before being made into Eiswein. Clearly the climate of an area will determine what can or cannot be done to concentrate the sugar content of the crop. For centuries the drying of grapes was a way of preserving the fresh fruit and the means whereby stronger and more stable wines could be produced. They became known as Passito wines (from the verb *appassire*, to wither or shrivel) and they were able to be kept for longer thanks to higher sugar and alcohol levels. Throughout Italy, when macerated together with herbs and other aromatic substances, wines of this style were thought to have medicinal properties and would serve as palliative roborants at a time when no other form of medication was available. They were the original tonic wines which subsequently evolved into the 'digestivo-style' products such as Amaro which still have a massive following in the south of the country. Gradually, though, the focus changed, with the aim of capitalizing on the extra richness and intensity of both aroma and flavour which the process delivers, to produce a more highly-prized wine which could typically accompany the sweet course or indeed act as a 'meditation' wine. In central and more northern parts of Italy an 'indoor' method of production was necessary owing to the drop in temperatures and rise in humidity levels that accompany the increased risk of inclement weather in the period following on from the harvest. Nowhere, however, is the practice of drying grapes to be processed into wine so widespread as it is in Soave and, in particular, Valpolicella. While originally the fruit was – as elsewhere – processed for the production of sweet or dessert wines, over the last century a much drier style has steadily evolved to meet more modern tastes and has proven to be a resounding success. As a result the operation has become big business during the last two or three months of the calendar year throughout the many villages of the Valpolicella area. Huge industrial-sized warehouses are crammed from floor to ceiling with layers of plastic crates filled with grapes. The drying process is fully automated, with giant fans to keep the air moving and the extra insurance of dehumidifying machines to protect against rot. This is the modern face of *appassimento*: it is of course a far cry from the traditional method which remained by and large unaltered for centuries.

As we have seen, the art of grape drying in the Veronese has been practised since Roman times when fruit was left to shrivel on fibre matting. By the sixth century the process had become more sophisticated; Cassiodorus described the painstaking operation of suspending each individual grape cluster from strings or threads hung vertically from the ceiling, a procedure which anticipates the modern obsession with avoiding the onset of rot. Whether the two systems continued side by side is not recorded, nor when, potentially to save space and to some extent labour, the Veronesi reverted back to the original method of laying the grapes out horizontally. This development may well have occurred as a result of the arrival of the silkworm-farming industry during the latter half of the sixteenth century and was certainly in common practice by the eighteenth. Racks known as *arele* were used to bring on the silkworm larvae when they became active in the spring. The larvae would feed on their staple diet of mulberry leaves spread out over the *arele*, making the later operation of 'harvesting' the cocoons of silk spun as the animal entered its pupal phase more practical. Over the winter months, before the eggs had hatched, it is logical to assume that the *arele* may well have been put to another use: it is entirely consistent with the resilient and resourceful character of Veronese farmers that the few tools of the trade they possessed would have been used in as many ways as possible. Stacking the racks one on top of another would have been a simple and straightforward way of optimizing storage space. Drying the grapes by laying them out is, in a way, less efficient than suspending the grapes from netting where the laborious task of frequently turning the fruit over to expose each side of the bunch to the passage of air is bypassed and a quick visual check is sufficient. However, turning the bunches regularly these days is not always a practical reality and perhaps not even strictly necessary given the almost industrial scale of the operation where 'controlled' *appassimento* is employed. Where plastic crates are used, and they are by far the most common container, the bottom is usually a perforated diagonal lattice which will therefore permit some air to circulate.

Nowadays bunches are once more laid out to dry, though racks or more commonly wooden or plastic crates are used instead of mats. Those wineries which stick with the traditional system of using the *arele* champion bamboo as the best material for its construction. The canes are lashed together and the gaps between them allow for some passage of air to help maintain the fruit in a healthy state. The hard, round surface of bamboo means that any leakage from the grapes therefore runs off the material rather than being absorbed, thus minimizing the subsequent risk of spoilage. In addition, bamboo is an extremely durable wood and will not need to be renewed with any great frequency. Some however argue that wooden crates are useful precisely because they absorb humidity and thus reduce the risk of infection by grey rot. Meanwhile other wineries prefer plastic to the flimsier wooden crates as not only are they more durable but, crucially, much easier to sterilize and keep clean. Whichever material has been chosen, these plateaux – as they are also known – are stacked together sometimes within an open framework, stretching almost from floor to ceiling in a designated *fruttaio* or drying room often situated on the top floor of the winery building. The time-honoured preference for siting the *fruttaio* in small buildings adjacent to hillside vineyards is still widely in evidence: producers point to the fact that these are ideal locations in order to benefit from the drier and windier positions higher up the slopes. During the initial phases of *appassimento,* when the fruit is most at risk from infection, the simple expedient of opening windows during drier spells and then closing them again when humidity levels threaten to rise maximizes the chances of maintaining the integrity of the crop throughout the process. The fruit is considered to be at its most vulnerable in terms of infection by grey rot during the first fifteen days. Often the *fruttaio* will be equipped with fans, and sometimes with dehumidifiers as well, as growers look to safeguard the health of the harvest they have spent the previous eight months or so working hard to realize.

Many producers rely on a very practical combination of the two approaches: the 'natural' or traditional, artisan way and 'assisted' *appassimento* which incorporates the use of machines to control the drying conditions. A classic example of this pragmatic modus operandi would be Masi's so-called NASA method (Natural *Appassimento* Super Assisted). Having collected and studied the effects of data relating to temperature, humidity, weight variations and ventilation over a number of favourable vintages, Masi looked to reproduce the conditions which can ensure an ideal environment for the drying grapes. Basically the idea is to measure and monitor ambient conditions and then modify them when necessary through the use of fans and dehumidifiers which kick in automatically when required. Masi developed this computer-operated system at their drying room at Garganago and the firm have a further twelve drying lofts at different locations. At the same time, Masi are adamant that the best conditions for the process include the storage of fruit on the classic *arele,* and furthermore are strong advocates for the influence of another 'natural' phenomenon which also continues to divide opinion.

The movement towards 'mechanically assisted' *appassimento* can, in real terms, be traced back to the early 1990s and in particular to the mercurial Franco Allegrini, owner and oenologist at the eponymous Fumane-based wine house. Franco identifies 1990 as the first great modern vintage for Amarone: 'In terms of climate, 1990 was an extraordinarily good vintage with no rain during the harvest and a dry autumn too. As a result, we had a crop of perfectly healthy grapes and we were able to maintain their integrity through to the finished product. That's the sort of wine I was looking for! But how could I continue to work at that level even in less favourable years? High humidity is almost standard in our area in the autumn months. The only solution was to try and control the drying process. That's where the idea of constructing a dedicated *fruttaio* came from. No more leaving things to chance! We could take charge of the whole process and get rid of rot.'

Having lost the entire *appassimento* crop of the 1987 vintage owing to an outbreak of grey rot, Franco was determined not to let that happen again. Roberto Ferrarini had completed his doctorate thesis at the University of Bologna at the end of the 1970s on the very topic of a new system of *appassimento* designed to protect the integrity of the raw materials. He built upon the pioneering studies into the subject in the 1970s of Professor Luciano Usseglio Tommaset, director of the oenological research centre at Asti in Piedmont. Under Ferrarini's guidance, Franco and a group of like-minded producers set about creating the first controlled *appassimento* warehouse close to the centre of the village of Fumane.

However, the presence of that same mould which destroyed Franco's crop can, in certain very particular conditions, have a potentially positive effect on the drying fruit according to a number of die-hard producers, Masi foremost among them. In its fully developed form as grey rot, the fungus can only have negative implications and any grapes showing telltale signs must be discarded immediately to stop the infection spreading. However, if the pathogenesis is limited it may take the form of so-called noble rot or *muffa nobile*, famous for its role in the creation of dessert wines like Sauternes and Tokaji Aszù. According to wine writer and researcher Dr Ronald S. Jackson, latent infections of the pathogen occur predominantly during the spring but may remain inactive. Under cool and dry storage conditions such as *appassimento*, the infection in its so-called 'larval' form is slowly rekindled. With the nascent infection there is little visible surface sporulation (unlike in the vineyard environment) and as well as further shrivelling, the colour of the infected fruit gradually becomes paler, changing from a deep, dark red and taking on more of a translucent lilac hue. In Soave, the colour of Garganega also modifies and the distinctly pink tinge typical of the ripe fruit will intensify. This 'larval' stage of *Botrytis cinerea* is kept in check by cool temperatures but, above all, by low humidity with the risk of the infection reaching its fully 'efflorescent' form more likely to occur under milder and rainier conditions.

One of the main effects of *muffa nobile* on the composition of the fruit will be the formation of higher than average levels of glycerol, evident in the finished wine as a luscious mouthfeel and an illusory sense of sweetness as many of the bitter and astringent qualities will seem softer accordingly. Modification of the aromatic components will also occur with the development of dried fruit notes and the classic 'honeyed' quality associated with botrytis, though this will be accompanied by a certain loss of freshness owing to a negative effect on monoterpenoids, esters and thiols. There are numerous other potential drawbacks including the formation of acetic acid, acetaldehyde and ethyl acetate, all of which are potentially damaging, as well as the production of laccase by the botrytis, one of the principal factors behind colour change and aroma loss. This oxidative enzyme acts on both anthocyanins, causing a certain browning of colour, and phenols, leading to the development of oxidative style aromas. *Muffa nobile* can then be a double-edged sword and its presence must be carefully limited to restrict the effect of its negative features. Overall, an Amarone which has experienced the effect of *muffa nobile* will display the round and luscious mouthfeel referred to above, along with sensations of extreme ripeness and preserved or macerated fruits; those wines without and which depend on maintaining the integrity of the grape skins, will typically have a deeper colour and a more structured and austere style with greater freshness of fruit characters. The production of the natural phenol resveratrol by the fruit as a form of protection against the pathogen is often talked up, though whether this stilbenoid has the health-sustaining properties some claim is open to debate.

It is of course tempting to buy into the somewhat romantic notion of a fine red wine which derives some of its character from partially botrytized fruit. 'Extremists' who defend the old ways argue that modern *appassimento* results merely in a concentration of aroma and flavour, and the nuances associated with the 'natural' method and *muffa nobile* are lacking in the final wine. There is some body of evidence to support such claims. Various experiments have seen grapes inoculated with botrytis and then stored under humidity- and temperature-controlled conditions before going on to produce creditable botrytized wines (see Batt et al.'s *Encyclopedia of Food Microbiology*, 2014); this would seem to demonstrate that the precarious task of managing botrytized fruit successfully is more than just a fantasy. However, many Amarone producers prefer not to expose their fruit to the risk of spoilage, embracing instead the security of controlled *appassimento* and the elimination of rot.

In some ways it's a similar story in Soave, though on a much reduced scale, of course; the two issues of how the grapes are stored and whether or not any presence at all of botrytis should be tolerated remain of critical importance. However, while the tradition of working with semi-dried grapes in Soave has roots that are as deep as those in neighbouring Valpolicella, the focus is more on keeping the tradition alive. While most of the major wineries in Soave continue to produce Recioto, it is usually in tiny quantities (currently around 0.25 per cent of the total of the various different Soave DOC and DOCG wines produced). The wine remains very much a niche product even though it deserves far greater recognition. Recioto di Soave and Recioto della Valpolicella share that common lineage which can be traced back at least as far as the sixth century AD and the Roman statesman Cassiodorus, though a parallel tradition, recently undergoing what might be termed a micro-revival, evolved in the small *frazione* of Brognoligo, part of the township of Monteforte d'Alpone. According to author and painter Massimiliano Bertolazzi, who hails from Monteforte, references to a local wine known as Vin Santo may be traced back to the early eighteenth century. The production of Vin Santo di Brognoligo has been maintained at very much a local family level with 'recipes' handed down from generation to generation. Gelmino Dal Bosco, owner and winemaker of Le Battistelle, explained his family's approach: 'The best grapes we would leave to dry and make Vin Santo. Every family would make some and save it for important occasions such as a marriage or the birth of a child. So we'd choose the best fruit from the oldest vines and dry the bunches until January or February until they looked just right, not too shrivelled. Then we'd press them and put the juice into *damigiane* and they'd be left there for six or seven years.' Sadly the production of Vin Santo di Brognoligo, which can only be sold as an IGT wine, has dwindled since Recioto di Soave was included in the Soave DOC discipline and became a more important focus of attention. In 2008, for example, the Dal Bosco family made just 108 litres of the wine divided between two demijohns. Tasted in spring 2016, the 2007 was still remarkably fresh, luscious and perfumed. A more studied example of Vin Santo is available commercially, albeit in minuscule quantities (250 bottles a year) from the well-known Ca Rugate winery. Michele Tessari outlined how their Corte Durlo is made: 'We dry carefully selected Garganega grapes on strings known as *picai* which are hung from the rafters for three or four months. We ferment in wooden casks and with some contact with the air so the wine develops a type of protective flor we call the *teralina*. Then we transfer the wine to smaller barrels to finish the fermentation. Finally we seal the bung hole with cement and leave it to mature for six years.' Corte Durlo is produced as a Veneto Bianco Passito IGT wine and only in favourable years. Proceeds from sales go to the parish of Brognoligo: 'When my great-grandfather died in 1918, the church was a great comfort to my family,' explains Tessari. 'Firstly my grandfather, then my father and now me, we've always honoured our debt of gratitude.' Azienda Agricola Portinari, another small Brognoligo-based winery, also produce a version of Vin Santo which the family refer to as a Passito d'Oro (golden Passito), named Anna Giulia after Umberto's granddaughter.

Meanwhile in wineries like Coffele and Pieropan it is still possible to see nets of drying bunches suspended from the rafters in the time-honoured manner (Pieropan also make use of the traditional *arele*). Here the question of *Botrytis cinerea* is also dealt with in a much more relaxed fashion: for example, Pieropan see noble rot as an important element in the production of their DOCG Recioto Le Colombare. A mid-2000s study carried out by E. Tosi, R. Verzillo, A. Marangon and G. Zapparoli – *The effect of Botrytis cinera on the quality of Recioto di Soave* – was reported in the Informatore Agrario periodical in 2006. The researchers conducted a series of 'microvinifications' on musts obtained from both botrytized and 'non-infected' fruit with interesting results. Clear differences in the colour, smell and taste were recorded: the so-called 'clean' must producing a paler wine with fresher, less evolved fruit aromas and less evident richness and sweetness on the palate, whereas those containing proportions of must from 'infected' fruit were of a deeper golden colour, with more nuanced and honeyed aromas and a greater sensation of sweetness. A subsequent study by many of the same group published in 2013 came to similar conclusions, noting that noble rot had a marked effect on the volatile components of the wine (notably various esters, phenols and lactones) which in turn influence aroma, flavour and structure. The positive side of noble rot is, it must be pointed out, generally much more closely associated with white wines so a more obvious 'match' is immediately apparent. Relatively free from the pressure of commercial incentives and logistical considerations, wineries like those mentioned above can devote as much time as they see fit to the production of a truly authorial style of wine.

Aside from the issues of botrytis and drying methodology, and irrespective of the colour of the fruit, the primary effect of drying grapes is the substantial loss of weight which the process brings about.

It is estimated that the grapes will lose on average between about 40 to 60 per cent of their weight through evaporation during *appassimento* as the water content in the pulp and juice of the fruit is slowly lost. The production regulations that cover both Amarone and the two forms of Recioto all specify a strict maximum volume of wine, not exceeding 40 per cent (or 42 for the rare Recioto di Soave Spumante), which can be extracted from the original mass of fruit that has been set aside. Such a substantial decrease can only be arrived at over a considerable length of time: in both Soave and Valpolicella pressing the semi-dried fruit for conversion into the DOCG wines is not, under normal circumstances, permitted to take place before 1 December following the vintage, a minimum of around two months, though in real terms the process will frequently last much longer. Some may argue that the decision of when to press should be based on a more precise chemical analysis of the components of the fruit, but the rules enshrine a principle which most uphold: the idea that such a highly-nuanced wine cannot be hurried and requires time in the cellar and patience on behalf of the producer in order to achieve its full potential. What distinguishes Recioto and Amarone from other *passito* wines made elsewhere is indeed the length of time for which the fruit is left to dry. Many wineries will, in the case of red varieties, delay pressing until the beginning of the New Year if possible (which equates to a period of approximately three months), whereas it is common with Garganega to put off the start of the winemaking process until March, or even in some extreme cases Easter, when the grapes will have been drying for six months and may have lost as much as 70 per cent of their original weight. The final decision will always be determined by a combination of climatic conditions and the level of 'readiness' of the concentrated fruit the winemaker is searching for. This is why the real success of a vintage in Verona cannot be measured merely in terms of the health of the fruit at harvest time: weather patterns during the autumn and early winter play a major part too and will either compromise or confirm the quality of the crop that has been set aside for drying.

The main changes brought about by *appassimento* are the increased levels of sugar and glycerol; the balance between glucose and fructose sugars is tilted in favour of the latter which are sweeter tasting as the glucose sugars are partly transformed into glycerine and gluconic acid. Many of the other components of the fruit such as aromatic substances, acid levels and colouring materials, are also affected. For example, as the ratio of skin to pulp will be higher – up to as much as 35 per cent in some cases by the end of process – so the level of normally stable anthocyanins increases proportionately as the water content diminishes. This same principle will apply to other constituent elements, one reason why the acidity levels in these wines give such a remarkable sense of freshness.

The speed of *appassimento*, as regulations recognize, is governed by the three variables of temperature, humidity and air circulation. Higher temperatures speed up the process, as does greater ventilation, while a rise in humidity levels will slow things down (with a correspondingly increased risk of grey rot infection). The production discipline is once again designed to cover these potentially contentious issues: where ventilation and dehumidification is practised, neither may take place at any other than ambient temperatures. Low temperatures are indeed vital for maintaining constant levels of polyphenols and anthocyanins which become less stable in warmer conditions when the added danger of ending up with slightly cooked or caramelized flavours also applies. For the record it should also be noted that the various grape varieties will react differently to the *appassimento* process. Corvina will dry more quickly than Corvinone, though it is also more susceptible to rot; Rondinella is by comparison much more resistant to rot; Molinara on the other hand lies somewhere between Rondinella and Corvina. With the white grapes, Garganega is again quite easily affected by rot; Trebbiano di Soave too though as we have seen, the fact that the bunches are typically quite compact makes the variety less of a suitable candidate. All in all, *appassimento* is an extremely complex process and managing the many variables discussed above means that the final months of the year in the winery are rarely tranquil ones!

Fermentation

The early stages of the fermentation of these sugar-rich musts take place during the coolest times of the year between December and March. Following pressing the must will generally undergo a two- or three-day pre-fermentation maceration with the solids before the yeasts become active. Ambient conditions (cool temperatures) will usually make the fermentation relatively easy to control though the use of various strains of yeast types (*Saccharomyces bayanus* in particular), some more capable of operating at lower temperatures, some more alcohol tolerant, are normally used as an insurance policy to ensure a linear and stable fermentation. Wild yeasts which form part of the microflora of the cellars are also generally less active in the colder winter temperatures. With Recioto di Soave the alcoholic fermentation will often take place in small wooden barrels (usually new French oak) to underline richness and texture and thereby enhance the sweetness of the wine. Pieropan, which uses larger and older barrels for both fermentation and maturation, is one of the few producers that continues to aim for a deliberately traditional style. In the case of red grapes, fermentation will take place in either stainless steel or wood often with skin contact through till completion, which typically may be as long as forty days or so. A protracted period of wood ageing is then likely to follow for the wines to stabilize and harmonize. With the white or sweet red wine this may be for around twelve months, while an Amarone can remain in wood for three or even four years before bottling. The traditional large old Slavonian oak *botte* is the classic vessel for maturing Amarone to continue the process of slow evolution, though plenty of growers like to add notes of spicy complexity to the finished product by incorporating a period in barriques into the ageing process. Though there is much to be said for the more subtle and seasoned notes that the use of older and larger wood imparts, it seems for now that the toasty vanillin tones which derive from newer and smaller barrels have become an integral part of the story for a number of ambitious wineries keen to make their reputation on the international scene.

Recioto della Valpolicella

The classic method of production of this, the most ancient of Veronese red wines, is a surprisingly sophisticated process. Traditionally the grapes were always pressed in the cool ambient cellar temperatures of winter. The yeasts remained largely inactive until the weather began to warm up slightly, allowing the gradual conversion of the sugars to alcohol to begin. At the first sign of cooler weather returning, the must would be transferred into external containers, leaving behind the residue of solids – mainly the skins – and thus slowing down the activity of the yeasts. The must was racked once more and then moved back onto the remaining solids in the original containers. The process of racking and returning was repeated over a period of perhaps two months up to as many as ten times. On each occasion a proportion of the nutrients was thus removed slowly nullifying the action of the yeast. The final racking was therefore of pretty much 'clean' wine which had arrived at between 12 and 14% abv depending on the original sugar content of the must, bearing in mind the fact that the colder outside temperatures would facilitate the precipitation process. Decisions would be taken along the way as to whether to add sulphur during the racking process or to allow for some exposure to oxygen to ward off reduced aromas, etc. Finally the wine would be left for a further month 'under surveillance' before being transferred to wood to complete the maturation process. The period of maturation, either in wood or cement, would last usually for around twelve months or so. The wine was typically racked at least twice more during this period. With a wine still relatively high in residual sugar the risk of the yeast becoming active again and starting off a second fermentation was a constant one, so the earlier rack and return process to remove all the nutrients left in the liquid had to be carried out with extreme care. The use of sulphur dioxide following the final pre-bottling filtration acted as a further insurance policy against successive movement – for example, during transportation of the finished product. The key steps in the method have by and large remained constant and been handed down from parent to child with the gradual introduction of slightly more refined techniques helping to bring increased stability to the wine over the generations. Most Recioto continues to be made along these lines.

CROSSOVER WINES

Ripasso

Despite the new-found and enthusiastic following, Amarone's documented history dates back little more than a century or so and the wine has in real terms only developed a clear identity since the middle of the twentieth century. Prior to then, when the *appassimento* process was still very much a cottage industry, semi-dried red grapes were made almost exclusively into Recioto della Valpolicella, a dessert or meditation wine. But if a red wine made from semi-dried grapes which can be either sweet or dry, and may even also be affected by noble rot, is a strange enough concept already, the idea of recycling the by-product to make yet more wine is indisputably a unique take on the production process! Valpolicella Ripasso was only granted its own denomination as recently as 2010, though it has been a part of the story of Veronese red wine for much longer than that. Attention has already been drawn to the resourcefulness of the Veronese grape farmers so typical of rural economies: Valpolicella Ripasso is an excellent example of this capacity and has its roots deep in *mezzadria* culture. Ripasso is actually the name of a technique of production rather than, as is usual with Italian wine, a reference to an area, a grape variety or alternatively, a brand name. It refers to one wine being 'passed over' – coming into contact with – another; in this case the pumping of a young red Valpolicella onto the lees or *vinacce* of a Passito wine. Even oral tradition traces the emergence of the practice back no more than two or three generations and one such example relates back to the supposed 'discovery' of Amarone in between the two World Wars. An article in the daily newspaper *L'Arena di Verona* written by Camilla Madinelli and published on 3 March 2008, records Francesco Quintarelli's memory of Gaetano Dall'Ora's account of how Ripasso was produced back in those lean years between the wars. Quintarelli himself spent some seventy years working in the wine trade while Dall'Ora was a founding member of the Cantina Sociale di Negrar in 1933 and the cooperatives' first president. 'We'd rework the autumn's new wine using the lees of the *passito*. There were two or three different "passages" and we'd make a "half" Recioto amongst other things. The last "Ripasso" was with water to make "la graspia", a rather sour and murky beverage which had to last us throughout the winter.' Amongst the current crop of producers, Tiziano Accordini of Fumane's Azienda Agricola Stefano Accordini recalls La Graspia as the classic drink of the local *contadino,* while Carlo Boscaini of the eponymous winery at Sengia close to the village of Sant'Ambrogio talks of how a 'Second Recioto' was regularly produced using the *ripasso* technique and then sold on. In order to survive, the typical *mezzadria* worker would have had to make the most of whatever was available, including recycling the lees of his precious Recioto; quite simply, next to nothing was thrown away.

While no one is sure how long the technique has been in use, Ripasso might even have gradually faded from the picture were it not for Masi and their one-time oenologist Nino Franceschetti. With the backing of Masi's owner Guido Boscaini, in the early 1960s the young winemaker decided to explore what the technique might be capable of delivering. Franceschetti told author Burton Anderson (as reported in his book *Vino*): 'Some people thought that was a stroke of genius ... but if you want to know the truth, I started doing it because I didn't want to waste those good Amarone lees. It was an economically motivated experiment that produced a very pleasing result. I understand some other wineries are doing the same now.' He was referring to Campo Fiorin, a wine first produced commercially by the Boscaini family in 1964. In fact they were reinventing a technique already commonly employed locally, but Campo Fiorin was to take the concept to a whole new level. The term Ripasso had no legal status at the time and though the wine was therefore not labelled as such, it was originally made in this way. Masi were to abandon *ripasso* some years later in favour of what they refer to as the Masi double-fermentation method, whereby wine made from freshly-picked grapes is refermented with 25 per cent of whole grapes of the same varieties which have been dried for about six weeks. But they had started the ball rolling back in the mid 1960s and, some fifty years later, such is the popularity of Valpolicella Ripasso that it has become a standard and indeed vital line for the vast majority of wineries in the area.

The current interpretation of the *ripasso* technique differs little in practice from the above accounts except that these days it is the lees of the Amarone rather than those of Recioto which are most commonly used. In commercial terms, as Franceschetti implied, it makes perfect sense given the shift in balance of production between Amarone and Recioto: currently the amount made of Recioto totals no more than 2.5 per cent of Amarone's production. Nonetheless, purists continue to insist that 'true' Ripasso is made using the lees of Recioto only as they have a much higher residual sugar content which will correspondingly make a more obvious difference to the final wine. The work begins when the *appassimento* wine is drawn off its gross lees, usually in February or March, to be replaced by a young Valpolicella. The subsequent refermentation can last anything between a couple of days and a couple of weeks, one of a number of variables which allow winemakers to make their own preferred style. The overall effect of the technique is to increase the alcohol content (usually from 1 to around 2% abv) and by taking on some of the character of the *appassimento* wine, to boost extract, body and richness. The typically lean and elegant style of Valpolicella is transformed by the high glycerol content of the lees into a much rounder and softer wine. The duration of the *ripasso* step has a marked effect: the general principle being the shorter the period the more fruit characters are accentuated and the more immediately approachable the wine will appear, while longer contact will result in a more structured, phenolic and drier style. The law prohibits the volume of Ripasso from exceeding twice the amount of Amarone or Recioto produced (the so-called 'double Ripasso' rule) so the lees from 1,000 litres of Amarone can be used to produce 2,000 litres of Ripasso, though some prefer the traditional one to one ratio. Furthermore up to 15 per cent of 'wine destined to become' Amarone can be added back into the wine 'in order to improve the quality of the product'. Additionally an extra 10 per cent of wine following the final pressing of the solids is these days added back into the new Ripasso wine. For the purposes of illustration the system customarily worked in the following way: if 1,000 litres of Amarone were racked off the lees to be replaced with 1,000 litres of Valpolicella, a resulting 1,000 litres of Ripasso would subsequently be produced – though of course the original quantity of lees would remain. Up until recently, those lees would remain in theory, a part of the Amarone even though 'diluted' by the addition of Valpolicella. The law is now being tightened up so that the press liquid of those lees becomes in future part of the Ripasso wine.

The producer may also ramp up the proportion of lees to achieve extra richness or even add whole or a pressing of dried grapes for a similar effect. Subsequent wood ageing will also vary but on the whole follows the parameters discussed earlier, not so much in terms of length of time in barrel, but more its size, age and wood type. A Ripasso will not spend anywhere near as long in wood as an Amarone: a period of up to two years – rarely more – can take place, though twelve months is perhaps more common. An unusual version made without any oak ageing is produced by the Tezza family based at Poiano in the Valpantena valley: 'Ma Roat' spends some eighteen months in stainless steel and a further three in bottle before release so that its defining aromas and flavours of black cherry and raspberry remain very much to the fore, an unusual and not unwelcome variation.

An increasing number of wineries in both Soave and Valpolicella favour a combination of fresh and semi-dried fruit for the production of premium wines. Grapes in most instances dried for a shorter period (often around four weeks) are pressed and the must added back to the wine to provoke a secondary fermentation (which can coincide with the MLF). Alternatively they are fermented separately before the two wines are blended together; the technique is known as 'double fermentation' and is sometimes seen on labels. On the whole, these wines show higher alcohol and greater intensity of structure and flavour with an increase in ageing potential. As limited bottlings they broaden a producer's portfolio and can help raise the cellar profile. Examples across the various Soave denominations and in Valpolicella, with the Superiore category in particular, are relatively common and their extra weight and richness offers an alternative proposition to the use of the *ripasso* process.

5

AROUND THE DENOMINATIONS

THE ESSENCE OF SOAVE

Enigmatic though it may be, one of the best and certainly most colourful descriptions of Soave was penned by the English author Charles G. Bode in his book *Wines of Italy*. As well as noting that 'Soave has a soft, velvety taste with a faint recollection of sweetness … so clear and dry that nothing of its subtle bouquet is ever lost', Bode also maintains that 'It tastes as a very clear, sunny sky might taste if one could drink it!' Sadly this rather fanciful turn of phrase has rather less currency some sixty years on, but to describe the aromas of Garganega as deriving mainly from a combination of terpenoid, norisoprenoid and benzenoid compounds doesn't have quite the same ring. Moreover, an analysis which identifies the chemical compounds that give rise to certain varietal characteristics probably does less to distinguish a good bottle of Soave from other dry white wines than Bode's recourse to synaesthetic imagery. Despite the rather arcane comparison, the author nonetheless managed to capture an essential truth about the wine: the fact that Soave's true character defies easy definition.

Bode stops short of mentioning the colour of the wine he was so enthusiastic about but from his description of how it is made ('the wine needs oak around it') it is an easy assumption that it would have been a pale golden colour. Perhaps even more so than with a red, the colour of a white wine will reflect the methodology of its production. Pale, almost water-white tones are associated with anaerobic, low-temperature fermentation in inert materials. The varying degrees or depth of darker, more golden tones are the result of carefully restricted exposure to small amounts of oxygen during fermentation and either extended skin or lees contact, and wood/bottle ageing – or both. The colour of a typical Soave will lie therefore somewhere along the spectrum from water white through straw yellow to a bright, medium gold.

Most wines, though, are defined by the most clearly recognizable fruit characters of their principal grape varieties and Soave's identity is definitely derived from Garganega. Its subtly pervasive aromas are those of orchard fruit and, in particular, the russet apple which smells exactly as it tastes, like a cross between an apple and a pear with lightly nutty overtones. Supporting this are a distinct note of apricot and citrus inflections of mandarin zest and preserved lemon. Floral tones are evident too, above all the clear and fresh scents of white flowers, particularly fruit-tree blossom (apple and the lightly spicier cherry) plus hints of jasmine and a faint camomile fragrance. A gentle sensation of creaminess is often apparent. These sensations carry through to the palate where they are sustained by balanced and often crisp and lively acidity. However, the essential quality which comes across on the palate in particular, and which remains one of Soave's principal defining features, depends on another issue which provokes great debate.

The word 'minerality' when applied to the aroma or flavour of a wine is a relatively new though very fashionable term. It seems to have crept into accepted wine vocabulary as recently as this millennium and still remains something of a hot potato. While frequently used it is also imperfectly understood, not least because it is not easy to pinpoint what a mineral sensation smells or tastes like. Descriptions vary from flinty, stony, salty and chalky to comparisons with graphite or, more evocatively, 'licking wet stone'. Beyond this lies the uncertainty about how such sensations can be present in the wine in the first place. It is true that dissolved mineral ions will be absorbed by the roots of the vine: for example there will be nitrates (used by the plant to make amino acids and proteins), magnesium (for chlorophyll) and phosphates (for DNA). As these are converted by the plant into other compounds and in any case are present in limited quantities, they are thought to have little if any influence at all on aroma and flavour. To try and get to grips with the subject, numerous studies have been carried out, all of which so far seem to conclude that there is no clear, direct link between soil composition and the aroma and flavour characteristics of a wine. Some point to the vinification process and the creation of thiols and esters as the source of 'the mineral element'; others to the use of certain yeast types and extended periods of lees ageing. There are those who maintain that geological and topographical conditions which affect such considerations as altitude and exposure have a part to play, too. The depth and texture of the soil will determine its ability to retain water and thus have a substantial impact on the nutrients the plant is able to assimilate, and those same nutrients will have a degree of influence on aroma and flavour. The logical inference is that a combination of different chemical compounds, which derive from growing conditions through to oenological practices, allow a taster to perceive what we recognize as the mineral element. On the whole, minerality does seem to be most closely associated with white wines that come from cooler growing conditions and vineyards with stony soils that have typically higher than average acid levels and are not blessed with overtly expressive fruit aromas. Soave certainly ticks all these boxes with a flourish. In the glass shadings of iodine, saline notes, smoke and ash have a 'seasoning' effect and give tone to the fruit flavours described above. It is surely more than wishful thinking to note that such sensations are so strikingly redolent of the mixed marine and volcanic geological origins of the area. For anyone wishing to understand the mineral aromas of Soave, simply rub two black basalt stones from one of the vineyards together and inhale.

These various elements define the aromas and flavours of Soave while the intensity with which they are expressed and the weight and texture of the wine in the mouth can be attributed to other factors, principally vineyard yields and winemaking methodologies discussed elsewhere. In general terms, wines from a smaller crop which has been reduced either through conditions during the growing season, by hard pruning or from a later harvest, will display greater concentration on both the nose and the palate. The fuller texture and greater weight that such wines also carry can be enhanced in the cellar through the use of wood or lees ageing, etc. Further and rather more subtle variations in style may be ascribed to the individual characteristics of the vineyards (such as altitude, exposure, microclimate, soil type) as well as the nature of the individual vintage.

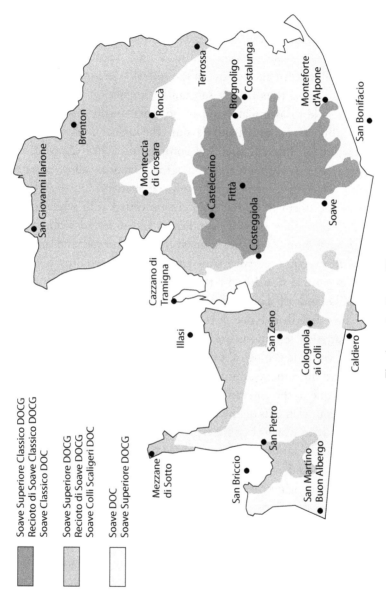

The denominations of Soave

Soave Superiore Classico DOCG
Recioto di Soave Classico DOCG
Soave Classico DOC

Soave Superiore DOCG
Recioto di Soave DOCG
Soave Colli Scaligeri DOC

Soave DOC
Soave Superiore DOCG

San Giovanni Ilarione

Brenton

Terrossa

Roncà

Brognoligo

Costalunga

Monteforte
d'Alpone

San Bonifacio

Monteccia
di Crosara

Castelcerino

Fittà

Costeggiola

Soave

Cazzano di
Tramigna

Illasi

San Zeno

Colognola
ai Colli

Caldiero

San Pietro

San Briccio

Mezzane
di Sotto

San Martino
Buon Albergo

THE SOAVE TERRITORY

The area under vine within the delimited DOC Soave territory is 8,000 hectares of which fractionally under 7,000 hectares are used for the production of Soave itself – the other 1,000 hectares are where Soave overlaps with the neighbouring DOC areas of Valpolicella and Durello. The genesis of the denomination came with the official recognition of the Soave Classico area in 1931 for 'Vino Tipico' and subsequently the Soave DOC itself was created with the introduction of the Denominazione di Origine Controllata system at a national level in 1968. This restored parts of the original area of Roman times, retained Recioto di Soave as a separate category and made Soave Classico a 'premium' sub-zone of the overall denomination. Subsequent modifications took place in 1998 when Recioto di Soave was promoted to DOCG and in 2001, with the addition of the Soave Superiore and Soave Superiore Riserva DOCG categories; in 2002 a second sub-zone, Soave Colli Scaligeri, was recognized.

Giuseppe Benciolini and Roberto Zorzin, contributors to Lorenzoni's *Il Soave: Origine, Stile e Valori*, divide the Soave production territory into four areas: limestone plains, limestone hills, volcanic plains and volcanic hills. The dorsal ridges of Lower Lessinia form the hillside vineyard sites while the valley bottoms between them, gently inclining towards the alluvial flatlands of the Adige, form the so-called plains. Happily this helpful breakdown acts almost as a template for the various denominations of Soave, as above. The limestone plains of the western sector are formed of the alluvial fans of the Mezzane, Illasi and Tramigna valleys and, of course, the valley floors themselves. The limestone hills above and between them continue as far as the Classico zone and so make up parts of both the Colli Scaligeri and Classico itself. The volcanic hills begin where the limestone recedes in Classico and also, as the Colli Scaligeri, arch across the Alpone valley at San Giovanni Illarione, merging into the ridge on the eastern boundary of the Alpone valley. The volcanic plains of the east are an extension of the Alpone valley and are separated from the limestone plains by the confluence of limestone and volcanic hills that forms Soave Classico. The two 'plains' areas form the simple Soave DOC production, while the Colli Scaligeri are formed of limestone hills to the west and volcanic hills in the east.

SOAVE DOC AND DOCG WINES

In simple terms, current production parameters specify differing release dates, minimum alcohol content and vineyard yields for each of the denominations as well as defining the growing area.

A regulation common to most is that the maximum percentage of the original weight of the grapes that can be produced as wine (the *resa in vino*) is 70 per cent (the *appassimento* wines have a more complex set of measures). With all of the wines produced under the Soave umbrella, Garganega is the main grape variety and must make up at least 70 per cent of the blend though a great many examples of all the categories are in fact pure varietals. A maximum of 30 per cent of Trebbiano di Soave is permitted throughout, though the variety has a very minor role to play in the *appassimento* process given the compact nature of its bunches. A maximum of 5 per cent of other authorized varieties (see the section above on other white varieties) can also – at least in theory – be included. With the non-*appassimento* wines only, Chardonnay can replace Trebbiano di Soave at up to 30 per cent.

Soave DOC

Distinguishing production regulations

- *Minimum alcohol content: 10.5%*
- *Release date: from 1 December of the vintage year*
- *Vineyard yields: 15 tonnes per hectare*

The Soave DOC vineyard area was fully mapped out in 1968 to include large tracts of land surrounding the Classico district. To the west this area overlaps with the Valpolicella DOC in parts of the municipalities of San Martino Buon Albergo, Lavagno, Mezzane di Sotto, Illasi, Colognola ai Colli and Cazzano di Tramigna; and to the east with the Lessini DOC in parts of the municipalities of San Giovanni Illarione, Montecchia di Crosara, and Ronca. A slice of Valpolicella vineyard is also to be found along the western edge of Montecchia di Crosara. The extension of the area to include the 'new' vineyards that sprang up in the 1950s and 1960s to meet the booming export trade ratified a development based on the economic needs of the agricultural community in the difficult post-war years. The decision, though a controversial one, brought recognition and desperately needed money to the area.

To the west towards Valpolicella, the plains above the Adige have predominantly limestone-based soils mixed with sand and pebbles which drain well and are perfect for growing fruit trees and grain as well as vines. The area begins around the small town of San Martino Buon Albergo at the mouth of the Marcellise valley skirting the spur which separates Marcellise from the Mezzane valley to the east. It occupies the broad plain below Lavagno between the village of San Pietro and the urban sprawl that borders the northern edge of the A4 motorway to the south, and over as far as Colognola ai Colli and the *frazione* of San Zeno lying at the bottom of the Illasi valley to the east. The area continues on the eastern side of the hills occupied by Colognola ai Colli where the floor of the Tramigna valley below Cazzano di Tramigna makes up the final section. Where plantings of Soave grapes are sometimes relatively sporadic, this is partly because the land overlaps in places with the Valpolicella DOC and, these days, red grapes fetch a significantly higher premium than the white varieties. Apart from the few hectares of Valpolicella vineyard in the commune of Montecchia di Crosara no such competition applies on the eastern side of Classico, and Garganega in particular takes over where the flatlands of the Val d'Alpone begin. Here in the eastern part of Soave the hills are primarily volcanic in origin so while the soils of the valley floor that reach down to the plains below are also alluvial in origin, they are formed of volcanic debris – much of it basalt – bound together by loamy clay.

Throughout the recent history of what is now the DOC area, the choice of crop has always been determined by market demand. The importance of a cash crop to suit the needs of the time dates back deep into the history of the *mezzadria* system. To this day most of the territory remains a patchwork of small parcels: the vast majority of vine growers own less than a hectare of vineyard and have customarily sold off their fruit historically to bottling houses or, more frequently these days, to the local cooperative. Cooperatives continue to be the driving force in the area: mergers and political manoeuvring over the last couple of decades have seen the powerbase concentrated in the hands of ever fewer players. Over the last twenty years the giant

Cantina di Soave has taken over its rivals in Tramigna, Illasi and Montecchia di Crosara. Meanwhile Cantina di Colli ai Colognola is a founder member of the large Collis Veneto group which produces a wide range of wines from across the Veneto (including Soave and Valpolicella); in addition the cooperative acquired a 40 per cent share in the well-known Arbizzano-based *negoziante* house of Sartori at the turn of the millennium in order to gain wider distribution. As Andrea Sartori, the current CEO of Sartori explains, 'They had the wine and we had the customers.' Other vineyard owners in both the Classico and DOC areas are members of the Cantina di Gambellara based in the neighbouring province of Vicenza. Cantina di Gambellara is a part of Vitevis, a union of three cooperatives, all of which are based in the province of Vicenza who decided to pool resources and join together in 2015. The independent Cantina di Monteforte, also very active in the area and whose 600 members farm around 1,300 hectares of vines, seems tiny by comparison!

To illustrate the importance of the cooperative movement across the Soave denomination, with the 2015 harvest (the latest statistics available), 90 per cent of the area's 2,927 growers sold off their grapes to the various cooperatives and another 7 per cent sold their fruit to bottling firms, leaving just 3 per cent who vinify the produce of their own vineyards. Given these conditions, it comes as no surprise that the plains are the source of the volume Soave which came to be such a force back in the 1960s and 1970s and which still dominates the bulk of production: there is over three times as much simple Soave DOC produced as the sum total of all the other white DOC(G) wines put together, nearly 290,000 hectolitres in 2016. Much of it is colourless and neutral-tasting – 'frankly vinous with a squeeze of lemon' would be a fitting description – and sells for a pittance. Production is trapped in a vicious circle: most growers have a few rows of vines and aim for them to be as productive as possible while the market that eventually buys the product has no intention of paying anything above the lowest conceivable price. The cooperatives are caught in the middle and have to try and somehow keep both their members and their customers happy. There is precious little room for manoeuvre in the commodity market and even less incentive to upgrade quality. The long-term answer, according to Bruno Trentini of the Cantina di Soave, is to develop your own good-value brands: 'Ten to fifteen years ago, we sold off 85 per cent of our production in bulk to bottlers and for private labels. Now we have our own brands for each sector of the market. With our new facilities at Viale Vittorio, we're aiming to up the numbers to eighty million bottles over the next few years.'

The story of the limestone plains might end there were it not for a small group of producers determined, each in their own highly individual way, to show the world the true potential of the area. Close to the north-western limits of the denomination, Marco Sartori produces an excellent Soave La Broia from vines grown on the valley floor at 100 metres just south of the village of Mezzane di Sotto: growing conditions 'on the flat' are, according to Sartori, fine for the production of quality white grapes – it's the reds that need the hillside sites. Marco maintains that vigorous though his Garganega vines may be, the key to good quality is to manage them properly in order to contain their yields. Further proof that Soave DOC is about more than just cheap and cheerful is evident with the wines of Ilatium, whose winery lies further down the valley, or the promising young Marco Mosconi whose vineyards lie just south and west of Illasi. Around Colognola ai Colli, Fasoli Gino make a Soave that ages particularly well from the Piave Vecchia vineyard – local records show that vines have been grown close to the old parish church since ancient times. The improving estate of Villa Canestrari also lies nearby. Just a few metres up the road, Agostino Vicentini produces a range of Soave using stainless steel only, even for his intense and bittersweet Recioto di Soave. Agostino, the fourth generation of a family of grape growers, believes that the vanillin flavours of wood compromise the *tipicita* of the local white wines. His two dry versions of Soave, Terre Lunghe and the Superiore Il Casale, nonetheless show an uncommon degree of richness and nuance. Agostino thinks the pursuit of quality rather than the quantity-focused production of his father's generation has been a major step forward. Even so *diraddamento,* the reduction of the crop by bunch thinning, was a difficult lesson for people used to a much more frugal way of life: 'My father suffered from Alzheimer's in the latter stages of his life. When he saw what we were doing in the vineyards he tried to tie the discarded bunches back on the vines!'

Though grown on the slopes of Monte Ceriani just north of Colognola ai Colli at up to 200 metres (so hardly 'plains' wine, by any stretch of the imagination), Tenuta Sant'Antonio produce over 100,000 bottles of Soave DOC in a range of different styles. Though the wine could conceivably be labelled as Colli Scaligeri the Castagnedi brothers prefer to stay with the simple DOC. It's a similar story with the Corte Adami winery on the outskirts of Soave, where the Adami family produce not only a fresh, fruity and eminently drinkable everyday Soave DOC but also a single vineyard cru version called Vigna delle Corte. This vineyard is adjacent to the vines which produce Filippi's Soave Colli Scaligeri Vigne della Bra' at Castelcerino but once again the wine is marketed as a regular Soave DOC. These wines are 'exceptions to the rule' in that they are produced from hillside vineyards in privileged positions, yet at the same time they serve to bring a little lustre to the humbler denomination.

On the eastern side of the hills of Colognola ai Colli and a little to the south of Cazzano di Tramigna, the Tamellini brothers produce a fine example of Soave DOC from vines grown around Costeggiola – some on the valley floor, some in the foothills – that straddle the border with the Classico district. Production is up to over 250,000 bottles, but nonetheless the Tamellini Soave maintains a balanced, perfumed and peachy style of wine which promises to hold up well in the bottle. The merchant house of Benanti is also based in this area but the municipality is again largely dominated by Valpolicella vineyards and over three times as much land is given over to red grapes as white.

The volcanic plains extend from just north of the town of Montecchia di Crosara for some 10 kilometres to the south around Monteforte d'Alpone and the A4 motorway. This is a large, broad and flat area bordered to the west by the hills of Classico and to the east by the volcanic ridge that separates the provinces of Verona and Vicenza. Also known as the Monteforte plain, the land is almost wholly given over to viticulture these days though, like nearby Colognola ai Colli, it was previously renowned for growing peas. Composed of sedimentary volcanic material from the erosion of the the volcanic hills mixed with loamy clay, the soil structure is far more uniform than in most other parts of the denomination. This broad and open area suffered especially badly from the freezing temperatures of the icy 1985 winter when many vines were lost. Subsequent replanting means that the vineyards have a higher plant density than elsewhere and most of the vines are no more than thirty years old. Once again the cooperatives are extremely active and only a handful of producer bottlers stand out from the crowd. The largest of these is La Cappuccina founded in 1890 and with almost 40 hectares of vines partly in the hills around Costalunga and partly on the Monteforte plain. The Tessari family produce good quality organic Soave in a range of different styles. Tessari is a very common surname around Monteforte and another family of that name, whose I Stefanini estate is also based at Costalunga, sold their fruit off to the local cooperative until 2003. They own some 15 hectares including land in the Classico district but make an excellent example of Soave DOC grown in a 6-hectare vineyard above Sarmazza on the Monteforte plain. Soave Il Selese refers to the original use of the land (the name means threshing floor in dialect) when growing grain was still a viable enterprise and the wine itself is fresh, full and juicy in an eminently drinkable style. Umberto Portinari, an even smaller-scale producer from neighbouring Brognoligo, makes an unusually rich and full version of Soave DOC from his Le Albare vineyard a stone's throw further to the east and right at the edge of the delimited area. It involves a technique called Doppio Maturazione Ragionata whereby half the crop is left to wither after picking and the rest left on the vine to gain *sovramaturazione* before the two separate batches of fruit are pressed and vinified together.

At the very eastern edge of the Soave DOC area a very different set of growing conditions exists around the village of Ronca where a series of small valleys running from north to south tumbles down the slopes of Monte Calvarina. A recent study undertaken between the growers' consortium and the Agricultural Genetics Laboratory at the Department of Viticulture of Verona University has come up with evidence that suggests Ronca may have a head start over many other parts of the Soave DOC territory. Working with the same clone of pergola-trained Garganega planted in four locations across the entire area (at Colognola ai Colli, in the lower-lying parts of the Pressoni vineyard of Classico, on the valley floor at Sarmazza on the Monteforte plain and at Ronca itself), they monitored the ripeness of the fruit in each over a five-week period leading up to harvest time. Results, amongst the wealth of data collected, showed that the accumulation of sugars especially in the crucial period immediately prior to harvest was significantly slower in the fruit grown at Ronca than in the other areas. The experiment is ongoing so a more exhaustive report will no doubt throw greater light on the matter; nonetheless, the idea that the wines of Ronca have their own distinct personality could in fact have some scientific basis.

A dozen or so wineries operate in and around the area, many of them quite small and fairly new to the world of bottled wine, but real promise is already being shown by the Dal Cero family's Corte Giacobbe estate, Corte Moschina and Gianni Tessari close to Ronca itself, Fattori and Franchetto Antonio at nearby Terrossa, and Sandro De Bruno at Montecchia di Crosara. All own hillside vineyards on or around Monte Calvarina and Monte Crocetta. Gianni Tessari notes that there is always a breeze along the eastern side of the valley especially in the evenings which helps to keep temperatures down. Diurnal differences are often more marked as a result, an increasingly important feature as the effects of climate change become ever more apparent. The wines do show a particularly fresh and scented character and combine fragrant fruit aromas and flavours with strongly evident mineral tones. Indeed Giulia Franchetto, who looks after export sales at her family's small Terrossa-based winery, singles out freshness and minerality as the two features which distinguish the wines of Ronca from their rivals.

Though Soave from the so-called plains can often 'make a virtue of its neutrality', what becomes clear on tasting the better-quality wines from these areas is that they do not lack backbone, a criticism often levelled at the more simple wines of the denomination. Instead they display broad but well-defined aromas and the sort of structure which promises scope for development. A commitment to quality that combines careful vineyard management with appropriate cellar practices, demonstrates that even the supposedly lesser areas of Soave are capable of delivering some great wines.

Soave Colli Scaligeri DOC

Distinguishing production regulations
- *Minimum alcohol content: 11.0%*
- *Release date: from 1 February of the year following the vintage*
- *Vineyard yields: 14 tonnes per hectare*

The Colli Scaligeri DOC was launched in 2003 as an attempt to address a fundamental imbalance in the 1968 regulations which failed to distinguish the multitude of excellent hillside sites in the territory which lie outside the Classico district from the low-lying plains vineyards. The 'sub denomination' was named after the noble della Scala family, so influential in the area in the thirteenth and fourteenth centuries. The vineyards are pretty much one continuous belt which begins in the west between San Martino Buon Albergo and Lavagno, though a small vineyard area just below the village of Mezzane di Sotto is also part of the denomination. The area continues eastwards through the low lying hills between Illasi and Colognola ai Colli, then arches north above Classico at the western side of the Val d'Alpone to where the valley starts to narrow significantly, and then extends down the eastern side of the valley to just below the village of Terrossa. The mix of different altitudes, soil types and exposures takes in most of the variables within the overall territory therefore, more or less replicating many aspects of growing conditions in Classico. Indeed the decision was taken to apply the same production framework to the Colli Scaligeri as Classico so the two denominations could – in theory at least – be viewed as equals. Given the lack of history and prestige relating to the former this seems to have been a bridge too far, encouraging growers to aim for similarly high standards only without the cachet and therefore the higher prices the Classico area commands. Since its inception fifteen years ago figures have dropped dramatically from nearly 26,000 hectolitres in the first year of production (2003) to less than 1,000 in 2016. The Colli Scaligeri denomination is clearly not working. Aldo Lorenzoni, Director of the Consorzio Tutela Vini Soave, believes this may be because there are so few growers with vineyards on the area who see the process though from bud to bottle so the ambition simply isn't there. Even so, given the opportunity to shine, the handful of producers who do take the denomination seriously are producing some of the most interesting and innovative wines in the area.

Though a widely available example is available sourced through the Cantina di Colli ai Colognola, quality is patchy and two names stand out head and shoulders above the rest: Cantina Filippi and Sandro De Bruno. Coincidentally both wineries have chosen to adopt a similar approach to production, giving their wines an extended period of ageing on the fine lees (in both cases up to eighteen months) to highlight the richness and nuance characteristic of the better examples of ageworthy

Soave. In terms of absolute quality they are clearly on a par with many of the finer wines of the Classico district and, as both wineries already enjoy an international reputation, pricing is not so much of an issue. While the Filippi estate lies right on the boundary of Classico, the De Bruno vineyards occupy positions at up to 600 metres on the slopes of Monte Calvarina near Ronca. Other growers in the area could conceivably also market their wines as Colli Scaligeri but prefer the simpler Soave DOC classification instead, a rather damning indictment of a category which, despite the good intentions upon which it was founded, is dying on its feet.

Soave Classico DOC

Distinguishing production regulations
- *Minimum alcohol content: 11.0%*
- *Release date: from 1 February of the year following the vintage*
- *Vineyard yields: 14 tonnes per hectare*

Soave Classico is where the two main soil types of the viticultural Veronese converge. There is no neat division between them although, in general terms, it is fair to say that the western part of the area close to the town of Soave itself is for the most part situated on a bedrock of stratified limestone of marine origins while the eastern sector sits mainly on a substratum of volcanic rock which is principally basalt and basalt-based breccia. The vineyards begin at an altitude of just 30 to 40 metres near the main settlements of Soave, Monteforte d'Alpone, Brognoligo, Costalunga and Costeggiola, which lie on the periphery of the area, to just under 400 metres at the highest point of Castelcerino at the very north-western tip. Classico is really the very southern extension of the ridge complex which divides the Val Tramigna and, further to the north the Val d'Illasi, from the Val d'Alpone. It is composed of two small, diminishing chains of hills both of which begin close to the hamlet of Castelcerino. One stretches in an easterly direction and forms the northern border of the denomination while the second runs approximately from north to south and makes up its western edge. The gently shelving land in between these two 'arms' is divided by three small valleys also extending in an easterly direction down towards the Monteforte plains. From north to south, these are the Val Rugate, the Val dell'Acqua and the Val Ponsara; two small, low lying ridges divide Rugate and the Val dell'Acqua and the latter from the Val Ponsara. Vineyard planting is highly intensive with just a few areas that are too rocky to sustain the vine, the main example of which lies close to Soave's castle where a small forest of cypress is clearly visible. Otherwise a few copses and the occasional tiny village are the only outposts in a sea of vines.

The western chain begins just west of the small *frazione* of Castelcerino with a long, winding south- to south-east-facing hill which merges into the vineyards of Costeggiola just above the village itself. The soils here are mainly a calcareous clay with basalt substrata in the more westerly parts. Apart from Coffele, Pagani and the Cantina di Soave, the main vineyard owners are Tamellini, whose Soave Classico Le Bine di Costiola is sourced from fruit grown in south-west-facing slopes, and Guerrieri Rizzardi whose Costeggiola bottling is from a south-facing 15-hectare plot west of the village. Two other important vineyard areas lie a little further over to the east from Costeggiola, though still just below Castelcerino. Adjacent to Costeggiola and just below Recoareto are the steeply sloping vineyards of Campagnola where most of the land is owned by members of the local cooperative. Directly beneath Campagnola is the well-known Carniga vineyard, made famous through its association with Arturo Stuchetti's Cantina del Castello winery. Though the vineyard is quite low lying, the stony, calcareous soils produce a wine with a reputation for being particularly long lived. To the west, the vineyards of Sengialta and the up and coming Balestri Valda winery abut one of the area's most celebrated vineyards, Calvarino, where the steep slopes with their basalt substrata are the source of the original 'single vineyard' Soave Classico bottling from Pieropan. Calvarino lies in the lee of what is probably Classico's best known vineyard area today, Foscarino. Championed from the outset by Roberto Anselmi, who still owns land there, a number of other important wineries such as Inama and Montetondo owe much of their reputation to the excellent growing conditions that Foscarino provides. The hillside becomes increasingly steep near the summit and dominates much of the central area of Classico; it is composed of a number of different expositions – south, east and west – and altitudes between roughly 100 and 300 metres. The lower reaches to the south and west occupy the area known as Roaro, where the Pieropan family are building their new winery. Unlike the stony basalt soils of Foscarino, much of the bedrock at Roaro is a sparkling white limestone which construction excavations have exposed. With due respect for the environment and a careful eye on the area's growing potential, the building will be covered over again once work is complete and replanted to vines.

The next hillside to the south of Foscarino is Pigno where once again a basalt substratum is evident. Corte Mainente and Gianni Tessari both produce bottlings of Soave Classico from the south- and south-west-facing slopes. Where the hill inclines down towards the northern edge of Soave town, the vineyards of Mondello mainly belong to members of the cooperative. The vineyard immediately behind the castle is another illustrious name, La Rocca, where both Pieropan (famously) and Guerrieri Rizzardi own vines. Fornaro also produce a tiny quantity of Capitel del Tenda from the highest part of the hill. Close by is the impressive Piazza Scheeti where the ground is littered with tiny, disc-shaped nummulite fossils which clearly dates the formation of the area back to the Eocene epoch when these marine creatures inhabited the shallow parts of the Tethys ocean. ('Scheeti' is the name in local dialect for small coins.) The eastern edge of the 'Square' enjoys a splendid view over the vineyards of the Val d'Alpone. Moving south again, the next hillside is known as Monte Tenda but, because of the limestone outcrop referred to above, there are few vineyards here, though Gianni Tessari produces a particularly aromatic single vineyard bottling. Lying below Tenda, the vineyards of the area known as Cengelle border Soave town. After Tenda, the final hillside of the western chain is Monte Tondo which lies at the southernmost tip of the Classico area. Monte Tondo is low lying with south-facing vineyards. At the foot of the hillside sits the Magnabosco family's Montetondo winery. The firm's regular Soave Classico is made from fruit gathered on Monte Tondo. Other producers including Nardello and Bertani also work vineyards in the area.

The northern chain takes in part of Castelcerino, the area around Fitta and the tiny settlement of Monte, through into the conical hill of Castellaro and then Tremenalto, a series of ridges which face north towards Montecchia di Crosara and Ronca, finishing up above the *frazione* of Costalunga. The more eastern parts of Castelcerino around Monte Ovo at 335 metres show a closer tie with the volcanic origins which characterize much of the rest of the hills of Classico's northern boundary. Coffele, Le Mandolare and the Cantina di Soave are the important landowners in this area which straddles the two communities of Soave and Monteforte d'Alpone. Just along from Recoareto, where most of the growers are *conferenti*, as the members of the local cooperative are generally referred to, lie the vineyards of Menini at up to 280 metres, facing from south to south-east. The calcareous clay topsoil lying on a bedrock of basalt and the position are major contributing factors to the distinctive character of two single vineyard wines produced by Le Mandolare from the contiguous sites of Roccolo and Corte Menini. Much darker brown soils, clearly formed mainly of basalt, are typical of Fitta where Suavia are based; indeed their Massafitta vineyard, the source of the Tessari sisters' varietal Trebbiano di Soave, is a classic case in point. The other vineyards around Fitta belong mainly to smaller growers who sell their grapes to the cooperative. Further east the hills are somewhat lower; Tremenalto, for example, has an average altitude of up to 230 metres. Nonetheless, the mainly north- and east-facing vineyards are an important source of fruit for a number of firms who appreciate the cooler growing conditions of the area – Lenotti, Fattori, La Dama del Rovere, Le Battistelle and Classico's two cooperatives among them. Tremenalto gradually merges into the vineyards above Costalunga and the area's north-eastern tip where I Stefanini and La Cappuccina are notable growers. On the south-facing aspect of these hills, the steeply sloping vineyards of Brognoligo overlook the main part of the Rugate valley. A small cluster of hillside sites lies at the end of the valley just below Fitta, including the important vineyards of Monte Carbonare, the source of Suavia's top bottling of Classico as well as Ca Rugate's impressive Monte Fiorentine and Le Battistelle's Roccolo del Durlo, all of which have the classic soils of clay over basalt typical of the eastern and central section of the Classico area. The southern side of the Rugate valley comprises the mainly north- and north-east-facing vineyards of Coste and Boschetti. On the other side of the ridge, facing south again, lies Monte Grande, the source of Pra's flagship Soave Classico; two smaller wineries Le Mandolare (Monte

Sella) and Le Albare also have holdings here. The hillside converges into the Costalta area where the grapes for the T.E.S.S.A.R.I winery's premium Soave Classico Le Bine Longhe di Costalta are grown (the word *bine* – also used by the Tamellini brothers – refers to a row of vines). On the other side of the road which leads from Monteforte to Costalunga and Brognoligo lie two further vineyard areas, Casotti and Casarsa, home to the cellars of Terre dei Monti and Tenuta Faltracco respectively. Both Monte Grande and Costalta overlook the Val dell'Acqua to the south, and nestled at the head of the valley below the eastern slopes of Foscarino are the vineyards of Pressoni where Cantina del Castello own a terraced amphitheatre containing some very old vines. The lower-lying Val di Ponsara is another area of intensive planting though, since the Carlo Bogoni winery sadly stopped producing Soave Classico a couple of years ago, there is no privately owned estate to fly the flag for the valley's potential. The Val Ponsara divides two prestigious *monti*: to the north Foscarino and to the south Frosca. La Frosca is a lower-lying (up to 150 metres), mainly south-facing vineyard site which brothers Carlo and Sandro Gini have elevated to 'grand cru' status in recent years through the family's lengthy history of fine wine production. These are mainly basalt-based soils with a vein of limestone covered with a topsoil of tufaceous clay in the central area known as Salvarenza. The vineyards lie in a sheltered bowl just behind the town of Monteforte d'Alpone bordered by the north-facing Fontana to the south and Croce just below the final peak of the Classico area, Monte Zoppega. This south-to south-east-facing hillside is right at the edge of the south-western part of the town; the main vineyard owner here is Nardello whose winery lies at the foot of the hill.

A few additional vineyards complete the full picture of the Classico area – Bassanella is a low-lying vineyard just outside of the town walls to the north of Soave, close to the Santuario di Santa Maria della Bassanella church and owned by Bixio, while around Monteforte d'Alpone, the Colle Sant'Antonio and Monticello vineyards are practically a part of the town itself.

With such a diverse array of expositions and altitudes there is little reason why two examples of Soave Classico should ever taste quite the same, notwithstanding the differing techniques of production. Nonetheless, clear styles do emerge even within such a relatively small area as Classico and which, by and large, tie in with the two types of terrain present. The western vineyards where the bedrock is primarily limestone tend to have a more direct and linear quality, particularly in their youth. The distinguishing aromas are inclined to favour the more floral aspects of Soave with lightly 'greener', predominantly orchard-fruit characters though notes of white peach are also present. On the palate, the wines appear a little leaner, often with a slightly more pronounced acidity, hence the more 'linear' structure – though with age, as the wine softens, it also fattens out to take on extra richness of both texture and flavour. The more eastern parts of Classico where basalt becomes the dominant substratum produce wines which when young are more expansive and fleshier in style. The aromas are more closely akin to more exotic fruits, with notes of yellow peach and nectarine in particular. The palate will typically appear richer and with a slightly more luscious texture and the lingering aftertaste more reminiscent of ripe and mature fruits rather than floral tones. While, clearly, stylistic traits can be blurred by winemaking techniques, it is at the same time a source of never-ending fascination to compare and contrast these two interpretations of the Garganega grape. Though the comparison tells only a part of the story, a signpost towards the distinction is to think of the differences in aroma, flavour and texture between a white and a yellow peach. One factor which should never be overlooked when considering both the worth of Soave Classico and what makes it such a special area is the amount of older vines to be found, particularly in the more central and sheltered areas of the denomination. Cantina del Castello, Gini and Le Battistelle all own good stocks of these venerable plants, some of which have never been grafted onto American rootstocks and are over a century old. The quality of fruit they provide can only be described as the stuff that the wines of dreams are made from!

Soave Superiore DOCG and Soave Superiore Riserva DOCG

Superiore DOCG – distinguishing production regulations

- *Minimum alcohol content: 12.0%*

- *Release date: from 1 April of the year following the vintage*

- *Vineyard yields: 10 tonnes per hectare*

Superiore Riserva DOCG – distinguishing production regulations

- *Minimum alcohol content: 12.5%*

- *Release date: from 1 November of the year following the vintage*

- *Vineyard yields: 10 tonnes per hectare*

Note: In both instances regulations stipulate that vineyards used to produce these wines planted following the introduction of the discipline (that is, new plantings) must have at least 4,000 vines per hectare.

These two categories, elevated at the beginning of the new millennium to DOCG status, can be applied to any of the three areas already outlined above – Soave, Soave Colli Scaligeri or Soave Classico. Provision for a Superiore version of Soave or Soave Classico was already written into the 1968 DOC classification (the Riserva option was a new departure) but, in real terms, had come to mean little more than a minimum 0.5% higher alcohol content and a later release date than for the regular or generic wine. With the added weight of Italy's quality-driven DOCG status behind them, the new categories were an opportunity to truly boost the wine's image. But the modified regulations proved to be the most contentious of all the territory's production disciplines. One particularly unhappy consequence of their implementation was to cause one of the area's leading producers to turn his back on the name Soave, seemingly for good. Roberto Anselmi was utterly convinced that Guyot and Guyot alone was the only form of *allevamento* for the production of quality Soave. When the idea of the new Superiore category was first mooted, he saw a chance to force the issue and campaigned for one of the qualifying conditions to be the obligatory use of his preferred training system. He didn't receive the support he was hoping for and vowed to stop making Soave as a result, marketing his wines as IGT Veneto instead. Dissenters complained that Anselmi's proposal was unrealistic without a detailed programme of research to demonstrate its validity, and the debate continues though without Roberto's input; he feels he has made his position perfectly clear. Ironically, one legacy of the argument is the inclusion of higher-density planting in future Superiore vineyards than is possible under the old *tendone* system, one of the very factors that so riled Anselmi to begin with. Indeed the intelligent application of the principle is to allow for vineyards containing old vines (as referred to above) to remain part of the equation. Even so, other objections were to follow including the rather haughty view that the denomination should only be applied to wines from the Classico zone. Few producers have chosen to take advantage of the Superiore category, though, unlike with Colli Scaligeri, numbers have at least remained fairly stable. Yet Soave Superiore might have become the default denomination to define the fuller style of quality wine produced throughout the entire territory. While the opportunity exists for producers in Classico to make use of the category, examples are seen only infrequently: Superiore and Superiore Riserva can virtually by definition only apply to wines of extremely limited production owing to the lower yields specified by the production discipline. Hence, for example Azienda Agricola Montetondo produce a number of bottlings from within the overall denomination: a Soave DOC, a 'generic' Soave Classico DOC and two single vineyard bottlings of Classico, one of which is bottled as Soave Classico Superiore.

For now the Superiore category would seem to offer greater scope for those producers outside Classico in particular who are determined to focus on quality production. Some of the rising stars of Soave are produced under the denomination: for example, the Dal Cero family's splendid Soave Vigneto Runcata from vines grown on the ridge between the two volcanoes, Monte Calvarina and Monte Crocetta, overlooking Ronca. Agostino Vincentini's Soave Superiore Il Casale, made from mainly 40-year-old vines grown near Colognola ai Colli, provides another example of how a producer's 'top' wine fits neatly into the framework. With vineyard yields set at a lower level than those for Classico as well as a later release date (therefore encouraging growers to give the wines more time on their fine lees or in barrel), the ambitious Superiore denomination has provided growers with an 'official' vehicle for maintaining the neglected tradition of producing ageworthy Soave, irrespective of whereabouts in the overall territory the fruit is grown.

This provides an extra incentive for growers like Dal Cero and Vicentini to keep faith with what is after all a core feature of Soave's identity.

Recioto di Soave DOCG

Distinguishing production regulations

- *Minimum alcohol content: 12.0% for the still wine, 11.5% for the Spumante*

- *Minimum residual sugar content: 70 g/l*

- *Release date: from 1 September of the year following the vintage*

- *Vineyard yields: 9 tonnes per hectare*

- *Maximum proportion of wine extracted from the grapes set aside for appassimento: 40 per cent (42 per cent for the Spumante version) of their original weight*

Note: Producers in the Classico zone are entitled to label their wine as Recioto di Soave Classico DOCG.

Recioto di Soave is a wine of tremendous pedigree. With a history which can be traced back over 1,500 years to Cassiodorus's references to the Acinatico Bianco popular at the royal court, and as the first wine in the Veneto to be granted DOCG status in 1998, it is little wonder that this distinctive and voluptuous wine is held in such esteem locally. As with the other white wines of the overall Soave denomination, Garganega makes up at least 70 per cent of the blend; up to 30 per cent of Trebbiano di Soave can also be included along with a maximum of 5 per cent of the other authorized white grapes. A high proportion of Recioto di Soave relies solely on Garganega. Like Corvina in the Valpolicella, the variety has winged bunches and traditionally these 'ears' were selected for the *appassimento* process. That age-old custom continues in Soave and thus harvesting can only be carried out manually. The selected grapes are picked relatively early in order to maintain the necessary levels of acidity which will balance out the residual sugar content in the finished wine. Grape drying is carried out in the time-honoured fashion with scant regard for the practice of 'assisted' *appassimento*. As a consequence, the presence of noble rot is widely accepted as a valid part of the process.

What really makes Recioto di Soave stand out, however, is the unique way in which it is made. While the drying of grapes and the presence of noble rot are both established ways of concentrating sugars and extracts in the production of dessert wines, in this instance the two methods are combined: a 'double bubble' which renders the wine peerless in terms of richness and concentration of flavour and aroma among the wonderful world of unfortified 'stickies'. The effect on the liquid in the glass is pretty remarkable: the nose is all candied fruits, honey, wax and wildflowers while the palate teems with apricot and mandarin flavours and the oily and almost unctuous texture is held in check by coursing acidity. Successful dessert wines often rely on the interplay between sweet and sour, and the relevant knobs are certainly turned up to eleven with Recioto di Soave! Most examples of modern Recioto are either fermented and stored or at least matured in wood, usually smaller new barrels, to enhance richness and texture as well as adding vanillin notes and structure-boosting tannins. As a result the wine has exceptional ageing potential. Inevitably produced in tiny quantities, over the course of the last few years little more than an annual average of 400 hectolitres of Recioto di Soave, 500 hectolitres of Recioto di Soave Classico and 90 hectolitres of the Spumante version have been produced. Sadly sweet wines are not at their peak of popularity; nonetheless, most 'serious' Soave producers keep the ancient tradition alive and continue to make this oenological treasure when conditions allow.

LESSINI DURELLO SPUMANTE

Main production regulations
- *Grape varieties: a minimum of 85 per cent Durella, and up to 15 per cent of Garganega, Pinot Bianco, Chardonnay or Pinot Nero either singly or in combination*
- *Minimum alcohol content: 11.0% for the Spumante (metodo charmat) and 12.0% for the Riserva (metodo classico)*
- *Release date: the Riserva version must spend a period of at least thirty-six months on the lees beginning from 1 January of the year following the vintage*
- *Vineyard yields: 16 tonnes per hectare*

The Soave vineyards on the eastern side of the Val d'Alpone occupy the same slopes as the lower reaches of the Lessini Durello denomination. This distinctive sparkling wine has, over the last few years, become the default glass of quality fizz in the fashionable eateries and bars of Verona. While the DOC discipline allows for a tank-fermented Spumante version, a perfectly enjoyable fresh, fruity and fragrant bubbly, it is the *metodo classico* wine which has captured the imagination of discerning fans and smaller-scale producers alike. The variety has some history both as a base for spumante and a blending or 'cutting' wine thanks to its often searingly high acid content. It was also frequently (and surreptitiously) included alongside Garganega amongst the grapes set aside for *appassimento* and destined for the production of Recioto di Soave, not just because of its acidity levels but also because, as the name suggests, the grape has a remarkably tough skin and is thus highly resistant to attacks of rot. In the last few decades through the efforts of two wineries in particular, Fongaro and Marcato, its potential as the source of a fine *metodo classico* wine has begun to be recognized.

For now, quantity levels are quite small. In 2016 some twenty wineries produced 400,000 bottles of the tank-fermented wine and some 200,000 of the bottle-fermented version. These figures have tripled since the beginning of the millennium and at the moment there are just under 500 hectares of vineyard registered for production. There is also a Monte Lessini DOC for both red and white still wines but the amount of land under vine is much smaller again and the wines are rarely seen apart from an excellent if unusual still version of Durello produced by the Sandro de Bruno winery. A large proportion of Durello Spumante is made by the Cantina di Soave using the *charmat* method, although they have also recently released a Riserva aged for thirty-six months on the lees which is bottle fermented. Some of the emerging wineries around Ronca and Terrossa, as well as those of the nearby town of Montecchia di Crosara, have an extra string to their bow these days as well: Ca Rugate, Corte Moschina, Fattori, Franchetto and Sandro de Bruno have all begun to market Lessini Durello Metodo Classico in the last few years. Tasting the wine, it is not difficult to see what all the excitement is about: the breadth of aroma and flavour conferred by long periods of lees ageing is most impressive. The denomination would seem to have a very promising future.

THE ESSENTIAL VALPOLICELLA

Talk of Hemingway's Valpolicella is steeped in nostalgia. However, the stories told about the writer's love of the wine, aside from being in all probability apocryphal, were often mere testimonies to his prodigious consumption. We know that he was briefly in the Veneto as an 18-year-old volunteer ambulance driver in 1918 though he spent most of his time in hospital recovering from shrapnel wounds to both legs. His next visit was thirty years later when he spent several months in Venice and found the inspiration for his novel *Across the River and into the Trees*. He spent time there again in the winter of 1949 to 1950 revising the newly finished novel and finally returned in mid-1954, following the two plane crashes in Africa which nearly killed him, for his renowned 'Scampi and Valpolicella cure'. Given that the novel was published in 1950, his observations about the wine draw on the time he spent there at the end of the 1940s: not the most propitious of times for wine production in Italy! Hemingway's comments about Valpolicella are voiced through the mouthpiece of its central character, the cantankerous Colonel Richard Cantwell. His first two observations are not particularly complimentary: 'I believe the Valpolicella is better when it is newer. It is not a *grand vin* and bottling it and putting years on it only adds sediment', and 'This wine gets awfully dreggy at the end.' His attitude has mellowed somewhat later in the book by the time he has found an example he seems happier with: '… the light, dry, red wine which was as friendly as the house of your brother, if you and your brother are good friends'.

This last quotation is the one which is continually referred to and which clarifies Hemingway's more charitable feelings about Valpolicella. Even so, the wine's main virtue seems to have been the feelings of comfort and security it inspires, its very conviviality. What little we do know about the Hemingway Valpolicella must be pieced together from the scant information we have about wine production at the time. The principal grape varieties behind the wine would have been Corvina (including possibly a proportion of Corvinone), Rondinella and Molinara. It would have been fermented in either wood or, possibly, cement and may have had a brief period of wood ageing. It would have been very much a rough and ready (and relatively unstable) style. If its prize attributes could be therefore defined as those of a reliable, everyday wine, the trail had gone cold by the time Mario Soldati made his first 'oenological journey' at the end of the 1960s. By then the defining example was probably closer to the Belfrage model: the wine's identity was largely moulded to suit the prevailing tastes of the time and sold at a price point which only companies of an industrial size could hope to sustain. While there seems to have been little substance behind the mythical status of the Hemingway Valpolicella, the stardust of international recognition and via such a charismatic figure proved to be a real lifeline. With the practical model of Bepi Quintarelli, who began realizing his own distinctive take on Valpolicella in the 1950s as their guiding light, smaller growers saw a glimmer of what could be achieved through focusing on quality production. So began the development of a new style of Valpolicella which could compete on an international stage in terms of more than just price. Meanwhile larger, merchant-style houses were working hard at upgrading the quality of their offer and their image, aware of the longer-term advantages such a policy might bring.

Today's youthful Valpolicella comes in a variety of styles. It spans a range of colours from the palest cherry red to a much deeper violet-toned ruby. The former tends to be a more accurate reflection of 'the real Valpolicella' while the deeper, darker and more structured styles are primarily made with a nod to the perceived fashion for that style of wine. The recent emergence of Oseleta amongst other dark-skinned grapes and subsequent demise of Molinara has brought about a shift in focus towards what some growers identify as a more 'important' style of wine, a somewhat pompous point of view which does the more playful and sympathetic style of Valpolicella a great disservice.

Just as Soave's distinguishing characteristics depend on Garganega, so Valpolicella's are defined by Corvina and the other varieties – although in theory allowed to make up more than half of the blend – invariably play a supporting role. Corvina's determining fruit characters are clearly those of cherry, mainly red but also black, with notes of raspberry and plum; background shadings of hedgerow fruits, blackberry, damson and sloe confer depth of aroma. Violet scents are often evident as well as a restrained measure of herbal tones, especially mint and sage. Many Italians pundits identify *mentuccia* (lesser calamint) which grows wild in many parts of the country. (*Calamintha nepeta* or *nepitella* as it is also commonly known has an aroma that straddles mint and oregano and is commonly used in cooking – it is an essential ingredient of the classic Roman dish *carciofi alla romana*, for example.) A clearly defining element is a twist of aromatic black pepper; mainly associated with the French variety Syrah, this quality is a trademark characteristic of Corvina as well. Altogether these different elements add up to a fresh and penetrating fragrance which is as appealing as it is nuanced. The palate is typically lively with brisk, at times bracing, acidity which underlines the wine's appetizing and savoury quality. A light to medium body is to be expected. Fruit flavours are ripe and juicy and underpinned by sapid or saline notes; while some producers prefer to maintain a gram or two of residual sugar to give a sense of roundness and smoothness, others aim for the palate-cleansing dryness which seems perhaps more appropriate for a wine with a consistently low pH. Light but fine tannins are just enough to give a degree of firmness to the finish and, in combination with the acidity, keep the exuberant fruit characters in check. It is entirely typical of the wines of the area that a degree of minerality is also part of the equation. Few wines are quite so immediately satisfying and at the same time so subtle and refreshing. At its best Valpolicella is above all a joyous wine: a celebration of the two key elements of freshness and elegance.

VALPOLICELLA DOC AND DOCG WINES

Variations on these defining characteristics come about through a unique set of production regulations: winemakers are able to make five different wine styles from the same vineyard using the same mix of grapes. Throughout all three zones of the Valpolicella, the options are the regular DOC version, Superiore DOC, Ripasso DOC (or Ripasso Superiore DOC), Amarone DOCG and Recioto DOCG plus the addition of the name of the sub-zone (either Classico or Valpantena). Many of them choose to make all five, staggering the harvest, the various winemaking tasks, the length of *appassimento* and wood ageing accordingly. Similarly the choice of grape variety can be adapted, within the regulations, to suit the individual product and the winemaker's objectives.

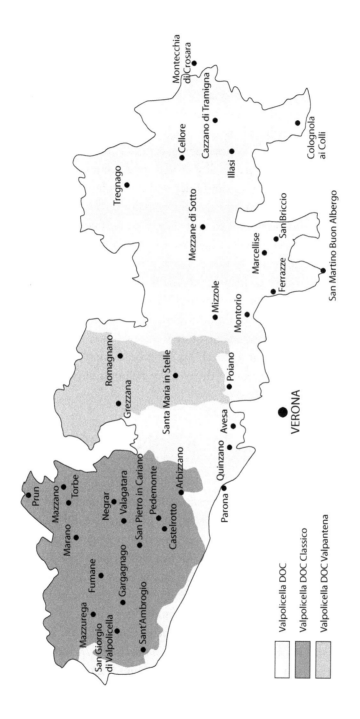

Montecchia di Crosara
Cellore
Cazzano di Tramigna
Illasi
Colognola ai Colli
Tregnago
Mezzane di Sotto
San Briccio
Marcellise
San Martino Buon Albergo
Ferrazze
Mizzole
Montorio
Romagnano
Santa Maria in Stelle
Poiano
Grezzana
Avesa
VERONA
Quinzano
Parona
Arbizzano
Prun
Mazzano
Torbe
Marano
Negrar
Valagatara
San Pietro in Cariano
Pedemonte
Castelrotto
Fumane
Gargagnago
Mazzurega
San Giorgio di Valpolicella
Sant'Ambrogio

Valpolicella DOC
Valpolicella DOC Classico
Valpolicella DOC Valpantena

The denominations of Valpolicella

Unlike Soave, the vineyards of Valpolicella resist easy categorization into different sections and the soils of the main growing areas are relatively homogeneous throughout. While basalt of volcanic origin is the main underlying rock formation in a few places, on the whole a substratum of marine limestone is typical of the higher hillsides. Where the slopes become less steep, calcareous marls are evident (Scaglia Rossa and Biancone) with some presence of degraded grey limestone. Where the lower slopes descend towards the valley floors, the rocky, calcareous clay gives way to a looser, pebbly clay of alluvial and colluvial origins. Finally, along the Adige river, alluvial fans are characteristic of the western part of the area giving way to the rich sedimentary plains common in the east. It is thus more helpful when trying to define stylistic traits throughout the Valpolicella territory to think more in terms of the effects which altitude, exposure and microclimate have on growing conditions and, correspondingly, on aroma and flavour profiles. Thus a Valpolicella grown at lower elevations may tend to have lower levels of acid, riper fruit characters and higher alcohol than the leaner and more aromatic versions from higher and steeper hillside sites (provided, of course, that sensibly contained crop levels and winemaking methodology permit a like-to-like comparison). The other main variable is the exact mixture of the component grape varieties.

The area under vine in Valpolicella totals just under 8,000 hectares or roughly a quarter of the entire delimited area. In addition to other crops (fruit and olive trees, etc.), plenty of forested land still breaks up the scenery though gaping scars of exposed rock on some of the higher hillsides, especially around Classico, remind the visitor that quarrying for stone is still an important activity for the local economy.

The viticultural area is split into three sectors. Classico in the west is made up of the following municipalities: Fumane, Marano di Valpolicella, Negrar, Sant'Ambrogio di Valpolicella and San Pietro in Cariano. The Valpolicella DOC begins beyond the eastern slopes of the Negrar valley and though the additional geographical sub-zone of Valpantena is often described as being sandwiched in between the other two (i.e. Classico and DOC), in fact a smaller area comprised of the land above the suburb of Parona plus the two valleys of Quinzano and Avesa is officially recognized for the production of the Valpolicella DOC(G) wines and separates Classico from Valpantena. The rest of

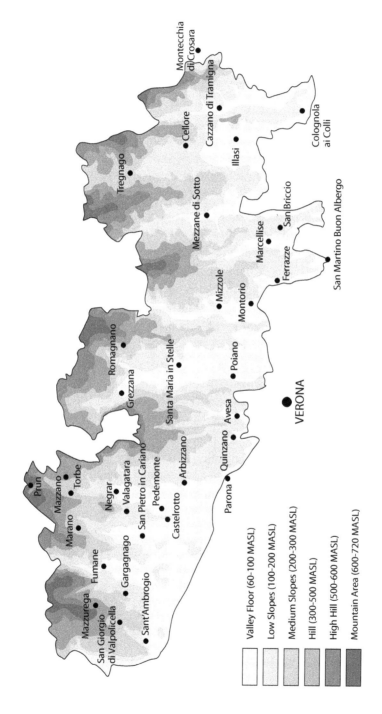

The topography of Valpolicella

Valley Floor (60-100 MASL)
Low Slopes (100-200 MASL)
Medium Slopes (200-300 MASL)
Hill (300-500 MASL)
High Hill (500-600 MASL)
Mountain Area (600-720 MASL)

the Valpolicella DOC territory stretches from the eastern limits of the Valpantena valley to the eastern edge of the Val Tramigna where the Soave Classico area begins. It includes all or part of the municipalities of Dolcè, Verona, San Martino Buon Albergo, Lavagno, Mezzane di Sotto, Tregnago, Illasi, Colognola ai Colli, Cazzano di Tramigna, Grezzana, Pescantina, Cerro Veronese, San Mauro di Saline and Montecchia di Crosara. As with Soave, the overall area was granted DOC status under the regulations passed in 1968 when Italy's new system of controls over wine production was implemented.

The component grape varieties are the same for all five different types of wine produced within the area. Corvina makes up between 45 and 95 per cent while Corvinone may replace Corvina up to a maximum of 50 per cent of the total blend. Rondinella is present of between 5 and 30 per cent while a maximum of 25 per cent is also permitted of other recognized varieties. If the logic seems a little convoluted, it is in fact not quite as complicated as it appears. To illustrate the point, a blend of 50 per cent Corvinone, 40 per cent Corvina and 10 per cent Rondinella would be allowed under current legislation as that 50 per cent of Corvinone replaces the same percentage of a potential total of 95 per cent of Corvina, etc. The other grape varieties are as discussed in Chapter 3. The idea, though, of any single variety other than Corvina making a substantial difference to the overall character of the wine is rarely if ever borne out; any effect is more to be seen as a nuance or shading rather than delivering a fundamental change to the wine's personality.

The vineyards described below in the Valpolicella DOC, Valpolicella Classico DOC and Valpantena DOC areas are where all five styles of wine listed above are produced.

Valpolicella DOC

Distinguishing production regulations

- *Minimum alcohol content: 11.0%*

- *Release date: No minimum ageing period specified*

- *Vineyard yields: 12 tonnes per hectare*

The many vineyards of Valpolicella are identified by names which have been handed down through generations. Most of them are toponyms or place names, which can refer to geographical features such as hillsides (or particular parts of hillsides), *frazione* or small sections thereof (the Italian word *localita* is a really useful term but has no obvious single-word translation). The list of vineyards named is anything but comprehensive and, rather, represents those likely to be fairly widely commercially available at the time of writing.

The DOC territory of Valpolicella is made up of both plains (or lower lying) and hillside vineyards. The topography of an area has a profound influence on the style of wine produced as do the varying microclimates of the different valleys the area encompasses. While it is a mistake to assume that fine wine is produced only in hillside sites, exposition and altitudes are fundamental in determining the precise nature of a wine's identity. The DOC zone has a multitude of highly suitable sites at every level. In general terms, the area has a slightly warmer climate than both Classico and Valpantena as the cooling influence of Lake Garda gradually diminishes in an easterly direction. The wines are often riper tasting, with lower acidity and higher alcohol than their neighbours, though at the same time they can struggle to compete in terms of elegance, finesse and, above all, breadth of aromatic profile. A frequently heard point of view amongst growers is that while the hillside sites in Classico are the finest in the overall area, the lower-lying vineyards there are planted on extremely rich and fertile soil which produces wines of lesser quality than the stonier and less fertile plains of the wider DOC area. On the whole, wines from the DOC territory tend to be warmer, more alcoholic and muscular than those from Classico.

The most westerly section of the DOC area begins at the eastern edge of the ridge that borders the valley of Negrar. Being just a couple of hundred metres outside the Classico zone, however, doesn't deter the Piccoli sisters Veronica and Alice from making wines which certainly show the structure and intensity for which those of the neighbouring valley are renowned, even though labelled as 'straight' Valpolicella DOC. Their south-facing vineyards lie in a well-ventilated spot on Monte della Parte which overlooks Parona. Just beyond here to the east lie the two small and peaceful valleys of Quinzano and Avesa. Much of the land is covered in forest, and though there are plenty of vineyards planted, most of the fruit is sold off. Just one small producer bottles and sells wines specifically from the area.

Based at Zovo in Quinzano, Pietro Zanoni owns vineyards in both steep-sided valleys (plus a little more land under vine in nearby Parona), where the coolish microclimate gives the wines a particular freshness without compromising their ageing potential. Even Pietro's 'simple' Valpolicella DOC is a reliable and consistently well-made wine and worth seeking out. Clearly there is real potential for fine wine production hereabouts.

The story is a similar one after the eastern limits of Valpantena where the Val di Squaranto is surprisingly, given its great length, relatively bereft of major vineyard areas and the hills are as likely to be covered with fruit trees as they are with vines. It is early days for La Giuva, a new wine-producing enterprise based at Trezzolano high up in the northerly reaches of the valley, whose first vintage was in 2011. Football and wine fans alike will be keeping an eye on progress as the estate is owned by Alberto Malesani, the ex-professional footballer turned football manager. At the other end of the valley, due west and above the town of Montorio – famous for its castle, Austrian fort and *progno* springs – another new producer is already starting to make waves. The elegant Villa San Carlo is set in the middle of an oasis of some 70 hectares which includes around 23 hectares of vineyard, though the Pavesi family vinify fruit from only a very small section. Early signs bode well as their Amarone has won instant recognition in various international wine competitions. As with neighbouring Qunizano and Avesa, the Squaranto valley appears to be ripe for development.

According to Cristiano Saletti of Terre di Pietra, Marcellise was known as the Valley of Cherries until a few years ago because that's all there was back then. The tiny winery was established ten years ago; the Campodelle family have been around a little longer and their Marion estate (named after the noble family who used to own the villa where the firm is now based) has already built up quite a reputation. Their vineyards lie in the area known as Borgo, just west of the village. Other names have been attracted to the area: both Torre d'Orti and La Brigaldara have extensive holdings on the clay and limestone hillsides which lie just north of San Martino Buon Albergo. At the southerly edge of the hills that form the western side of the valley, not far from the town of San Martino, lies another oasis. Close to the small *frazione* of Ferrazze, Enrico and daughter Maddalena Pasqua have transformed the 400-hectare Tenuta Musella estate into a country Relais and winery.

From approximately 25 hectares of biodynamically farmed vineyard and, guided by of one of biodynamic's early pioneers and Steiner disciple Alex Podolinsky, the wines produced by this branch of the Pasqua family are starting to make others sit up and take notice. Ironically Marcellise, one of the shortest valleys in the entire Valpolicella area, tended to be generally overlooked until the Amarone boom alerted interested parties to promising vineyard sites.

The next valley to the east (Mezzane) marks the western boundary of the Soave DOC area and, perhaps for this reason, vineyard plantings become immediately much more evident.

It is worth remembering that into the 1980s and 1990s, Soave was just as popular if not more so than Valpolicella and vineyards in areas where both wines could be produced were the most sought after. Ironically the picture has totally changed over the last twenty years: these days Soave houses are keen to invest in Valpolicella while there seems to be precious little traffic the other way. The emerging importance of Mezzane di Sotto as a production area for red wines can be seen in the roll call of both established and up and coming names who work vineyards there: Corte Sant'Alda, Dal Cero, Ilatium, Massimago, Mosconi, Provolo, Roccolo Grassi, San Cassiano, Tedeschi, Tenuta Sant'Antonio, Villa Erbice, etc. It is reassuring to note that many of them continue to produce Soave. Vineyards cover both sides of the valley, though on the east-facing slopes these tend be focused more on the southern reaches of the ridge that separates Mezzane from Marcellise. The area above Lavagno, in particular, is densely planted on the clay and limestone soils between Castagne and San Briccio. The impressive Tenuta Sant'Antonio is based here on the summit of the Monte Garbi vineyard. On the west-facing side of Mezzane a number of smaller wineries are also producing some first-class Valpolicella and Amarone: San Cassiano, Massimago and Corte Sant'Alda in particular, though further up the valley – indeed overlapping the two municipalities of Mezzane di Sotto and Tregnago – Tedeschi's splendid Maternigo estate sits on the high marl hillsides overlooking the length of the valley below. Riccardo Tedeschi's painstaking work in identifying the differing characteristics of the various vineyards (31 hectares planted) has led to the production of some highly promising, super-charged wines that show the classic mix of tremendous freshness and great potential longevity.

At some 40 kilometres long, the Val d'Illasi is the longest of the valleys that runs south from the Monti Lessini to the floodplains of the Adige, and it finally opens out to meet the A4 motorway some 20 kilometres to the east of Verona. It is divided into various sections, though the Valpolicella vineyards begin mid valley in the municipality of Tregnago, taking in Illasi itself, and finally Colognola ai Colli. Together, the three communes form the largest single area for the production of the Valpolicella reds throughout the entire DOC territory, even though the southern reaches around Colognola ai Colli are primarily given over to Soave with over five times as many white as red grapes planted. The village of Tregnago sits at just over 300 metres above sea level and the valley shelves slowly down towards Colognola ai Colli some 12 kilometres and more than 200 metres lower down. As with Soave the presence of the main cooperative looms large over the valley, and Cantina di Soave dominates red wine production. There is however a growing number of other wineries of major significance, notably Romano Dal Forno, a modern legend of Valpolicella, whose vineyards around the small hamlet of Cellore d'Illasi are planted on the alluvial, pebbly soil that characterizes both the floor and lower slopes of the valley. The family's higher vineyards occupy the upper slopes around Monte Lodoletta at around 370 metres where the terrain is more based on limestone. Cellore seems to be turning into something of a mecca for lovers of fine wine: directly opposite Dal Forno, Flavio Pra – whose uncle Graziano owns the famous Pra winery in Soave – has built his new cellars. Flavio foresees a big future for Illasi and his vineyards occupy both the pebbly terrain close to the valley's famous *progno* and, higher up the valley, the marl soils of Tregnago. The Palazzo Maffei estate of the Cottini family lies just over the crest of the hill from Tedeschi's Maternigo estate in neighbouring Mezzane; its south-east-facing vineyards around Roccolo on the western side of the valley overlook Tregnago below. Also based at Tregnago and founded in 2003, the 16-hectare Tenuta Chicherri estate lies on the opposite side of the valley over the ridge from San Giovanni Ilarione. While their winery is situated in Tregnago itself at Villa Cipolla, the Pieropan family acquired vineyards on Monte Garzon on the eastern slopes of the valley in 1999 close to Cellore. At 400 metres and facing south, growing conditions on the limestone and clay soils seem perfect for a combination of elegance and richness. More recent investment has seen the Pasqua family buy up 26 hectares of vineyard on the opposite side of the valley at Monte Vegro for the production of their Mai Dire Mai ('never say never') range. Illasi is famous for its medieval castle which dates back to the Scaligero period of Verona's history. It dominates the valley from its position on the ridge separating Illasi from the Val di Tramigna, overlooking important vineyard sites including the nearby Tenda hillside where the Trabucchi family cultivate around 22 hectares of land.

East of Illasi, the final valley of the Valpolicella DOC, the Val di Tramigna, also forms the border with Soave Classico. Despite this proximity, red grapes once again dominate the valley: there are just 74 hectares registered for Soave and over 200 for Valpolicella. The local cooperative was the Cantina di Soave's first major acquisition more than twenty years ago and so much of the fruit grown in the valley is incorporated within their range. Soave producers Coffele are one of the very few to fly the flag for 'growers' wines' in the area and produce some delicious DOC(G) reds from their smallholding above the town of Cazzano. Otherwise Ronca-based winery Fattori own a 12-hectare property at Bastia which lies on the boundary between the Val di Tramigna and Montecchia di Crosara and from where they produce a range of Valpolicella-based wines. Ca Rugate and a number of other Soave-based producers are the other important vineyard owners in the area.

Valpolicella Classico DOC

Distinguishing production regulations
- *Minimum alcohol content: 11.0%*
- *Release date: No minimum ageing period specified*
- *Vineyard yields: 12 tonnes per hectare*

If the Valpolicella DOC is – like the Soave DOC – an area dominated to a large extent by cooperative interests, then Valpolicella Classico is the land of the *negoziante*. These firms represent the recent history of commercial wine production in the Veronese, when growers customarily sold off their fruit or wine to larger concerns who would then sell on the finished product. Though there has been a huge increase in the number of smaller grower/bottlers over the last couple of decades, the presence of *negoziante* houses remains strong. Masi, for example, while owning vineyards also work with some forty-two growers across the Veronese, some of whom have been supplying the Boscaini family for over three generations. 'We're looking for commitment from both sides,' explains Raffaele Boscaini. 'Ours is a serious project and it has to work for everyone involved.' Bolla work with some 400 hectares of land in Classico and thirty families depend on them for their livelihood. In the valley of Marano, Campagnola – who produce a million bottles of the Valpolicella wines a year – rely on some 75 hectares in the valley of Marano farmed by *conferenti*, while owning a much smaller area of vineyard themselves. Similarly Pasqua and Sartori own significant areas of vineyard but supplement their production through networks of growers. The *negoziante* system has roots deep in the culture of Veronese wines with strong ties to the *mezzadria* way of life. It continues, in a way, in a modified form with the cooperative movement. The two can even work together: just as Sartori work closely with the Cantina di Colognola ai Colli these days, so Bolla's involvement in Classico is largely conducted through their association with the Cantina Sociale San Pietro in Cariano, one of two Classico-based cooperatives. The other, the Cantina Sociale di Negrar, remains staunchly independent.

Sant'Ambrogio di Valpolicella

The Valpolicella Classico zone begins in the northern suburbs of Verona itself and stretches up as far as the lower reaches of the Lessinia mountains covering an area of just under 3,500 hectares of vineyard (the extended zone totals over 4,000 hectares). Classico is often thought of as the three principal valleys of Fumane, Marano and Negrar though locals always include the 'semi-valley' of Sant'Ambrogio which is where – running from west to east – the zone actually begins. The hills below Monte Pastello separate the Adige valley from those of Valpolicella and right at the northern edge of the commune lie the vineyards at Monte, a windy spot at some 400 metres, overlooking the Adige. The Cantina di Negrar produce one of their Espressioni range of Amarone from fruit grown here. Where the hill chain descends to the flood plain of the river lies the village of Sant'Ambrogio itself: a number of smaller wineries such as Aldegheri, Corte Aleardi and Corte Benedetti are based here. Due south of the village is the small hillside area of Montindon and the 35-hectare estate from where the well-known Zenato winery produces a range of Veronese reds. Just west of the village is the flat-topped conical hill of one of the area's most famous vineyard sites, La Grola, really an outcropping extension of the ridge to the north and indeed the most westerly vineyard area of Classico itself. La Grola has a long local history of producing wine, but its fame has reached new heights over the last few decades since the Allegrini family bought a 30-hectare site there and began producing the wines which have been instrumental in redefining the area's image. Sadly the Allegrini family no longer market La Grola as a Valpolicella Classico, however. Carlo Boscaini and the Tommasi family both own vines on or around the hillside. Just above La Grola lie the south-west-facing vineyards of Costalunga and two other important sites also occupy the western flanks of the bottom of the ridge. Both Sengia and the Conca d'Oro are small amphitheatres that lie below San Giorgio di Valpolicella (or San Giorgio Ingannapoltron, as it is also commonly referred to). The main vineyard owners here are Carlo Boscaini, Le Salette, Monte Dall'Ora, Corte Rugolin, Quintarelli and Tommasi. At the southern tip lies the ancient Serego Alighieri estate set amidst its own vineyards close to the area known as Vaio Armaron, and just above the central offices of Masi at the *frazione* of Gargagnago. Near neighbours Villa Monteleone also produce a range of good-quality wine. The style of the Sant'Ambrogio wines is a particularly voluptuous one: the wines are fleshy and seductive with ripe and round fruit flavours and many of the vineyard sites lie at lower elevations where the slightly warmer growing conditions make their presence felt. Beyond Sant'Ambrogio, the vineyards of the Fumane valley begin.

Fumane

The vineyard area of Fumane is clustered largely around the mouth of the valley and split into two main sections by the presence of the Colle Incisa. This steep-sided limestone spur is mainly planted to vines on its summit – an area known as Costa delle Coronne – and is otherwise well known for the Madonna de La Salette sanctuary which is plainly visible partway up the hillside as you enter the valley from the south, passing the Secondo Marco winery. To the west of the hill, the road snakes up past Allegrini's Palazzo della Torre estate, flanking Marega and Zeno Zenigli's Monte dei Ragni vineyards, towards Mazzurega. The village is surrounded by vineyards and Cottini own some 15 hectares at their Campiano estate.

Mazzurega is also a source of grapes for another of Cantina di Negrar's Amarone Espressioni. Higher still lies Cavarena, the source of Allegrini's Amarone, and above which their premium Amarone vineyard Fieramonte is located. The Tedeschi family's 7-hectare La Fabriseria sits close by and partially overlaps into Sant'Ambrogio as do the vineyards at the top of the Monte Solane ridge where Tenute Ugolini and Gamba Gnirega both own land. Lower down the slopes and between Mazzurega and the Colle Incisa, the Custoza-based winery, Monte del Tra's estate is located in the 'Lena di Mezzo' area. At nearby Cavolo, are some of the highest vineyards in Classico. Though only a short distance as the crow flies from Fumane itself, the *frazione* of Cavolo (less than four hundred inhabitants) also sits at 600 metres, an indication of just how steep this western side of the valley can be. The main vineyard owners around Cavolo are Accordini and Scriani. The most southerly extension of Cavolo lies just above the Costa delle Coronne vineyards. The style of the wines produced on the western slopes of Fumane is clearly affected by the altitude of the vineyards and the cool, well-ventilated growing conditions: salient characteristics are the broad, intense, spicy aromas and lively acidity of these typically elegant and sometimes rather lean wines.

To the east of the Colle Incisa, the Via Progni heads up towards the village of Molina in Lessinia and on the eastern side of the valley opposite the hill, the vineyards begin on the south-facing slopes of Monte Santoccio. The vineyards below at Maghi and Osan occupy the steep incline which drops to the very edge of the village of Fumane itself. Two smaller wineries, Monte Santoccio and Ca dei Maghi, own vines in the area. This hillside curves round into one of Fumane's most prestigious vineyards, Monte Sant'Urbano, a long south-west-facing ridge (Speri are the major landowners) which tapers down into Monte Gradella from where Santa Sofia and Sartori both produce limited edition bottlings. The gradients on this side of the valley are usually rather more gentle and the land lower lying, which gives rise to an elegant, balanced and riper style of wine. Adjacent to Monte Gradella are the vineyards of Casterna where the Valentina Cubi winery is based.

Marano di Valpolicella

Fumane borders on Marano to the east and the Monti Sant'Urbano and Gradella form part of the western side of the ridge which separates the two municipalities. A rather longer and narrower though in places barely less steep valley, Marano is famous for its fragrant and fruit-driven style of wine: it's luscious, ripe cherries all the way. There are two main villages in the valley: towards its mouth, Valgatara and, much higher up at over 300 metres and towards its northerly limits, Marano itself. Inevitably most of the vineyards are focused around these two areas. Most of the better-known areas around Valgatara are clustered along the eastern side of the valley and the long Masua hillside which, at up to 400 metres, offers a variety of sites and expositions on the chalky clay soils and separates much of the two valleys of Marano and Negrar. Both Tommasi and Venturini produce Amarone from the central section of Masua. Just north of this part of the hillside, Le Marognele and Le Bignele are both smaller-scale cellars making the local red wines from grapes grown on the surrounding land. Similarly Gamba Gnirega, owned by the Aldrighetti family, have vines in Gnirega, adjacent to Masua, as well as Fumane; their Le Quare range comes from the Marano-grown fruit and shows a full, rich style. Below the highest part of Masua to the south and again bordering on Negrar (where they are based), Villa Spinosa produce an intriguingly aromatic wine from the Figari hillside. In Valgatara, small cellars such as those of Fratelli Degani, Aldrighetti Lorenzo e Cristoforo and Corte Rugolin make convincing versions of the local wines. Masi's bottling plant is located on the edge of the village on the site of the old Paolo Boscaini winery. A little further up the valley, just above the Giuseppe Campagnola cellars and on the western slopes opposite Masua, the Ravazzol vineyard has a longstanding reputation for the production of fine wine. The principal vineyard owners, Ca La Bionda, continue this tradition with real distinction. Ravazzol lies just south of the small village of Prognol where the Antolini winery sits surrounded by vineyards, and from where it's a short drive up to Marano itself.

Lying below the village to the west, the Vaona family's estate at Novaia covers 10 hectares of land with some 7 hectares of mainly south- and south-east-facing vineyard at between 250 and 400 metres. The soils up here are a clay rich marl with some presence of tufa and basalt: the area above the village to the north was, during its formation, the source of significant volcanic activity and the land surrounding Marano is one of the relatively few spots in Classico where volcanic soils are clearly evident: a contributory factor to the fleshy yet elegant style of the wines. Just above Novaia is Camporal where the recently constructed

Albino Armani winery blends in seamlessly with the many dry-stone wall terraces that cover the slopes; the roof garden offers a commanding view over the valley below. Two other wineries also worth seeking out are based in Marano itself: close to the centre of the village, and proprietors of the local restaurant Da Bepi, the Lonardi family produce the classic wines of the Valpolicella in an unpretentious and authentic style, while Terre di Leone have a more ambitious range. Their vineyards are beyond the village to the west partly overlooking Fumane, where the volcanic soils particular to the higher parts of the valley continue. A significant number of important vineyard areas occupy the slopes above and below the sanctuary at Santa Maria in Valverde on the Castelon hill. The present-day church was built in 1682 though the site was thought to be home to a fort back in Roman times which was later destroyed under the Scaligeri family. This is a wonderful setting from which to gaze out over both the Fumane and Marano valleys; some of the higher parts of Negrar are also visible in the distance. The sanctuary is just outside the small village of Pezza where Corte Zardini produce a range of honest, authentic and rather rustic wines. A short drive from Pezza takes you up to the northern limit of the Marano valley at the village of San Rocco, the source of Cantina di Negrar's San Rocco Amarone from fruit grown at 510 metres. To the east of Pezza, Purano is another elevated vineyard position where the Borghetti family makes wine at the Corte Fornaledo estate. Below Purano the beautifully positioned Tenuta Santa Maria Valverde (the cover photo of the book) is run by Ilaria and Nicola Campagnola – cousins of the homonymous *negoziante* further down the valley; the charming old farm sits just above the renowned Gaso or Gazzo vineyard. Marano-based San Rustico, owned by another branch of the family, makes a range of premium wines from fruit grown in this south-facing amphitheatre. Shortly after Gaso, the road winds back down into Fumane at Santoccio.

Negrar

The last valley of Classico is Negrar, much the longest and most densely planted to vines of the three. Indeed, along with the suburbs of Verona and San Pietro in Cariano which also boast over 1,000 hectares of vineyard each, Negrar has the largest surface area given over to vineyards in the entire Valpolicella DOC territory. The wines of Negrar have the reputation of being the fullest, most structured and long-lived of the Classico denomination; while this is generally true, the wines produced in the northernmost parts of the valley in particular where altitudes exceed 500 metres can, not surprisingly, show a decidedly lean and austere character. The western side of the valley which flanks Marano (and therefore the Masua hill) has a high concentration of well-known vineyards starting at Moron which also borders on to the *frazione* of Pedemonte (part of the commune of San Pietro in Cariano). Moron is a relatively low-lying, south-east-facing part of the hillside, characterized by colluvial soils at its feet with clay and limestone above. Cantina di Negrar's Recioto is produced from grapes grown in Moron while La Dama also own vines in the area and Cantina Salgari are located nearby. To the north, Moron merges into one of Classico's most prestigious and celebrated vineyard sites. The chalky clay soils around the *frazione* of Jago occupy the long hillside at between 200 and 300 metres overlooking the small town of Negrar itself. Close to the wooded summit of La Masua a cave carved into the tufa was, according to local sources, still inhabited at the end of the Second World War. There are three main sections of Jago: di Sotto (lower), di Mezzo (middle) and di Sopra (upper) which form the south-east-facing slopes on the eastern side of the La Masua ridge. Fratelli Recchia own almost 50 hectares of vines here while Damoli have a vineyard in the middle section and Villa Spinosa are based in Jago di Sotto. Members of the nearby Cantina di Negrar and Corte Merci also have land in and around Jago. Below the northern section lies the impressive Villa Bertoldi, a famous loggia and portico construction dating back to the fifteenth century, in the area known as Palazzo. The palace was the headquarters of the Gestapo during the Second World War and the new owners, the Recchia family, have long-term plans to restore the building. The vineyards of Torbe begin just above Palazzo, below the road which connects the village with Jago. The southernmost vineyards, around the areas known as I Toari and Colombare di Torbe, are composed of similar tufaceous soils as the contiguous hills on the other side of the ridge in Marano. Wines of note produced from fruit grown at Torbe are the Amarone Campolongo from Masi, Cantina di Negrar's premium Ripasso Classico Superiore and Terre di Pietra's Valpolicella Classico Stelar. The south- and south-east-facing vineyard slopes of Torbe are mainly concentrated below the road which leads up to the village of Prun, famous for its quarries of Lessinia Stone. At around 500 metres the vineyards mark the northern border of the DOC boundary. Tenute SalvaTerra have acquired the sixteenth-century Villa Salvaterra which sits just below the village. The villa itself is being restored although the surrounding vineyards have already been replanted and are in production for both versions of Amarone from Salvaterra, the regular Classico and Riserva Cave di Prun.

On the other side of the Progno di Negrar below Provale, the vineyards of Panego face mainly southwest at between 400 and 500 metres and fold into those of Mazzano below. Claudio Viviani owns vineyards in both areas and Masi produce their premium Amarone Mazzano from vines at the edge of the village. The vineyards of the eastern flank of the Negrar valley are situated below the road through Mazzano which leads up through Fane and, beyond, to the Ponte de Veja and Sant'Anna d'Alfaedo. They begin at San Ciriaco from where they slope down towards the village of Costeggiola. The Boscaini family produced a Valpolicella Classico San Ciriaco until a few years ago and Masi continue to manage vineyards in the area, as do Corte Merci. The next fold in the hillside has west- to south-west-facing vineyards at Villa which directly overlook Negrar, and where another of the cooperative's Espressioni range of Amarone comes from; Mazzi also produce an Amarone from grapes grown in Villa. The chalky marl soils give way to a substratum of basalt around the tiny hamlets of Preperchiusa and Palazzin above the area known as San Peretto where the two main grower/bottlers are the Mazzi brothers and Tommaso Bussola. The next major vineyard area is Monte Cere. The steeper slopes on the north-eastern side are, for most wine lovers, the real focus of interest: this part of the hill is known as Monte Ca' Paletta and is where the legendary Bepi Quintarelli's winery sits surrounded by vineyards. Further up and over to the west of Ca' Paletta is another famous vineyard. The south-facing Tramanal, at around 400 metres, has a great reputation though at the moment there is no wine labelled as such available on the market. Much of the land due south from Ca' Paletta and Tramanal dropping down towards Arbizzano is forested as far as the Novare estate, wrapped around the imposing Villa Mosconi Bertani. The Bertani family still own the villa and have started a new venture in the wine business: Tenuta Santa Maria di Gaetano Bertani. The beautifully preserved valley is wedged in between the two *frazioni* of Santa Maria di Negrar and Arbizzano but retains an almost timeless atmosphere of peace and tranquillity.

Directly above Novare to the west at between 250 and 400 metres, the Galli family's Le Ragose winery lies right on the eastern border of the Classico zone. The vineyards are planted mainly in a south-west-facing amphitheatre next to the cellars. Just above their estate, Villa Spinosa owns vines on the Costa del Buso hillside.

San Pietro in Cariano

The final commune for the production of Valpolicella Classico shares a border with all the others but while San Pietro in Cariano cannot lay claim to even 'semi-valley' status, it nonetheless has its fair share of excellent if lower-lying vineyard sites and well-respected producers. Much of San Pietro is fairly flat land and occupies the northern flood plain of the Adige. The rich and fertile soils are heavily planted to highly productive vineyards which on the whole give soft, simple wines which are low in acid and designed for early consumption. However, a number of gentle hillsides form more highly prized sites. At the lowest extension of the western flank of the Fumane valley below Marega, the vineyard area of Bure Alto surrounds the old Benedictine monastery which is now the headquarters of Tenute Ugolini and where grapes for the firm's Valpolicella Classico Superiore San Michele are grown. Villa Girardi, owned by a member of the Tommasi family, also produces a Valpolicella Ripasso Classico Superiore from Bure Alto. A short distance away, in the area known as Ambrosan, are two further family-owned wineries, Azienda Agricola Nicolis and Cantina Spada. Due south on the other side of the village, four wineries – Brunelli, Montecariano, Tenuta Pule and Fla Tio – are grouped around the perimeter of the south-facing amphitheatre of vines at Monte. The finest example of this small area, and indeed a real indication of the undoubted potential of San Pietro in Cariano in general, is the Valpolicella Classico Superiore Camporenzo made by Monte Dall'Ora. Diagonally opposite at the eastern edge of the village, are the contiguous vineyards of Tenda and Vajol. Vajol is of particular interest and is where the Rubinelli family farm 10 hectares of vines surrounding their Corte Sant'Anna farmhouse. The winery sits at the end of a track which connects to the road between San Pietro and nearby San Floriano at precisely the point where Celestino Gaspari's eye-catching Zyme winery is located. On the other side of the road, sitting on top of the gently sloping Squarano hillside, is the Cantine Marchesi Fumanelli with 28 hectares of surrounding vineyard.

As with Tenda, Vajol and Squarano itself, the lower-lying hills immediately to the south at Castelrotto merging into Corrubio can be seen as an extension, or a series of outcrops, of the ridge which separates the valleys of Fumane and Marano at Monte Sant'Urbano and Gradella. A clutch of wineries are based or own vineyards here – for example, Cantina di Negrar's final Amarone from the Espressioni range is produced from their member's vineyards in Castelrotto. Entering the village, Monte Dall'Ora is the first winery you come across. Their vineyards occupy the tip of the low-lying hill complex; in addition to the classic clay and limestone soil structure there is a vein of sandstone on the property. Just below here to the west is the area known as Cengia where Begali are based, and Secondo Marco owns vineyards directly opposite the Begali cellars. A little further on the headquarters of Tenute SalvaTerra are within the Villa Giona complex: vineyards surround the early sixteenth century palace which is now a hotel. Cantine Buglioni's old cellars are very close though the operation will be moved to new premises under construction near the firm's accommodation and restaurant facilities in neighbouring Sant'Ambrogio. Both SalvaTerra and Buglioni lie close to the foot of the southern part of the Corrubbio hillside which is known as Monte Sacchetti: the small family winery Luciano Arduini also own vineyards here. The larger production plant of Rino Sartori lies just further over to the west on the outskirts of Pescantina.

The final vineyard area of San Pietro is at the north-eastern edge of the municipality. Here the lower section of the Masua hill meets the flatter land between the two *frazione* of San Floriano (famous for its twelfth-century church) and Pedemonte. These particular parts of the hillside are known as Semonte, Olmi and Fontana, names which can be found on bottlings by Tedeschi and Venturini, both of whom are based close by. Other important wineries such as La Brigaldara and Tommasi have their main cellars in the area, as do smaller concerns such as Manara and Accordini Igenio. The lower slopes of Masua have a great reputation for both Amarone and Recioto. Indeed many excellent wines are produced within the territory of San Pietro: they generally show the ripe, palate-flattering style which is typical of the lower-lying vineyard areas, with red fruits and the scent of violets especially evident.

Valpolicella Valpantena DOC

Distinguishing production regulations
- *Minimum alcohol content: 11.0%*
- *Release date: no minumum ageing period specified*
- *Vineyard yields: 12 tonnes per hectare*

Although vineyards have been recorded in Valpantena since at least the ninth century, local place names date back to Roman times. For instance, the village of Quinto where the cooperative is based is so-called because it lies five Roman miles from Verona. Some even claim the history of wine production within the valley might be traced back earlier still, to the Etruscans. While the wines from Valpantena do have a distinctive style, it can seem something of a mystery why they should merit their own separate denomination – not that the people who live and work in the valley are complaining and, of course, staunchly defend their privileged position. The hugely influential Bertani has been the name practically synonymous with Valpantena since the firm was founded at Poiano in the 1850s. The first firm to export the local wines on a large scale and to lay down a reputation for their quality, the importance of Bertani in the creation of this special status should not be underestimated.

A long valley, Valpantena marks a change from the shorter and rather more narrow valleys of the Veronese to the west. Unlike Fumane, Marano and Negrar, the valley stretches up to the heart of the Alta Lessinia to the north and therefore lacks the protection of any natural barrier before the high plains to mitigate temperatures and growing conditions below. The main vineyards begin around Grezzana. Fewer vines are grown on the steep and rocky gradients of the east-facing side of the valley and there is a greater concentration of vineyards on the more easily workable and gently sloping west-facing side, particularly between the village of Santa Maria in Stelle and the *frazione* of Romagnano. Otherwise the pebbly, alluvial soils of the valley floor, from Quinto down past Poiano to the northern reaches of the suburbs of Verona itself, remain the other most densely planted area. For many years the Cantina Valpantena cooperative and a tiny handful of producers, like Tezza in Poiano, were the only sources of the local wine apart from that one important name. But over the last decade or so investment in a new winemaking venture called La Collina dei Ciliegi up at Erbin beyond Romagnano, followed by the purchase of the Bertani brand by Tenimenti Angelini in 2011, has opened a new chapter in the valley's history. The most recent development is, however, possibly the most significant of all. In 2015 Genagricola, the agricultural arm of Italy's largest insurance group Assicurazioni Generali (the Generali Group) completed the purchase of the 35-hectare Costa Arente estate just above Grezzana. With the cost of land in the Classico area currently exceeding €700,000 per hectare (almost 300 per cent more than twenty-five years ago), it was only ever going to be a matter of time before quieter backwaters like Valpantena attracted the interest of big business.

The style of the wines in Valpantena looks like an interesting long-term proposition: they are often distinctly lighter in style, less structured and slightly less alcoholic than those from the other valleys. Locals claim the slightly cooler and windier climate of the valley has an important part to play. While 16% abv and above is not uncommon for an Amarone from either the Classico or the extended zone, its counterpart from Valpantena often remains around 15% abv. But what the wines might lack in structure they make up for in charm with appealing cherry and black pepper elements usually very much to the fore. Collina dei Ciliegi work with the same oenologist as the Cantina Valpantena and a similarity in style is clearly evident. It is likely, too, with Costa Arente – where the consultant oenologist is the well-known Riccardo Cotarella – that the wines will lean towards the sort of impressively polished and well-rounded commercial character that is geared to pleasing an international audience. Just as Bertani once blazed a trail for the area, so the 'new wines' of Valpantena seem set to continue the tradition.

Further denominations

Within these three adjoining vineyard areas, the production of another four types of wine are covered by disciplinary regulations under the Valpolicella banner. In essence they reflect the individual stylistic traits identified above.

Valpolicella Superiore DOC

Distinguishing production regulations
- *Minimum alcohol content: 12.0%*
- *Release date: a minimum of one year's ageing beginning from 1 January following the vintage*
- *Vineyard yields: 12 tonnes per hectare*

A clear indication of wine style is implicit in the production disciplines of the DOC and DOCG Veronese red wines with the sole exception of the Superiore denomination. What distinguishes the category from the 'normal' versions of Valpolicella (including Valpantena or Classico) DOC is simply a minimum ageing period and an extra degree at least of alcohol. While the creative winemaker thus has *carta bianca* to develop the raw material as he or she sees fit, the consumer is left not knowing what to expect unless of course the 'house style' is already a familiar one. The variables that the Superiore category opens up will of course have a fundamental bearing on what the wine smells and tastes like. Aside from the provenance of the grapes themselves, there are a number of factors to be considered. Firstly there is no stipulation as to the type of container in which the minimum ageing period is carried out – this could be cement, stainless steel, wood, bottle or even clay amphora. Secondly fruit for fermentation may just be freshly gathered, include a proportion of semi-dried fruit or even be entirely from semi-dried grapes; similarly there is no specification as to how any *appassimento* might be carried out, so the grapes could be partially dried on the plant (*sovramaturazione*), or for a couple of weeks or even a couple of months in the *fruttaio*. A third and often surprising consideration is the alcohol content which can swing upwards wildly from the required minimum of 12% abv: there is, for example, a reasonably well-known version of Valpolicella DOC Superiore on the market which regularly reaches at least 16% abv (Morari from Torre d'Orti), higher than many an Amarone. Indeed examples of this type – for instance, San Cassiano's Le Alene and the Verjago from the Cantina di Negrar, both Superiore wines made from 100 per cent dried grapes – make the most convincing case yet for the mini-Amarone style. The freedom of expression that the Superiore category offers can be a double-edged sword and the principle of caveat emptor most definitely applies!

Despite the potential confusion, the Superiore category can include some of the territory's most interesting and finest red wines. Most wineries will choose either a single favourable site or a selection of the finest fruit to work with in order to try and produce something different and special. Furthermore, fermentation is frequently modified: higher temperatures extract more colouring and phenolic substances and the use of wood ageing is common. The combination will make more of the darker fruit aromas and flavours such as the 'hedgerow' characters and herbal notes at the expense of the fragrance and immediacy of floral and cherry notes, and the wines generally show greater ageing potential. The interpretation of the category by the individual winery is, of course, key to understanding the nature of the beast and the question of fresh or dried fruit is at the heart of the decision. Some believe the unique character of the terrain itself is best expressed through the use of fresh grapes only so that the fruit and the land on which it grows determine the wine's identity rather than a particular process or method of production; this approach favours the freshness and elegance that some believe Valpolicella is all about. Others argue that the historical identity of Veronese red wine is tied inextricably to the use of semi-dried fruit and that this option provides the structure that the use of fresh fruit only lacks, leading to a wine that is richer, riper, more intense and capable of improving for longer in bottle. Many look for a compromise between the two positions and use a proportion of semi-dried grapes with the aim of combining the best elements of both camps. A treasure trove or a minefield? The answer is of course both. Further information can be found in Chapter 6.

Valpolicella Ripasso DOC

Distinguishing production regulations
- *Minimum alcohol content: 12.5% and 13% for the Superiore version*
- *Release date: a minimum of one year's ageing beginning from 1 January following the vintage*
- *Vineyard yields: 12 tonnes per hectare*

The rising volumes of Ripasso on the market today clearly go hand in hand with the rising popularity and volumes of Amarone: just think of all those extra lees. By the early years of the new millennium, Ripasso had started to attract enough interest to warrant some kind of formalization of the production process. Accordingly rules were drawn up and incorporated within the Valpolicella Production Discipline in 2007, the vintage from which the first officially sanctioned bottles appeared on the market. By 2010 Ripasso had become a denomination in its own right. Provision was made for the introduction of a Superiore version and both categories could be produced in all three geographical zones. Reference to the particular area of production on the label follows a precise model: firstly 'Valpolicella Ripasso', followed by the sub-zone (if any), followed by 'Superiore' when applicable – for example, Valpolicella Ripasso Classico Superiore. From being a way of 'boosting' basic Valpolicella (which is where its origins lie), Ripasso had been reinvented as, if not exactly a mini-Amarone, then a wine that offers the consumer some of the aroma and flavour of Amarone but at a fraction of the cost. Markets have welcomed the Young Pretender with open arms.

Current legislation points the producer towards this mini-Amarone style. An 'illustrative guideline' suggests that the base Valpolicella wine remains in contact with the lees of the Amarone or Recioto for a period of fifteen to twenty days in order to promote greater structure and potential longevity than a typical Valpolicella might offer. According to Article 9, this leads to a wine with a higher alcohol content, proportionately lower acidity, more roundness, and which is richer in phenols and extract. Purists remain unconvinced by the argument and continue to produce what they insist is a more accurate reflection of the traditional model by limiting lees contact to a matter of days rather than weeks, and this style can be the safer bet. Other producers make a Ripasso with a certain amount of reluctance, simply because it makes sound financial sense to do so and missing out on a glaringly obvious commercial opportunity is a luxury few can afford. Some turn their backs on the idea completely and remain indignantly dismissive about the true worth of the technique in the first place. If there are rumblings of discontent about Ripasso from a technical and/or professional point of view, there is some justification for the concern. While a glass of Ripasso can be an immensely pleasurable experience, not all examples are always as well put together as they might be. As Amarone, in particular, spends an extended period on its lees as a result of the lengthy fermentation process, the dangers of a second spell of lees contact can all too easily result in the development of bitter flavours such as the increased perception of dry tannins and 'off' aromas. The process needs super-attentive care in order to avoid the dangers of overextraction and to manage the oxidation/reduction process properly. Furthermore Ripasso can appear too much of a 'constructed' wine, almost as if assembled by a deluded oenologist named Frankenstein from different body parts which then have difficulty in knitting together! As ever, finding the right producer is vital, but thorough research can reveal that Ripasso at its best is a true hedonistic delight where richness, softness and velvety texture are all defining features plus, of course, the interplay between the fresher aromas of the base wine and the extra intensity of dried fruits.

Amarone della Valpolicella DOCG

Distinguishing production regulations

- *Minimum alcohol content: 14.0%*

- *Pressing date: not before 1 December unless otherwise authorized by the Growers' Consortium*

- *Maximum sugar content: 12 g/l at 14% abv, correspondingly 0.1 g/l for every additional 0.10% alcohol between 14 and 16% abv and 0.15 g/l for every additional 0.10% alcohol above 16% abv*

- *Vineyard yields: 12 tonnes per hectare of which a maximum of 65 per cent may be selected to be put aside for appassimento*

- *Wine yield to grapes ratio: a maximum of 40 per cent*

- *Release date: a minimum of two years' ageing beginning from 1 January following the vintage; for Riserva a four-year ageing period beginning from 1 November of the vintage year*

Amarone finally came into being in the period immediately after the Second World War following a gestation period of a mere seventy years and more, and the term Amarone seems to have been coined only a decade or so previously. Cantina di Negrar, certainly one of the firms instrumental in the wine's creation, conserve a bottle labelled 'Amarone Extra' with a vintage date of 1939 and a label featuring the Villa Mosconi where the winery was originally located at the bottom of the Negrar valley. They also have convincing evidence to suggest that they began producing Amarone on a regular basis in the early years of the 1940s. The story goes that the word was first used by their cellarmaster Adelino Lucchese in 1936; when tasting a wine with Gaetano Dall'Ora, the cooperative's president, he is reported to have exclaimed: *Questo non e un Amaro, ma un Amarone!* ('This is not an Amaro, it's an Amarone!') Use of the augmentative suffix '–one' refers to 'a bigger or more important' version of something in Italian, so the working translation of Amarone is 'a great big Amaro' or 'a great big bitter one'. Previously wine of this style had been known as Recioto Scapà (or a Recioto that 'got away'), 'Recchiotto Amaro' and even, in all likelihood 'Vino Rosso Austero', a term probably first coined by Scipione Maffei in the 1700s to describe a wine of this style. A catalogue entry from an exhibition of produce from the Veneto in 1871 lists a 'Vino Rosso Grola Austero' from the 1869 vintage which almost certainly relates to a 'serious' dry red produced on the La Grola hillside at Sant'Ambrogio. Lamberto Paronetto believed that surviving sets of analyses carried out around this time showed numerous examples of wine with high alcohol and low sugar levels, providing evidence of a burgeoning production of an Amarone style. In 1903 the Recchiotto Amaro from Cantina Antonio Quintarelli at San Vito di Negrar was a gold medallist at an oenological and gastronomical fair in Milan, for example. However, a sweeter style of wine similar to Recioto was still very much the main focus of attention for local winemakers with regard to maintaining the tradition of working with semi-dried grapes, even though, as Giovanni Battista Perez observed at the end of the century, tastes were beginning to veer away from sweeter towards drier styles of wine.

The lengthy gestation period came about as a result of a succession of events which effectively held the growth of the wine industry and the development of Amarone in check for decades: the arrival of peronospera in 1880, followed by oidium and, at the turn of the century, phylloxera. Then two World Wars put a block on thoughts of anything other than survival. Another pioneering firm strongly associated with the birth of Amarone is Bertani. During the time of the Austrian domination of Verona, Gaetano Bertani went into voluntary exile in Burgundy where he developed a keen interest in the local wines and methods of production. As a result he introduced French varieties into the area and planted Verona's first Guyot-trained vines – a photograph taken in 1883 shows a Guyot-trained vineyard planted in *ritocchino* fashion where the rows run up and down the hillside rather than following the contours. Another lasting legacy of Gaetano's time in Burgundy was the family's enduring taste for dry wines rather than the sweeter ones mainly produced in Verona at the time. Secco Bertani, a 'brand' developed in the 1870s, used a proportion of French varieties alongside local grapes and was vinified with little remaining residual sugar. The Bertani family claim the term Amarone was already being used in their cellars in the 1930s though the idea was brought to fruition after the War, when Cavaliere Guglielmo Bertani hired the Piedmontese oenologist Ernesto Barbero to evaluate and develop a series of Recioto wines that had fermented to dryness in their cellars. Barbero prepared a token quantity of the style from the 1958 vintage, though the successive vintage is generally acknowledged to be the firm's first official release of 'Amarone'. It was certainly during the period between the end of the Second World War and the early 1960s that interest began to grow and important firms like Bolla, Masi, Allegrini, Speri and the Tedeschi family began to produce Amarone on a regular basis. The idea that the wine came about as a mistake – from a cask of Recioto left unchecked which had fully fermented out – is subscribed to by many of the people who can remember back to those times. Renzo Tedeschi, for one, believes this to be the case.

When the DOC laws were drawn up in 1968, however, the wine was in its infancy and still viewed as a variation on the Recioto style. The legislation recognized Amarone only insofar as: 'Recioto della Valpolicella can also be produced as a dry wine with a maximum of 0.4 degrees of alcohol left undeveloped; as such it can be labelled "Amarone".'

Until new legislation appeared in 1990 which endorsed Amarone as a separate denomination the wine was still generally referred to as Recioto Amarone della Valpolicella. It is interesting to note that the original formula encompassed 0.4 degrees of alcohol undeveloped, and this gives a clear view of what the early versions must have tasted like. That proportion of undeveloped alcohol relates to a residual content of fractionally under 7 g/l, a far cry from today's potential maximum of around 16 g/l. While climate change over the past few decades has certainly produced crops of fruit with consistently higher sugar levels and correspondingly a higher potential degree of alcohol than would have been the norm before rules were modified, this does not tell the full story. Amarone was initially produced and sold as a 'vino da meditazione', or a post-prandial wine to be enjoyed on its own, in company and perhaps paired with a piece of mature hard cheese (Amarone has an astonishing affinity with *parmiggiano reggiano*, for example). At first Amarone was not an easy wine to sell; the well-stocked 'library' of older vintages which Bertani used to maintain shows that it was certainly no overnight success. But the giant step forward for production was the introduction of the 'controlled' approach to *appassimento* in the late 1990s which, in practical terms, eliminated the risk element of the process. All of a sudden it became possible to guarantee consistency of supply and Amarone was no longer a rarity. While in the 1970s some 5.5 per cent of the annual harvest was set aside for *appassimento*, in the 1980s the figure had risen to 7 per cent. In the 1990s this became 10 per cent and in the first decade of the new millennium it spiralled upwards to 28 per cent.

With an annual production of just a few million bottles, the idea of a wine to be sipped while discussing the finer points of life was a sustainable concept, but the potential to increase numbers dramatically required a fundamental shift in focus in terms of how the wine was to be brought to market. Indeed the dilemma that faces 'modern' Amarone is still to be resolved: how to find the best use for a wine with extraordinarily high alcohol and generous residual sugar levels. A number of producers are looking to take fermentation further towards full dryness, leaving a level of residual sugar of 2 or 3 g/l and thus aiming for a more food-friendly product. Others argue that a wine with such a high alcohol level becomes drinkable only when balanced by a certain level of sweetness and for now this seems to be the approach finding most favour with the consumer. However, the very sweetness that has helped to make Amarone so popular does make the wine extremely difficult to pair with many foods; sugar, after all, has the effect of 'dumbing' the palate. Imaginative suggestions such as drinking Amarone with Oriental and Asian cooking seem to have an eye on sales opportunities as much as meaningful gastronomic choices, though there is something to be said for the combination. There is no doubt that Amarone works really well with slow-roasted or braised meats (especially sweeter meats like pork, game and the local favourite, horse). While producers such as Marcello Vaona of Novaia feel that, with an annual production that has now reached some 18 million bottles per annum, Amarone must find a place at table, others – like Romano Dal Forno – prefer, somewhat ironically, not to drink Amarone with food at all and favour a return to its traditional, sociable role as a wine to enjoy in good company, over a game of cards, perhaps. In this sense Amarone is still finding its feet.

Today's Amarone has many different variations which are governed by several key factors. Location of the vineyards is, of course, the main consideration and altitude, exposition, soil type and microclimate are determining features. The differences between the wines from the Classico, Valpantena and the various valleys of the DOC Valpolicella areas mirror those distinguishing sylistic traits identified above. From the winemaking perspective, the presence or elimination of any evidence of botrytis has a significant effect on style. Where the presence of a small, carefully monitored amount of noble rot is encouraged and where the pathogen has not reached its efflorescent phase, the wines lean towards more tertiary and oxidative aromas and have a particularly high glycerol content which highlights their softness and expansive flavour. A classic exponent of this type is Masi. Those who prefer to avoid any trace of botrytis produce on the whole a more muscular wine with rather tighter structure and fresher fruit characters. Allegrini produce an exemplary version. Other notable variations are the length of the *appassimento* process which will affect concentration as well as fruit character and, of course, the use of wood. Amarone will always spend several years in cask before release and the size and provenance of barrel will play its part. While cherry and chestnut are still in use, oak is easily the most popular wood. Older, larger barrels (the traditional *botti*) will impart subtle and seasoned notes while newer, smaller ones (barriques and tonneaux) tend to have a more immediately apparent effect, imparting notes of vanilla and coconut and bringing sweet oak tannins into play. Though a departure that began as recently as the 1990s, the use of barriques seems to be here to stay.

Whichever path the winemaker chooses to follow, Amarone is above all an easy wine to appreciate. Bewitching aromas of black cherry, fig, dark chocolate, molasses, wood smoke, orange and clove are both immediately appealing yet have real depth. The palate is no less seductive with its rich, ripe, dense and velvety mouthfeel. A vein of acidity provides a surprising degree of freshness and prevents the wine from being cloying and, when well managed, the tannins are fine and not intrusive. Very few fine wines are quite so voluptuous and enjoyable at such an early stage (almost from its date of release) though the best versions can age for upwards of twenty years and more.

Recioto della Valpolicella DOCG

Distinguishing production regulations

- *Minimum alcohol content: 12.0%*

- *Pressing date: not before 1 December unless otherwise authorized by the Growers' Consortium*

- *Residual sugar content: expressed as a minimum of 2.8% potential alcohol (just under 50 g/l)*

- *Vineyard yields: 12 tonnes per hectare of which a maximum of 65 per cent may be selected to be put aside for appassimento*

- *Wine yield to grapes ratio: a maximum of 40 per cent*

- *Release date: no minimum ageing period specified*

Note: There is provision for the production of both Recioto della Valpolicella Classico and Recioto della Valpolicella Valpantena

Many of the longer-established wineries of Valpolicella recall that in the 1950s, 1960s and even 1970s, the main focus of *appassimento* was for the production of Recioto, a wine which they still hold dear. Indeed it is accepted unconditionally as the true mother of Veronese red wines, harking back to the times of wines such as Vino Retico and Acinatico. Until the middle of the nineteenth century the wine was often referred to as Vino Santo (holy wine), and there are abundant references throughout the eighteenth century to the production of Vino Santo in Verona (including Maffei). In all probability the name refers to its use in religious ceremonies, after the clergy had kept the art of wine production alive in the Middle Ages. The idea of Vino Santo is thought to have been popularized through Florentine wine merchants, though a number of what are more than likely apocryphal stories trace it back to Greek origins. Gradually the name spread and became accepted throughout the Italian peninsula as a generic term referring to a sweet wine made from semi-dried grapes. Giovanni Battista Perez is usually credited with being the first to refer to the local version as Recciotto or Recchiotto in the late nineteenth century, a name which was eventually to morph into Recioto during the next century. Perez himself was not a big fan of Recchiotto though admitted it suited market requirements at the time. By 1899, however, he felt emboldened to declare that sweet wine was no longer in fashion.

Despite the shift towards drier wines, producers in Valpolicella continue to produce the Recioto style, jealously guarding their heritage. Most continue to treat the product with the utmost reverence despite its decreasing popularity, but the product shows no signs of becoming a museum piece such is its hold on the hearts and minds of those who make it. Nonetheless where once Recioto came in a different set of guises, production tends to focus on one particular style these days. Journalist Elisabetta Tosi identified as many as six different interpretations of Recioto for the Cantina di Negrar-sponsored book, *Terra, Uomini e Passioni nel Mito del Recioto e dell'Amarone*, three containing some residual carbon dioxide and three still versions. Of the three 'sparkling' wines, 'Fresco' is a wine from the most recent vintage with only partial fermentation completed and 'Mosso' is an even rarer example which is refermented (and often refermenting) in bottle. These two styles have all but disappeared. The Spumante or fully sparkling version was once rather more common and, unlike the others, was incorporated within the DOCG discipline. This style has also dwindled and is only made by a handful of cellars. What little remains is usually produced according to the so-called Martinotti method which, when introduced soon after the Second World War, used the innovative technology of the autoclave. In all likelihood these three related styles came about in much the same way as Amarone – that is, from barrels of Recioto where the fermentation had been left unchecked and refermentation had begun once in bottle.

Similarly the style known as Amandorlato (or almond-like) derives from very particular circumstances where a Recioto has fermented out most but not all of its sugars. Paolo Galli of Le Ragose whose Ammandorlato [sic] 'Raghos' is a classic example, maintains that the fermentation ceases spontaneously at a level which is too dry for Recioto and too sweet for Amarone. Masi also produce a version called Mezzanella and a few other other wineries (Cantina di Negrar, Corteforte, Montecariano and Villa Canestrari) continue to make Amandorlato when conditions allow. The classic and defining characteristic is, of course, a strong almond-like flavour – as the name suggests – which contrasts in an intriguing fashion with the remaining sugars: the perfect illustration of a bittersweet wine. Another way of preventing an impromptu secondary fermentation is the common practice of arresting the fermentation process at the desired level of residual sugar with the addition of neutral alcohol (as in Port, for example). With the arrival of the know-how that more sophisticated technology brings, the practice has all but died out in Valpolicella – though until 1990 and the introduction of the new production discipline, reports Tosi, a few wineries were still making a Recioto Liquoroso, fortified at up to 19 to 20% abv. The final Recioto is the one which has come to define the denomination today: a still, sweet, red wine which accompanies 'dry' cakes such as *pandoro*, shortbread or *pissota con l'ua*. Two contrasting styles are produced: one made without any wood ageing which exalts freshness of aroma and flavour and is a burst of ripe and fragrant luscious red fruits all over both nose and palate, or a wood-aged version (often in small barriques) which adds notes of vanilla, spice and toffee to the more developed dried and candied fruit flavours and which can age remarkably well.

6

WHO'S WHO

The following winery guide is not comprehensive, though it attempts to cover the important bases and thus give a broad cross section of production today. The selection is restricted to producers I have visited at least once and have some knowledge of beyond merely tasting the wine; to assess a wine properly, it is essential to understand something of its background. References are made in the main body of the text to wines I have tasted from cellars which I may not have visited. The longer profiles are of producers who neatly illustrate some of the many different aspects of today's winemaking scene or who are particularly important to its recent history. Length of profile should not be confused with excellence of production standards: some of the area's finest wines are made at estates who may perhaps have been allocated only a shortish paragraph below. There are several hundred wineries in the Veronese, so if your favourite has not been included, this is simply because it has not been possible to visit all of them.

SOAVE (INCLUDING DURELLO)

Anselmi
Via San Carlo, 46 - 37032 Monteforte d'Alpone VR
+39 045 7611488
www.anselmi.eu
'I had a bonfire,' says Roberto Anselmi as he recalls the moment he turned his back on the Soave denomination in 2000, 'and I burnt all my old labels.' Roberto was used to a fight: his father was a *negoziante* selling millions of bottles of wine made from bought-in grapes. Returning from a world wine tour which changed his philosophy on wine production completely,

Roberto decided he was going to buy back his grandfather's vineyards (which his father had sold off to fund the building of the winery) and dedicate himself to producing top-quality wine. So he did, but admits he had a battle on his hands. His quest for quality was built on two founding principles: growing top-quality fruit which he insists is only achievable through high-density Guyot training and low yields (leaving just two or three bunches per plant from no more than four buds), and the use of modern technology in the cellars (in particular, anaerobic fermentation and the use of nitrogen). Before long he had established a reputation for being one of Italy's top white-wine producers.

He doesn't regret the decision to start selling his wines as IGT Veneto for one moment. He grins: 'No more bureaucracy.' His customers also seem happy enough to accept the names San Vicenzo and Capitel Foscarino instead of Soave, a denomination which has certainly had its image problems in the past. 'The key factors behind quality are air, sun and wind. And of course good viticultural practices – we don't use chemicals in our vineyards any more.' He seems a little less dogmatic these days, freely admitting that it is possible to achieve good quality using single pergola, but he has 'found his way' and sees no point in turning back. Current production runs to some 700,000 bottles, mainly San Vicenzo plus smaller amounts of Capitel Foscarino (around 60,000) and barrel-fermented Capitel Croce (40,000), a single vineyard wine from the Zoppega hillside, as well as his 'take' on Recioto di Soave, 'I Capitelli' IGT, and tiny quantities of Cabernet Sauvignon 'Realda'. Gazing into his crystal ball, Roberto foresees a great future for aromatic dry whites: 'Excellence is a concept which is still evolving, but one thing's for sure, it has to be grounded on the right viticultural systems.'

Balestri Valda

Via Monti, 44 - 37038 Soave VR
+39 045 7675393
www.vinibalestrivalda.com

Balestri Valda are in the throes of converting to biodynamics and Laura Rizzotto has discovered a new passion, beekeeping: 'They gather nectar from the local plants and give us a 360 degree vision of what's happening around us.' The family also produce a delightfully delicate olive oil, though their main driver is Soave. Father Guido and brother Luca make the wine to a simple formula: low fermentation temperatures followed by at least six months on the fine lees prior to bottling, and minimal use of wood. Their standard bearer is the generic Soave Classico, an archetypal example of the denomination. Two further cuvées are bottled separately: Sengialta and Lunalonga both contain a proportion of Trebbiano di Soave and continue the theme of great purity of style. There are also two versions of Recioto, one sparkling and one still, though they are not made every year. A new varietal Trebbiano di Soave, Libertate, made partly in terracotta amphorae, is in the early stages of development.

Azienda Agricola Le Battistelle – a growing venture

Via Monti, 44 - 37038 Soave VR
+39 045 7675393
www.lebattistelle.it

Italy has a rich agricultural heritage where wealth and reputation customarily go hand in hand with land ownership: it is a common feature in small, rural, farming communities to find a number of families sharing the same surname, especially in traditional wine-producing areas. In Brognoligo di Monteforte d'Alpone, or just Brognoligo as the village is mainly known, the names Dal Bosco and Tessari are frequently encountered.

Gelmino and Cristina Dal Bosco run the 9-hectare Le Battistelle estate: 6 hectares of vineyards belong to the family and a further 3 hectares are rented from other local smallholders, all of which are situated in the north-eastern section of the delimited Classico area. The vineyards are within just a couple of kilometres from the tiny but scrupulously neat and clean winery which lies just off the village centre. The family hails originally from the village of Giazza, high at the head of the Progno d'Illasi and situated just inside the Parco Naturale Regionale della Lessinia below the Carega peaks. Giazza is one of the few remaining municipalities of the area settled by German-speaking peoples (from the area around Munich) soon after the start of the second millennium, where a few old folk still speak the version of German known as Cimbro (or *tauć* in dialect) as a first language. The Dal Bosco family's ancestors moved down to the Monteforte area in the seventeenth century. Since then the descendants of Carlo, in 1642 the first of the family to be born in Brognoligo, have made the name a fixture hereabouts. Gelmino explained that his slightly unusual first name was chosen to distinguish him from the many other men in the family; traditionally, Giuseppe and Angelo have been the most popular choices.

Gelmino's grandfather Angelo was born in 1904 and was a grape grower prior to the founding of the local cooperative in the early 1950s, which he helped to set up. Gelmino explained that before then grapes would be sold to other producers and everything was done on a handshake: 'Sometimes you'd just never see the people again! So the co-op really saved our bacon.' Gelmino continued to sell his grapes to the cooperative until 2002 when the family took the plunge and started to vinify for themselves under the guidance of local oenologist Armando Vesco. The first couple of years were sold off in bulk and their first bottling was from the 2004 vintage.

Putting aside his new role of winemaker, Gelmino recollects how little life in the vineyards has changed over the last few decades and indeed since the days when he first began to help his father Gasparino who had carried on the family tradition of grape growing. 'We'd usually be in the vineyards by around 5.30,' he remembers. 'We worked with hoes for the most part. We rarely planted anything, in fact all we've ever done is to manage the vines we have. We would prune the shoots much longer in those days as the old vines were so much less productive than they are now. With the new rootstocks, the younger vines produce much more vegetation and fruit than the old ones ever did. We replanted when a vine died – just like today – but otherwise it was mainly maintenance work, building the ground back up where there had been a landslip, renewing terrace walls, etc. We trod the paths our forefathers made until the first roads up amongst the vines were built in the 1970s and '80s. The women would bring us breakfast at 8.00 a.m., usually polenta, salami and eggs. Luckily we have springs on the property so drinking water wasn't a problem. For treatments we would just use Bordeaux Mixture [a copper sulphate solution]. We'd store the water in an old cement tank or just dig a hole to make a pool if we had to and then mix in the powder. We'd strap the pump on the back and off we'd go, one person with the pump and the other following behind carrying the bucket of liquid [attached to the pump with a rubber tube]. We'd normally carry out around no more than three or four treatments over the course of the growing season partly because the hillsides here are well-ventilated but also because it was such hard work. In any case we'd never treat the vines after San Pietro's day [June 29th]. But there was still plenty to do in the summer months: we'd cut the poles that we used for the support systems, usually acacia or chestnut; it was all done by hand using a 'manarin' [cleaver]. We'd cut the poles under the waxing moon because they'd last longer and then stand them in a copper solution until they turned a silver-green colour. Because of their elasticity, we'd also gather willow shoots for tying the vine shoots up on to the training wires.

'Back at the cellar we'd clean out the wooden tubs, barrels and damigiane [demijohns] we used for making the family's wine. It was a pretty rudimentary approach! We'd crush the grapes by foot in oval wooden tubs which were 2 or 3 metres long and maybe a metre or so high. Then we'd pour off the juice into 'vedotti' [small wooden barrels of between 50 and 300 litres capacity] to ferment. We'd just leave it to its own devices. I suppose you could say we were already making "natural wines" in those days.' He laughs. 'We'd make six or seven containers a year: people drank much more back then too, a couple of litres of wine a day was normal. We'd keep the worst stuff for vinegar. We'd tend our other crops, too, we used every available bit of land to grow fruit and vegetables: peas, strawberries, salad, tomatoes, as well as olive and cherry trees. Our hills were one big garden then and everyone was happy: there'd be people in the vineyards all the time and we could hear them singing even hundreds of metres away. Sometimes we'd stay up in the vineyards for lunch too; we'd have a couple of glasses of wine then a nap for an hour or so before we got back to work.

'Harvest times were the busiest period, we'd have to carry everything down the hillsides on our backs.' Wooden yokes were wedged behind the neck and across the shoulders and held in place with outstretched arms. Suspended from each hooked end was a conical woven basket (the gerla) containing up to 40 kilos of freshly picked grapes. 'The women's loads would be lighter because they'd usually have their babies to carry too. It's just under 2 kilometres up to the top of the Durlo hill and we'd make the round trip three times a day. Then we'd load the grapes on to a cart to take down to the co-op cellars. We were still using the yokes into the 1980s. It was hard work but they were easier, less stressful times back then. It seems to me that the weather was more harmonious too: softer and milder. It all began to change in the 1970s and 1980s though in a gradual way. We got tractors and built roads. Then we started getting help and advice about what treatments to use and when. But nothing much has changed in the highest parts of the vineyards, especially at Le

Battistelle and Roccolo del Durlo. We're still using the same old tubes up there.'

The family's Le Battistelle vineyard (after which the winery is named) was first recorded in 1644. It lies on the hillside just above the village and the steep slopes form a natural amphitheatre. The soil here is partly a clay/limestone mix but with basalt present too. The company's first bottling (then called Sacripante, the name of a figure in Italian literature renowned as a boaster and a brigand) was the wine produced from this vineyard. However the Dal Boscos' most spectacular location lies a little further over to the west along the ridge between the peaks of Monte Carbonare and Monte Grande, and on the very crown of the hill. Roccolo del Durlo, or the Durlo hilltop, is one of the most delightful settings in the whole of the Soave area. It sits on the top of a ridge and offers a wraparound panorama of some of the region's best-known vineyards. To the north lies Castellaro, to the east Coste and Boschetti, to the south Monte Grande and Pressoni and, due west, Foscarino with Carbonare just above. In the early part of the 1400s the village of Brognoligo belonged to the noble Montanari family of Verona. The family and their representatives would visit Brognoligo frequently in September or October to check on the state of that year's harvest and at weekends would use this spot as a base from which to go hunting in the hills. The practice pretty much carried on until Napoleonic times when the family sold their land to the local Durlo family (Signor Durlo was not a nobleman but a rich *contadino*). The property remained in their hands until the early part of the twentieth century when, with no male heirs, the remaining daughters each claimed and then sold off a part of the estate. Angelo Dal Bosco bought land from them some time between 1920 and 1930. In 1960 he rebuilt a small dwelling on the very crown of the hill. The structure remains today and Gelmino and his family use the place as a summer escape or somewhere to take friends and visitors seeking solitude and a glass of cool wine. The surrounding vineyards contain some of the oldest vines in the area, including some centenarians which predate the arrival of phylloxera. The family are propagating a small experimental vineyard from the cuttings.

As well as tiny quantities of Vino Santo in the years that warrant it, the family produce three wines, all Soave Classico DOC. The simplest one is Montesei, made in lots of 15,000 to 20,000 bottles a year from holdings in the Rugate valley and Tremenalto. Like the other wines, Montesei is fermented in stainless steel at cool temperatures but then stays for just a month or so in contact with the fine lees before early bottling in the spring following the harvest. This charming wine is the essence of Soave Classico: with an ethereal lightness yet crisp and fragrant too, it is usually drunk young for its freshness and delicacy of flavour. The grapes that go into perhaps their finest wine Le Battistelle (6,000 bottles per year) are harvested later before a similar fermentation regime followed by up to one year in stainless steel on the fine lees. The point of difference for the final bottling, Roccolo del Durlo (4,000 bottles per year), is a two-day pre-fermentation crio maceration at even lower temperatures (around 10°C). While the Roccolo del Durlo is slightly richer and more structured than Le Battistelle, both wines mature well in bottle, continuing to improve for up to five to seven years.

Cantina del Castello

Corte Pittora, 5 - 37038 Soave VR
+39 045 7680093
www.cantinacastello.it

Owned and run by genial president of the Consorzio di Soave, Arturo Stocchetti, Cantina del Castello is located in a palace near the centre of town whose origins date back to the thirteenth century. Though the family produce small amounts of Valpolicella and two versions of Recioto di Soave, the main thrust is some 120,000 bottles of Soave Classico made in a ripe, full-flavoured and expansive style which shows decent ageing potential. The star of the show is Soave Classico Pressoni from a vineyard adjacent to Monte Foscarino which contains 20 per cent Trebbiano di Soave.

Cantina di Monteforte

Via XX Settembre, 24 - 37032 Monteforte d'Alpone VR
+39 045 7610110
www.cantinadimonteforte.it

Founded in 1952 by a group of eighty growers, the Cantina di Monteforte now has six hundred members owning a total of 1,300 hectares. The cooperative is the second largest producer of Soave Classico, drawing on 350 hectares. While the cellars produce some 15 million litres of wine annually, bottled sales account for 15 per cent and the rest is sold in bulk. The winery was fortunate enough to keep most of the cement tanks from the original construction and cement accounts for around 70 per cent of storage and fermentation facilities with the rest in stainless steel and some wood. The management team has introduced incentives for members to aim for quality fruit and set up a 'Quality Project' in the Pigno/Ponsara/Foscarino area above La Frosca where the use of insecticides has been eliminated while near Castellaro, further north in Classico, another group of growers are working to produce a Classico Superiore from reduced yields. Cantina di Monteforte seems to be heading in the right direction.

Such promising signs are certainly borne out in the tasting room with a range of well-made and honest wines particularly at the higher end of the quality scale. The simpler versions of Soave and Classico DOC are decent enough but three 'limited edition' bottlings slip smoothly through the gears. Both the partially barrel-fermented Vicario and Foscarino show good promise and need time in bottle to show their best while the Castellaro selection – aged in part in barrel – is a splendid wine by any standards. Nuanced and with good *tipicita*, the saline and candied-fruit flavours are backed up with good acidity and there is plenty of room for further development. Though Soave is the main focus, the winery also produces Durello (the *metodo classico* version spends around forty months on the lees) and the full range of Valpolicella from fruit grown mainly in Montecchia di Crosara including an attractive Ripasso.

Cantina di Soave – a sense of responsibility
Viale Vittoria, 100 - 37038 Soave VR
+39 045 6139811
www.cantinasoave.it

If only the prosperity of the local cooperative cellar were a suitable barometer for the wellbeing of a denomination, then Soave would be in rude health. Though its roots stretch back to the end of the nineteenth century, Cantina di Soave is nonetheless a thoroughly modern cooperative. This already massive operation has ambitious plans to increase production capacity over the next few years from the 6,000 hectares of vineyard owned by its 2,200 members. At the moment that annual output is already a figure of thirty million bottles. The hub of the enterprise is on Viale Vittorio on the outskirts of town, lying within easy reach of the motorway, and comprises the commercial and administrative offices, the bottling lines and finished goods warehouse. There are a further five branches. The historical home in Via Roma in the centre of Soave has been turned into a members' resource centre. The nearby Cantina Rocca Sveva is the main showpiece: restoration work was completed in 2003 and it is now a visitor centre as well as a vinification plant for the cooperative's premium range, and the impressive underground tunnels lie full of maturing wine. There are two production centres for red wines at Cantina di Cazzano di Tramigna (acquired in 1996) and Cantina d'Illasi (since 2005), which means that Cantina di Soave now controls 49 per cent of the vineyards in the Valpolicella DOC zone. Cantina di Montecchia di Crosara, where mainly Soave and sparkling wines are produced, was incorporated into the fold in 2005. This last arrival means that production levels of Soave Classico now represent 43 per cent of the sub-zone's total area under vine, 48 per cent of the Soave DOC area and 70 per cent of Lessini Durello.

The period just after the Second World War saw the cooperative start to become a truly major force in the area. The Italian economy was in serious difficulty and for countless grape growers their only hope of survival lay with the cooperative movement. In turn, the cooperatives' only realistic route to market ran along the line of least resistance: the pragmatic way to turn members' meagre resources into much-needed cash was to move large quantities at low prices. This meant selling a substantial proportion of the annual crop in bulk to other bottlers around the country and through private labels. Belfrage captures the mood of the times in his frank and clear manner in *Life Beyond Lambrusco*:

> … after all those years of war, depression and disease, Italians found themselves in the forties and fifties having to decide which way they were going to point their wine industry. Control (i.e. capital) lay in the hands of the big, private merchants who were gradually (thanks to liberal deployment of government and, later, EEC funds) equalled and outstripped in power by the even bigger growers' cooperatives or *cantine sociali*. Large-scale production of *vino bevanda* (beverage wine) was therefore favoured. The thinking was that since France had already captured the fine wine sector, Italy's future could only lie in taking up the low and middle ground, concentrating on attractively priced wines of an acceptable (or at least not unacceptable) and reasonably reliable standard. It was a decision made by bureaucrats and financiers

concerned with profit and loss ledgers, unemployment statistics and other political and economic considerations. Quality entered the equation only as a sub factor.

What may or may not have been foreseen at the time is that Italian wine producers would spend the next few decades trying to live down this image. Similarly it is all too easy to see the formative years of Valpolicella and Soave on European export markets in precisely this context; in fact, until the early years of the new millennium, some 85 per cent of total sales of the Cantina di Soave were via the two channels of private label and bulk wine. This figure is gradually changing and the cooperative has put in place a comprehensive range of different brands, all bottled at source, which aim to appeal to as broad a spectrum as possible of customers. While there are various different styles of frizzante and sparkling wine (Cantina di Soave owns the well-known *metodo classico* Equipe 5 brand) and other local IGT and DOC wines (a range of DOC varietals from the Garda area, for example), Soave and Valpolicella clearly remain at the heart of the production. At the simple, everyday level, the commodity products are clean, honest and soundly made – it would be unrealistic to ask for more – while the premium selection, under the Rocca Sveva label, has won awards at many international wine competitions. Both the Rocca Sveva Soave Classico and special selection version Soave Classico 'Castelcerino' are well done, the latter in particular. 'Castelcerino' is made from fruit selected in six vineyards of the homonymous area of Soave and left to wither slightly on the vine before harvest, the idea being to aim for a richer and fuller style. Similarly the Rocca Sveva reds are sound examples of the various denominations.

The upgrade in product quality is a reflection of careful and conscientious planning. Production facilities are thoroughly up to date and governed by management systems approved by the appropriate certification bodies in order to meet the most stringent food safety and hygiene regulations. Such diligence has allowed the cooperative to expand well beyond the domestic market and exports now account for 42 per cent of total sales. Cantina di Soave has strong representation in Northern Europe in particular, and a growing presence in South America and Japan. To demonstrate how seriously the cooperative takes the American market, offices have now been opened in Boston and a brand ambassador for the US appointed. According to CEO Bruno Trentini, the US was a particularly successful market thirty years ago, but has been mismanaged since. This attitude typifies the current regime: to do well in a particular market you first need to understand how it operates.

This is not to say that the Cantina di Soave does not have its critics, most of whom point to the massive political power the cooperative holds and the unmatchably low prices the wines sell for. There is, though, due recognition that with such power comes responsibility. There can be no doubt that the structure holds members' interests as the core of its values – accompanied, on the face of it, by a sense of commitment and obligation towards upholding the reputation of the denominations it represents. Faced with the burning issue of the times, that the recent success of the red wines deriving from the *appassimento* process (Ripasso and Amarone) threatens to spiral out of control and put the future of the wines of Valpolicella at risk, Trentini again favours a careful and considered approach. 'Basically we have two possibilities. Either we can reduce the proportion of the crop that we put aside for *appassimento*, or we can limit the production of Amarone to certain vineyards. The second option is a very difficult strategy because you must take either certain producers or certain areas out of the equation.' He is keen to insist that the cooperative has every intention of protecting the future of Valpolicella. Current policy favours the former approach and he maintains that no more than 20 to 30 per cent of the crop is set aside for drying. He points out that while helping to keep the numbers down, this also allows them to work with the best-quality fruit for the Rocca Sveva wines, in particular. Clearly this is a pragmatic and politically correct solution, as a lot of the area's smallholders, concerned about missing out on what might be considered as 'the gravy train', would agree. 'We have to learn how to manage our production disciplines properly, just as the French have done,' he concludes. It is a lesson other producers are also trying to give careful consideration to and their concerns should not be ignored: does the first option that the winery favours place the quality and integrity of the denomination or the interests of its members at the heart of the debate?

Cantina Filippi – an oasis in Soave

Via Libertà, 55 - 37038 Soave VR
+39 045 7675005
www.cantinafilippi.it

'Perhaps whoever drew the final line on the map bore a grudge against the people living here at the time,' is the only explanation Filippo Filippi can come up with. 'It used to bother me, but not anymore,' he grins. It's actually quite difficult to imagine the current owner of Cantina Filippi being too upset over very much at all let alone a tiny, geographical detail such as a line on a map: the description 'laid back' might have been coined with him in mind.

The issue in question is the road which divides his 35-hectare estate from neighbours Coffele – another top drawer Soave producer. The road marks the boundary between two zones of Soave Classico and Colli Scaligeri, and the Filippi estate lies on just 'the wrong side of the tracks'. Over half of the property is covered in original woodland – something you rarely see in Classico, which in some parts is a hill-to-hill carpet of vines these days. The estate originally belonged to a noble Tuscan family, the Conti Alberti, who sold it to the Visco family just over a hundred years ago (Filippo's mother's maiden name was Visco and she married into the Filippi family). It's a wonderful place for a leisurely walk, if you're lucky enough to be invited to join Filippo. You might want to take in the limestone caves from where the building materials for the thirteenth-century villa were quarried, the spring which provides good drinking water but, above all, as the woodland is preserved in its natural state, the abundance of unchecked flora and fauna. Apart from the profusion of wild flowers such as iris and peony, it's a forager's delight: within half an hour on a bright spring morning you can easily gather the basic ingredients for a healthy and tasty lunch. *Bruscandoli*, the early shoots of wild hop, make a delicious frittata when lightly fried and then set in a thin omelette. Then there are *bruscansi*, the tender stems of butcher's broom: these closely resemble asparagus spears (the two plants are related). They are purple in colour and have a lightly bitter, aromatic flavour reminiscent of liquorice, an excellent base for risotto. The plant is also known as *pungitopo* or 'mouse stinger': when mature it forms clusters of spiny-tipped leaves. Bunches would be suspended from the rafters around fresh salami hung there to season and mature slowly, and the sharp tips of the leaves helped to keep the mice away from an easy meal. On the lawn outside the *agriturismo* there is a plentiful supply of *sciopeti* (or *carletti*) which are good in salads; the unusual name mimics the sensation of biting into the semi-succulent leaves.

Of course the only wine to accompany such a splendid wild feast would be the Filippi Soave. Four variations on this theme are produced, plus two additional wines made from less traditional varieties. Montepulciano is a highly idiosyncratic choice in such northerly climes and is here fermented with brief skin contact to produce a tiny amount of rosato. Filippo's Chardonnay vines date back to the 1980s at a time when growers were being advised to plant early-ripening varieties, a decision he seems to regret somewhat now, though the Susinaro vineyard has a high basalt content which confers a luscious tropical-fruit character to the 5,000 or so bottles made on an annual basis. The other wines are all made from the classic white varieties of the area, either singly or in combination. A similar approach to fermentation is applied to each individual wine: spontaneous fermentation in stainless steel with minimal intervention and low sulphur levels followed by a lengthy period on the fine lees before bottling. The malolactic fermentation may or may not occur depending on ambient cellar conditions. Filippo's aim is therefore very simply to let the wines be an expression of the vineyard and the vintage, a brave choice but which, when it pays off, can result in some hugely impressive 'natural-style' wines.

Two versions of Soave Colli Scaligeri are bottled: Castelcerino (40,000 bottles a year) spends around eight months on the lees and is a pure varietal (Garganega). Vigna del Bra (10,000 bottles a year) is the highest vineyard on the property and contains approximately 10 per cent of the Trebbiano di Soave variety; when the wine is young it can appear quite lean and nervy but puts on flesh in bottle and seems capable of taking a decade or so in its stride. In particularly favourable vintages Filippo also produces a tiny amount of Vigna del Bra with extra, typically some eighteen months in total, ageing on the fine lees. This cuvée shows even greater ageing potential and is a remarkable balancing act between intensity and delicacy of aroma and flavour. The final two wines completing the range are both 100 per cent varietals, produced under the IGT (*indicazione tipica geografica*) banner and made in lots of around 2,600 bottles each in good vintages.

Turbiana is also one of several traditional local names for the Trebbiano di Soave grape while Monteseroni is a pure Garganega. The former is a very direct wine with a clear and clean linear style: leesy and penetrating with intense green fruit flavours and a vein of brisk acidity. Monteseroni, on the other hand, is much more expansive. Made from low-yielding vines, approximately 40 hectolitres per hectare, it undergoes a protracted fermentation of around sixty days without temperature control (thus the malolactic fermentation is inevitably completed). This lush and mouthfilling wine has an uncommon length and breadth of flavour with a highly nuanced and perfumed finish. It is a rather sad reflection of the current political climate that Monteseroni is not released as the Soave DOC, Soave Colli Scaligeri DOC or even Soave Superiore DOCG it is presumably fully entitled to be. Filippo is certainly unable to market the wine as a Soave Classico. Perhaps that arbitrary borderline continues to niggle after all?

Ca Rugate

Via Pergola, 36 - 37030 Montecchia di Crosara VR
+39 045 6176328
www.carugate.wine

This ambitious winery run by Michele Tessari includes 72 hectares of vines spread across Soave Classico and the Valpolicella DOC area (in Montecchia di Crosara), plus managed vineyards near Brenton for their Durello Metodo Classico Pas Dosé. Overall standards of quality are high and while Soave Classico Monte Fiorentine and Valpolicella Superiore Campo Lavei win most of the praise, Soave Classico San Michele and Valpolicella Rio Abo are both excellent examples of the simpler style. The spacious new winery at Montecchia di Crosara includes a charming small museum which recreates rooms from the old family home at Brognoligo.

Coffele - a family affair

Via Roma, 5 - 37038 Soave VR
+39 045 7680007
www.coffele.it

Cantina Coffele lies just off the main street of Soave across a quaint, cobbled courtyard. The rather cramped and seemingly chaotic production cellars are filled to capacity with gleaming stainless steel tanks. The overriding sensation is of a bustling, small- to medium-sized business, family-owned and run. In 1970 Beppino Coffele married into the Visco family who owned vineyards up at Castelcerino. Though a teacher by profession, his father owned a Durella vineyard close to their home in the Val d'Alpone so the decision to devote himself to wine production came naturally enough. With the thoroughness that befits someone of his background, he looked at many different types of training systems before settling on the traditional pergola and then began bottling in the early 1980s: 'I was the caterpillar back then, putting in the time in the hope that my children would eventually take wing.' His hopes were realized when Alberto and Chiara followed in their father's footsteps. Having studied oenology at one of Italy's top oenological schools, the Istituto Agrario San Michele all'Adige (now the Edmond Mach Foundation), Alberto took up the reins in 1995. His sister Chiara joined the firm six years later to manage the business side of the operation.

While the commercial hub of the enterprise is at the seventeenth-century Visco Coffele palace in town, a ten-minute drive past Costeggiola and Recoareto through an undulating sea of vines leads up to family vineyards below the small hamlet of Castelcerino, the highest point of the Classico district. Throughout the early years of the new millennium, the family gradually converted to organic production, receiving full certification in 2014. They have now acquired two splendid black carthorses which Alberto uses to plough the fields. The animals also help out in the most natural way of all: piles of well-seasoned manure are the source of the only fertilizer used in the vineyards these days. A donkey and a small herd of goats complete the menagerie. The buildings are slowly being refurbished and the first part of the project has seen the completion of a large airy room with floor to ceiling windows at the front looking out over the vines below. From early autumn and through the winter the room is full of drying Garganega grapes, their skins slowly turning pink as they begin to shrivel, suspended in the traditional way from the rafters: a splendid and increasingly rare sight nowadays.

Coffele produce some 130,000 bottles of wine currently, most of which is based on Garganega. The Soave Classico Castelcerino is a pure varietal and produced following a simple and straightforward pattern – fermentation at up to 16°C in stainless steel, no malolactic and early bottling. This simple but delightful wine has aromas of ripe pear and nuts and a fleshy palate with peachy notes and crisp acidity. Despite its lack of pretension, the wine can age beautifully as a bottle of the 2000 vintage ably demonstrated in autumn 2016: it was still extraordinarily fresh and had taken on lightly spicy tones to the flavours of candied fruits and fresh almonds. It is an instant reminder of what makes Soave tick: sixteen years old and still scintillatingly fresh (albeit that the wine had been stored in perfect conditions up at Castelcerino). Two other versions of Soave Classico are a little more ambitious in style. Ca Visco, also fermented in stainless steel, is from the highest terraced vineyards on the property. The only Coffele white containing any Trebbiano di Soave (25 per cent) and grown on volcanic soils, Ca Visco has a wonderfully ethereal perfume somehow reminiscent of high-altitude Müller Thurgau. The final dry white is Alzari. This again is pure Garganega, 40 per cent of which has undergone forty days' *appassimento* before fermentation in 1,500-litre French barrels (though the family's long-term plan is to use acacia barrels made from their own trees). This is a much richer and toastier style, though even the youthful Alzari shows those lightly perfumed candied fruit notes which only emerge with ageing in the other two wines.

There's a Vintage Brut (also 100% Garganega) made by the long charmat method and a Recioto di Soave Classico Le Sponde, less alcoholic though no less intense than other examples and where the sweetness is balanced by brisk acidity. A final 'folly' completes the range of Garganega-based wines: Aurea Retia is a sweet spumante also made from dried grapes. Once a popular style, sparkling Recioto di Soave is rarely produced anymore. Like Amarone, it may have come about by accident: the new Recioto, still high in sugar, would often begin a second fermentation around Easter as temperatures rose, and people grew to love the style. Coffele also make Valpolicella and Amarone from 5 hectares of vines at Campiano above nearby Cazzano di Tramigna. Like the 'regular' Soave Classico, their Valpolicella is a simple, fresh wine: full of plum and cherry fruit flavours and underscored by light saline and herbal notes. The Amarone is a spicy, almost spirity wine weighing in at around 16% abv.

This is a heart-warming story which the wines more than live up to. Beppino is a proud but humble man, delighted that his children have indeed learned to fly.

Corte Adami

Via Circonvallazione, 32, 37038 Soave VR
+39 045 6190218
www.corteadami.it

A small producer with a winery at the edge of town, Corte Adami make a number of variations on the Soave theme including a good basic version and Vigna delle Corte from the vineyard adjacent to Filippi's Vigne delle Bra above Castelcerino. More recent additions are the Classico Cimalta and a 'natural-style' wine bottled without filtration or the addition of sulphur. The Adami family also produce Valpolicella from vineyards at their Mezzomonte estate near Musella at the bottom of the Val Squaranto to good standards.

Corte Giacobbe

Via Moschina, 11 - 37030 Roncà VR
+39 045 7460110
www.dalcerofamily.it

Owned by the Dal Cero family, this small, dynamic estate has lofty ambitions. Good basic Soave demonstrates the classic characteristics of a wine fermented at low temperatures using selected yeasts, with aromas of tropical fruit to the fore. Soave Runcata from vineyards further up Monte Calvarina at 450 metres is marketed as a Superiore DOCG. Oenologist Davide Dal Cero likes to ferment and age the wine in acacia barrels: 'Acacia is less porous than other woods and with less oxygen present, the grape aromas retain their integrity and the wine stays younger and fresher for longer,' he claims. Acacia adds light notes of honey and beeswax rather than the vanillin tones of oak and these integrate well with the apricot, citrus and herbal inflections of Garganega. Runcata has the credentials to become an iconic Soave on the evidence of the last few vintages. The family also produces Valpolicella Ripasso and Amarone from the San Briccio hillside in Lavagno: as the wines are still in the early stages of development it is too soon to offer a meaningful evaluation.

Corte Mainente

Viale della Vittoria, 45 - 37038 Soave VR
+39 045 7680303
www.cortemainente.com

This small property, built in the traditional style around a courtyard which once served as a threshing floor, is full of memories. The old mulberry tree which still stands in one corner of the yard prompts Ugo Mainente to recall his mother's story of how the silkworm pupae were kept under the mattresses to hatch. Today Ugo's sons, oenologist Davide and agronomist Marco, make the family wine from 15 hectares of vines in Pigno, Monte Tenda and Cengelle. Good, fresh and zingy basic Soave Cengelle DOC and the vibrant and scented Classico Tovo Al Pigno are made in a very clean and modern style while the more aspirational Nettroir follows a quirkier path via extended skin contact and maceration, Ripasso style, on Recioto di Soave lees.

Corte Moschina

Via Moschina, 1 - 37030 Roncà VR
+39 045 7460788
www.cortemoschina.it

Corte Moschina is a family-run winery producing a number of variations on Durello, Soave and Valpolicella. Quality is sound across the range with a couple of ambitious versions of Soave: Evaos is made with whole bunch pressing and minimal sulphur while I Tarai, from a vineyard on Monte Calvarina, is based on late-harvested fruit from older vines.

Sandro De Bruno

Via Santa Margherita, 26, 37030 Montecchia di Crosara VR
+39 045 6540465
www.sandrodebruno.it

Sandro Tasoniero farms vines at up to 600 metres on the basalt soils of Monte Calvarina around Ronca and Terrossa, growing a mix of local and international varieties with pergoletta training for the former and Guyot for the latter. Sandro likes to ferment in stainless steel and then give his white wines plenty of time on their lees (in some cases up to eighteen months). He makes a rare example of still Durello, a broad but lean wine with candied fruit flavours and intriguing mineral and peach-skin aromas; similarly his two versions of Soave are richly flavoured, aromatic and develop well in bottle. The Superiore Monte San Pietro matures in wood and is a remarkably substantial glass of wine.

Fasoli Gino

Via C. Battisti, 47, 37030 Colognola Ai Colli VR
+39 045 7650741
www.fasoligino.com

The pioneers of organic wine in the Veronese (with certification since the 1990s), Fasoli Gino own 20 hectares of vineyard but also work with a network of like-minded growers to produce a wide range of Veronese wines from their slightly chaotic cellars at the village of San Zeno just above Colognola ai Colli. The wines reflect the larger than life character of brothers Amadeo and Natalino. Simple Soave Borgoletto is a good everyday example though Pieve Vecchia is far more ambitious; a staggered harvest from old vines, barrel fermentation and plenty of lees ageing combine in a singular, deeply coloured and rich wine that often attains 14.5% abv. The range of Valpolicella is also head-spinning, with 'basic' Valpolicella Corte del Pozzo weighing in at around 14.5% abv while Amarone Alteo can hit 17.5% abv depending on the vintage.

Fornaro

Via S. Matteo, 68, 37038 Soave VR
+39 340 3313477
www.fornarovini.com

You couldn't wish to find a simpler cellar: stainless tanks, a refrigeration unit and a few demijohns, not a sign of wood anywhere. 'My focus is on the grapes,' agrees oenologist Damiano Fornaro. Regular Soave Classico and even smaller quantities of Capitello del Tenda show real purity of style with the latter in particular demonstrating good ageing potential. Damiano's first vintage of Capitello, 2010, was still in great form six years later, a slightly austere and ethereal yet beautifully balanced wine. His latest experiment is with a Soave made in a terracotta amphora. His father Luciano and uncle Gianni help out in the vineyards.

Fattori

Via Olmo, 27, 37030 Terrossa VR
+39 045 7460041
www.fattoriwines.com

Antonio Fattori runs this enterprising winery at Ronca producing some 350,000 bottles of Veronese wines from vineyards on Monte Calvarina, in Soave Classico and the recently acquired 12-hectare Col di Bastia in Monteccia di Crosara for a range of Valpolicella. The family also has a parallel business as a *negoziante* for the production of Pinot Grigio and more 'commercial' wines. With soundly made still wines, Fattori are also ramping up their production of Durello.

Fongaro - head full of fizz

Via Motto Piane, 12, 37030 Roncà VR
+39 045 746 0240
www.fongarospumanti.it

When wine lovers decide to beat a path to Societa Agricola Fongaro's door, they will be rewarded with more than just a memorable view over the Val d'Alpone and beyond the town of Soave to Lake Garda shimmering in the distance. The winery lies along the winding road from the village of Ronca that heads up the western slopes of Monte Calvarina towards the *frazione* of Brenton, a rather unassuming, mainly single-storey building that melds into the surrounding vines at over 500 metres. The vineyards lie above and below the winery up to around 650 metres and are planted in *ritocchino* fashion or in straight vertical lines up and down the steep hillside in the dark basalt soils of the extinct volcano.

Born locally in 1914, Guerrino Fongaro came back home in the mid 1970s following a life as a successful entrepreneur in the wine business in Bergamo. Bergamo lies just to the west of the Franciacorta region where Guerrino was to find his inspiration. While it is the classic Champagne grapes – Chardonnay and Pinot Nero – that form the backbone of the Franciacorta DOCG sparkling wines, Guerrino decided on his return to keep faith with the local Durella variety, though it was practically unknown outside the immediate vicinity. Unknown that is except to the canny *spumantisti* (sparkling wine producers) from Verona and beyond who found the coursing acidity, low alcohol and apparent neutrality of the grape a positive boon in giving vigour and vitality to wines made from other less strident varieties. The history of Durella follows the familiar Italian path of wines sold in bulk as *vini da taglio* ('cutting' or 'improving' wines).

Guerrino began planting Durella plus tiny amounts of Chardonnay and Incrocio Manzoni mainly to the Guyot system he had become familiar with in Franciacorta, though traditionally local vineyards had always been trained high using the classic Pergola Veronese. The company's 10 hectares of vineyards have now all been converted to

Guyot. But his next innovation was to take Durello in a direction no one had previously dreamed of. His use of the *metodo classico*, as practised in Franciacorta, was to help transform what had hitherto been perceived as something of a sow's ear into a true silk purse. Though Guerrino sadly passed away recently at the ripe old age of 101, he lived long enough to see his dream come to fruition. His two grandsons – Alessandro who looks after the vineyards and winemaking and Matteo who handles the commercial side of the business – have taken up the reins and are producing some of the finest *metodo classico* to be found throughout the length and breadth of the peninsula. It seems that the rest of the world is slowly beginning to wake up to the massive potential of Lessini Durello Spumante DOC too: Fongaro have a good existing market in China and have made small inroads into Denmark and Germany as well.

The Fongaro wine begins fermentation in stainless steel before being transferred to bottle or magnum where it will remain for between three and seven years (in the case of the Riserva) on its fine lees until *sboccatura* or 'degorgement', and this is when the magic takes place. The wine's improvement as it rests on those lees is startling; indeed it can be fairly neutral when young (though always characterized by the clear if sometimes elusive aroma of hawthorn blossom) but becomes much more perfumed as it ages. If left long enough, notes of red apple, pear and apricot develop amongst hints of dried flowers, saffron and camomile, all against a backdrop of rich yeast-autolysis aromas. The Fongaro range is made up of six different wines, all produced by the *metodo classico* and each one carefully colour coded.

The white label Brut is a relatively easy introduction to Durello. Some 20 per cent of Incrocio Manzoni, the perfumed Riesling/Pinot Bianco/Chardonnay crossing, makes the wine instantly accessible despite the underlying vein of brisk acidity. The grey label Brut spends an extra twelve months on its lees (forty-eight in total) and contains 20 per cent or so Chardonnay. Though already a little less 'easy' than the white label wine, the Chardonnay provides a familiar note of ripe melon amid the aromas of bread crust and mature orchard-fruit flavours. Each of these two wines is produced in batches of around 9,000 or 10,000 bottles a year. With the violet label, we move into the inimitable world of pure Durello and aromas of apple and lime amongst the mature leafy and yeasty flavours that spread across the palate. Where there are approximately 20,000 bottles of the *Viola*, only 7,000 bottles or so are produced of the first of the two black label wines. The Brut Riserva spends at least sixty months on the fine lees; the wine appears almost 'sculpted' on the palate, so fine is the balance between ripe and subtle nectarine and pear flavours and the clearly evident though somehow seemingly gentle acidity which gives the wine its understated structure. Sandwiched in between this and the other black label wine is the green label Pas Dosé wine which spends thirty-six months on the lees. The only *liqueur d'expedition* added to this wine is a small dose from a bottle of the same product. Less time on the lees gives the green label a fresher style with flavours and aromas of hawthorn and camomile clearly present; some 20,000 bottles are made a year. The final wine of the range is the black label Pas Dosé Riserva of which just a few thousand bottles are produced. After between six and seven years on the fine lees, and with the *liqueur d'expedition* added as above, the full Durello story unfolds. Over the broad and ripe yeast autolysis notes, the wine maintains an incisive almost floral freshness and stays remarkably light on its feet despite the ripe and mature flavours of dried apricot and pear; the finish is tremendously long and tapers gently away to a final enticing mineral note.

These wines are not matured in cavernous underground cathedrals carved out of chalk such as encountered in Champagne, but in a few brick-built bins which lie in the simple cement-lined vault tunnelled below the winery. From such humble beginnings, Durello has now conquered nearby Verona where a glass of Durello is becoming the city's preferred aperitif. If you're lucky, it may even be coming your way soon.

Franchetto

Via Binelli, 22, 37030 Terrossa di Roncà VR
+39 045 7460287
www.cantinafranchetto.com

The sisters Giulia and Anna help out their father in the cellar and their mother to run the business respectively, as well as managing company sales. Their deliciously delicate and scented Soave stands out in a range which also includes good Durello and tiny quantities of Valpolicella from rented vineyards in Montecchia di Crosara.

Gini Sandro e Claudio – history in a glass

Via Matteotti, 42 - 37032 Monteforte d'Alpone VR
+39 045 7611908
www.ginivini.com

If Pieropan is the name that immediately springs to mind when talking about quality Soave, a few other estates can point to a similarly distinguished and, in some cases, even longer history of producing grapes and wine. Azienda Agricola Gini is run by brothers Sandro and Claudio Gini. The winery lies close to the centre of the 'Party Town' of Monteforte d'Alpone. 'That's the reputation we have to live up to,' says Claudio, smiling. Their grandfather was a well-known winemaker locally and would deliver the family's wine as far as the hostelries of Verona on a horse and cart. Sadly he died young and was succeeded by the brothers' father Olinto in 1945 when just 16 years old. Part of the load was always a small barrel containing an older wine – considered much superior to the more youthful and fresher style much in vogue today – a glass or two of which would play a part in helping to seal any deal. 'Dad carried on the family tradition but to start with, at such a young age, just wasn't used to drinking. Thank goodness the horse knew the way home!' Claudio explains, offering a clue as to where that notoriety comes from. While Olinto bottled wine, the family supplied Bolla too throughout Soave's heyday in the 1960s and 1970s. 'That was when we brought in cement tanks to replace most of the *botti*. But we always kept the best wine in barrels until the following year. It wasn't until the 1960s that younger wines came into fashion. Now everyone is looking for that style,' he says.

The Gini family have been producing grapes since the 1600s so history is hard-wired into their way of thinking. The brothers have replanted very little, renewing when they have to and preferring to work with the fruit from their older vineyards. They own 55 hectares of vineyard, 35 hectares in the Soave Classico zone (they have vineyards in Valpolicella too) including the famous south-south-east-facing La Frosca vineyard close to Monteforte itself where their most favoured plot is known as Salvarenza. Where La Frosca has a mainly basalt-based soil, Salvarenza also has a vein of limestone mid-slope with a covering layer of degraded tufa originating from the rocky summit higher up. The vineyard is named after the area where a young maiden called Renza, who lived close by, was under threat from a group of brigands but was 'saved' at the eleventh hour by a passing knight; the name stuck. The difference between the two wines shows through in both aromatic profile and structure. La Frosca is a typical 'volcanic' wine with a freshness and distinctive opulence of almost tropical fruit aromas and a fleshy, expansive palate; Salvarenza has less immediate breadth but greater intensity and a zesty and floral quality particularly in its early stages of development, while the palate is tighter and has greater persistence. A third Soave, the Gini Soave Classico, is produced from a further 12 hectares of vineyards which are a mixture of limestone and volcanic soils. As with both La Frosca and Salvarenza, the wine is made solely from Garganega grapes and, like them, the 'regular' Soave Classico also shows an uncommon capacity to take plenty of bottle age in its stride. Properly cellared bottles can keep for ten or twenty years and still have something to offer. While the ability to age is to be expected from the two 'premium' versions of Soave Classico, the supposedly 'lesser' wine is also built to last.

While it remains a moot point whether a wine like Soave truly benefits from being aged, it is possible to put the theory of longevity to the test thanks to producers like Gini. The wine 'puts on flesh', gradually becoming richer and fatter and at the same time allowing the aromas of wax, honey and candied fruits that are typical of an aged Soave to emerge. The aromatic profile thus broadens out and shows rather greater nuance and delicacy as the wine matures. Though modern tastes might lean towards the more immediate style of full ripe-fruit aromas and flavours with freshness, lift and vitality as the most prized attributes, there is of course room for both interpretations. Claudio compares tasting Soave as it matures to the gradual opening of a fan.

The first bottling with the family's label in 1980 was Soave Classico followed by La Frosca in 1985 and Salvarenza in 1990. The basis of the family's approach is to keep the juice as clean as possible. From 1985 onwards the brothers have cut back on the use of sulphur during the first stages of fermentation, adding a small dose only when the wine is first racked and then again on bottling. Indigenous yeasts are preferred whenever possible; they also favour refrigeration over filtration, avoid clarification and give their wines a light filtration just before bottling. La Frosca and Salvarenza are both produced from lower vineyard yields, spend longer on the fine lees and then time in 'seasoned' wood (at least three years old) reflecting their view that the microflora of a cellar is better maintained through the presence and use of wood. Approximately a third of the vines which produce the fruit for Salvarenza, harvested a couple of weeks later than La Frosca, date back to the late nineteenth century and have never been grafted on to American rootstocks. Some could be over 120 years old.

Gini produce a fourth Garganega-based wine, Recioto di Soave Col Foscarin, which contains a proportion of grapes affected by noble rot. Again this wine is somewhat 'retro' in style and aims for a luscious, rich and full-bodied character that is perhaps more typical of what Recioto di Soave was like until the 1980s. There are future plans to produce the traditional red wines of Valpolicella as well at their Campiano estate. Given such a painstaking approach to 'getting it right', they will doubtless be well worth waiting for.

Ilatium

Mezzane di Sotto - 37030 VR
+39 045 7834648
www.latiummorini.it

The Morini family crush the fruit from just over 40 hectares of vines (some owned, some managed) in their modern winery at the foot of the Mezzane valley. Several different cuvées of Soave (including one without added sulphites) are produced in a fresh, clean and simple style. Red wines favour the use of barriques and tonneaux and show abundant sweet, slightly jammy fruit flavours.

Inama

Località Biacche, 50, 37047 San Bonifacio VR
+39 045 6104343
www.inamaaziendaagricola.it

Inama's aim is to give maximum expression to Garganega grown in volcanic soils. The family work with around 30 hectares of vines in Classico mainly on Monte Foscarino but also at Tremenalto, Tondo and close to Monte Carbonara. The vineyards on Foscarino are close to the summit in a particularly well-ventilated spot with a commanding view over Soave's castle and the plains below. The vines are trained to the modern Pergoletta system which helps shade the ripening fruit from excessive sun. While the family will avoid using treatments if possible, they will intervene when necessary to safeguard the crop (and therefore the people they have working for them).

Inama first started bottling in 1991 and helped to pioneer the use of French oak barriques in the area. Until a few years ago it is fair to say that their use of oak could be rather heavy-handed but recent vintages have seen a movement towards more seasoned barrels with lower toast. Those creamy, vanillin and coconut notes play more of a background role these days allowing the aromas of Garganega to assume centre stage and the wines are much better for it. Inama produce around 250,000 bottles of a good, simple Soave Classico Vin Soave; between 30,000 and 35,000 bottles of Classico Vigneti di Foscarino which is fermented in used barriques and, from a 2-hectare plot on Foscarino, Classico Vigneto du Lot. Thirty per cent of Du Lot is fermented in low-toast new barriques where it remains for another six months followed by a further six in stainless steel before bottling; about 13,000 bottles a year are made of this impressively rich, Burgundian-style wine which shows excellent ageing potential. A Sauvignon Blanc called Vulcaia Fumé shows the benefits of fermenting the variety in oak and has the fat, ripe and rich character typical of Foscarino wines. The Inama family also produce a range of reds, mainly from Bordeaux varieties, from a further 30 hectares of vineyards in the nearby Colli Berici.

Le Mandolare

Via Sambuco, 180, 37032 Brognoligo di Monteforte VR
+39 045 6175083
www.cantinalemandolare.com

The Dal Bosco family produces around 70,000 bottles a year of white wines from 100 per cent Garganega grapes. The mother, Germana, makes the wine with her daughters Anna and Chiara helping out. Three styles of Soave Classico take in the fresh, fruit-driven Corte Menini, Il Roccolo which sees some wood and the more ambitious Monte Sella made in a fuller and richer style. A Recioto di Soave and a Passito Bianco complete the range.

Marco Mosconi – finding his feet

Via Paradiso, 5, 37031 Mormontea VR
+39 045 6529109
www.marcomosconi.it

Though he graduated as a surveyor, Marco Mosconi chose instead to become a wine producer. His great-grandfather founded the estate and subsequently his grandfather helped to set up the local Cantina d'Illasi cooperative and Marco's father continued to sell off the family's fruit. Marco currently owns 10 hectares of vines (and rents another 2 hectares), aiming for the magic number of 15 hectares of land, a level at which many smaller producers believe they can both spread their wings and cover all the necessary costs. He already had a role model in Romano Dal Forno through his friendship with one of the family's three sons, and subsequent visits to Piedmont during his student years had reawoken the family passion for wine. In 2006 he decided to expand the family home to include a small winery and start making wine.

For a year he worked with Michel Barbaud, the French agronomist whose organic forest concept is an inspiration to many biodynamic converts. Barbaud advised a programme of soil management in order to get the most out of vineyards. 'I have two main types of soil in my vineyards,' Marco explains. 'Here at Corte Paradiso [the vineyard at the back of the winery] where we make our Soave, we're on the pebbly, alluvial soil of the Illasi valley floor. The nitrogen content is high and the vines have so much vigour, so I've been mulching a carbon-based compost in between the plants. My yields have halved and I no longer need to practise *diraddamento*!' The vines, he believes, are really healthy now and there has been a notable improvement in the level of microflora. 'But it's a windy spot and I have to be really careful with my young Garganega plants. The shoots are extremely long and tender so they can break quite easily when the wind is up.' Next to the pergola-trained Garganega are a few rows of Corvina which he has planted using Guyot: 'The young shoots here are much easier to deal with; I can close two training wires together over them to clamp the shoots firmly in place and keep them stable. I don't think the system would work with Garganega, though.' Marco also owns land at nearby Monte Curto in the foothills of the eastern slope of the valley where the soils are a calcareous marl: 'The ground is low on iron so we add cow manure to improve the balance. We use both pergola and Guyot and I'm still getting to grips with the relative merits of both systems.' He also rents land in the Monte Vegro vineyard further to the north and in the commune of Lavagno on the east-facing slopes at Turano in the next valley to the west, Mezzane. The vines there are older and all pergola trained. 'One thing I have definitely learned is that it's better to work with older vines,' he adds. Marco has been just as active in the cellars, experimenting with different sizes and types of oak. 'While I like what I've done with barriques and tonneaux, I'm increasingly being drawn back towards larger *botti*. I'm a great admirer of Romano Dal Forno,' he confirms, 'but I need to find my own way.'

The simple Soave Corte Paradiso and Valpolicella Monte Curto DOC wines are fermented and stored in stainless steel and made in a round and approachable style which displays, in both cases, admirable freshness and breadth of aroma. Soave Rosetta is produced from a later harvest of his older vines and a Valpolicella Superiore comes in part from freshly picked grapes from his Monte Curto vineyard while the rest, from Mezzane, are semi-dried. 'I only make about 4,000 bottles a year of this one but I managed to win Tre Bicchieri [the coveted award from Italy's *Gambero Rosso* wine guide] with the 2012,' he says. Marco also makes a few thousand bottles of Amarone and tiny quantities of a Cabernet Sauvignon from rented vines at Turano. Tasting through the range, the potential for both red and white wines in the area is clearly apparent. Marco agrees: 'I started out focusing mainly on the red wines but I'm really enjoying myself with the whites at the moment.'

Monte Tondo

Via S. Lorenzo, 89, 37038 Soave VR
+39 045 7680347
www.montetondo.it

The Magnabosco family run their winery based at the foot of Monte Tondo as you approach town from the south and the Soave exit off the A4. A complete range of Soave begins with a basic DOC through a generic Classico and two single-vineyard wines from their holdings on Monte Foscarino. Casette Foscarin is a partially oak-aged basket of flowers while Foscarin Slavinius, made from whole bunch fermentation completed on the gross lees, is more Burgundian in style. There is an example of Soave Brut and three versions of Recioto di Soave: a spumante and two still wines. One is fermented in stainless steel and aged in oak while Nettore di Bacco is fermented in wood and aged in stainless steel. The family also make a full range of Valpolicella from vineyards in Cazzano di Tramigna. Accommodation is available at the winery.

Nardello

Via IV Novembre, 56, 37032 Monteforte d'Alpone VR
+39 045 7612116
www.nardellovini.it

Brother and sister Daniele and Federica run this family winery with around 14 hectares of vineyard on Monte Tondo and Monte Zoppega. The cellars lie just below Zoppega. Anaerobic vinification at low temperatures and minimal use of sulphur results in two crystal-clear versions of Soave Classico: Meredies is made from 100 per cent Garganega grown in both vineyards and Vigna Turbian, a part of Zoppega, contains around 30 per cent Trebbiano di Soave. The latter is a particularly exciting example of the denomination and shows tremendous balance and verve. A third Classico, Monte Zoppega, begins fermentation in stainless steel and is then transferred to barrel where it undergoes malolactic fermentation and remains on the lees for a further six months or so: more Burgndian in style, the wine ages well in bottle. Not to be missed is their excellent, barrel-fermented Recioto Suavissimus.

Pieropan - trailblazing

Via Giulio Camuzzoni, 3, 37038 Soave VR
+39 045 6190171
www.pieropan.it

With fifty vintages now under his belt Leonildo (Nino) Pieropan is indisputably the founding father of quality Soave. When he first took up the reins at the family winery in the mid 1960s, Soave was seen as little more than a cheap and cheerful, mass-produced wine beyond its predominantly local market. Nino cites the great Italian author and gastronome Luigi Veronelli as the man who finally convinced him that the family's wine from the Calvarino vineyard should be bottled separately with its name on the label. The first bottling was with the 1971 vintage, since when Calvarino has gone on to become the embodiment of the concept of Soave as a fine wine, able to hold its own on an international stage. At the time Pieropan had just started working with vitrified cement though his father first brought cement tanks into the winery in the early 1930s: 'We always harvested in October back then, it was much cooler and the must would stabilize on its own. I bought my first Vaselin press around the same time. Before that we were still using a basket press and the wines were pretty tannic!' He still uses cement and *botti* for storage and cement tanks will be installed at the new winery which is under construction on the outskirts of town; Pieropan admits he'd be happy enough to get rid of stainless steel altogether. He believes the arrival of technology has brought negative as well as positive changes: 'In general terms, Italian wine lags behind the field in terms of the quality of its raw materials. There's too much focus still on the cellar – technology is no guarantee of quality though it can certainly help.' Winemaking at the Pieropan cellars follows a simple and traditional formula with fermentation and storage mainly in cement.

In the vineyard, Pieropan is a great believer in the local varieties: when Chardonnay arrived on the scene in the early 1990s, he stuck with Garganega and Trebbiano. Plantings of the French grape were largely at the expense of Trebbiano which seemed for a while to be heading the same way as the Tocai and Malvasia vines that were still common in the area until the 1940s. 'Trebbiano works better in cooler years. As it matures around two weeks earlier than Garganega and the vines used to be mixed up together we'd have real problems harvesting in more difficult vintages. It wasn't until the 1980s that people began planting by rows and maturation times.' As Garganega is so vigorous it is an arduous task in the warm summer months to contain the plant's energy, so short pruning and pergola seem to suit the variety just as well as Guyot, he feels. The family's 40 hectares of vines in Classico are planted in roughly equal measure to the two systems. At the same time, he bemoans the restricted choice of clones available to growers: 'Everyone used to do it themselves – take cuttings from the best vines and propagate them. The nurseries have been pushed by market demands into focusing on the most productive clones and we're putting the microdiversity of the territory at risk as a result.' Not surprisingly, he remains convinced that good viticultural practice is the only starting point for the production of great wine.

Pieropan has gradually expanded the firm's vineyard holdings, buying up La Rocca, a south-facing 6-hectare plot on the hill behind Soave's castle, known locally as Monte Rochetta, in 1976 and the wine was first produced as a single vineyard bottling with the 1978 vintage. Following work experience in Tuscany at Isole e Olena and Poliziano, Nino's son Dario became enamoured of red wines and the family acquired land on Monte Garzon above Cellore d'Illasi in 1999. The first vines were planted in 2002, the same year that Villa Cipolla in Tregnano was purchased and refurbishment of the cellars was completed in 2005. There are currently 16 hectares in production including 4 hectares of rented vineyard. Dario is a trained oenologist and his brother Andrea an agronomist, so the future of the family wine business seems to be assured.

Pieropan does not come from a particularly long line of grape farmers. His grandfather Leonildo, a doctor with a keen interest in wine, established the firm in 1880 mainly selling Recioto in demijohns from the Palazzo Pullici close to the centre of town, still the hub of the business today. The family bought the Calvarino vineyard in 1901 and only started bottling following the end of the First World War. The products themselves hardly need much of an introduction. The regular Soave Classico is mainly Garganega with around 10 to 15 per cent of Trebbiano di Soave and is a classic of its type: a melange of floral-toned, orchard fruit flavours and aromas backed up by crisp acid and clear mineral notes. The Calvarino vineyard faces west at up to around 200 metres with predominantly basalt and clay soils. The Pieropan wine is fermented in cement and spends twelve months on its lees and several more in bottle before release. Low yields highlight intensity and structure and the relatively high proportion of Trebbiano di Soave (30 per cent) brings the steely acidity which plays a key role in the wine's great potential longevity. Calvarino's balance, concentration and ability to improve with age first brought Pieropan's Soave to the attention of a wider audience. La Rocca, on the other hand, is pure Garganega. A bigger wine thanks to later-harvested fruit from south-facing vines planted on the slightly lower lying and mainly limestone soils, La Rocca is fermented in used barrique these days before spending a further twelve months on its lees in *botti*. A fuller and richer style than Calvarino, it also ages well. Pieropan's Recioto Le Colombare is also made in a very traditional style. Dried on the classic *arele* for up to five months, the partially botrytized fruit is fermented and aged in old *botti* for that extra touch of authenticity; the wine's subtle sweetness is perhaps why Pieropan suggests the rather unusual pairing with anchovies! As they're made from young vines and with so few vintages released, it is perhaps too soon to offer a full assessment of the red wines from Monte Garzon fully, though the Pieropan family are to be applauded for producing the Valpolicella Superiore from fresh fruit only, and the Amarone already shows definite promise.

Flavio Pra

Via delle Pezzole, 3, loc. Allodola, Cellore VR
+39 045 6175915
www.icampi.it

When Flavio Pra's father retired from brother Graziano's well-known winery in Monteforte d'Alpone, the young oenologist worked alongside his uncle for a while before setting up his own consultancy business. However he missed having a winery and set up I Campi in Cellore d'Illasi in 2006. Drawing on twenty-five years' winemaking experience, he brings precision methods to bear on two versions of Soave and all five wines from the Valpolicella. A range of stylish wines of great purity, the Soave Classico Campo Volcano from vineyards in Monteforte and Amarone Campo Marna from a vineyard at 550 metres in the Val d'Illasi are both excellent though the Valpolicella Ripasso Campo Ciotoli also merits attention.

Graziano Pra

Via della Fontana, 31, 37032 Monteforte d'Alpone VR
+39 045 7612125
www.vinipra.it

A well-reputed producer whose modern winery lies on the outskirts of Monteforte d'Alpone below Monte Riondo, Pra makes a range of Soave and Valpolicella from family-owned vineyards in both territories. Soave Otto (200,000 bottles a year) is an excellent 'entry level' wine, though the firm are best known for their Classico Monte Grande which involves the *taglio del tralcio* technique of breaking the vine stems with the first waning moon of September and leaving the bunches on the vine for a further month. This modified form of *appassimento* brings weight and richness to the wine which also spends time in large French oak barrels. Colle Sant'Antonio also uses stem break while premium Staforte follows a more conventional route. Pra's Valpolicella is made from grapes grown on the Morandina estate on the higher reaches of the hillside dividing Illasi from Mezzane.

Tenuta Sant'Antonio

Via Montigarbi Italie, 37030 Lavagno VR
+39 045 7650383
www.tenutasantantonio.it

The four Castagnedi brothers have offices and warehouse facilities at Colognola and a winery at the top of the San Briccio hillside dividing

Mezzane and Marcellise. They supplement the fruit from their 70 hectares of vines in Soave and Valpolicella with another 30 per cent from managed vineyards for three separate ranges: while the Telos wines (made without added sulphites) are an interesting departure, the main Tenuta Sant'Antonio label forms the core of their production and exhibits a consistently high standard. Two versions of Soave DOC from the Monte Ceriani vineyard to the west of San Zeno are both classic examples of their type. In Valpolicella, the excellent Superiore La Bandina is a regular award winner and, of the three versions of Amarone, Campo dei Gigli is a particularly palate-flattering example.

La Suavia

Via Centro, 14, Fittà, 37038 Soave VR
+39 045 7675089
www.suavia.it

The sisters Alessandra, Meri and Valentina, the fourth generation of the Tessari family to work the land at Fittà, produce some 200,000 bottles of wine a year from their 25 hectares of vineyard. The focus is on Garganega for Soave Classico, Monte Carbonara and IGT Le Rive while highly rated IGT Massafitta is made from 100 per cent Trebbiano di Soave. Clean, particularly aromatic wines which conjure up notes of camomile, citrus fruits and flint are made with great conviction.

I Stefanini

Via Crosara, 21, 37032 Monteforte d'Alpone VR
+39 045 6175249
www.istefanini.it

Francesco Tessari produces approximately 100,000 bottles of Soave a year from 15 hectares of land around Costalunga, all made from 100 per cent Garganega grapes vinified in stainless steel. The differences between them are determined by the vineyards themselves. Selese from the DOC area is the simplest wine with appealing fresh, ripe-fruit characters, while Classico Monte di Toni is much fuller with rich, leesy flavours and an expansive, floral-toned finish. Monte di Fice, from the highest vines of the property, is more intense and luscious. They are classic examples of the Monteforte style.

Gianni Tessari (Marcato)

Via Prandi, 10, Roncà VR
+39 045 7460070
www.giannitessari.wine

Gianni Tessari took up the reins at Marcato, one of the leading lights behind the emergence of Durello Metodo Classico, in 2013. Also owning vineyards in Soave Classico (as well as the Colli Berici), the Tessari signature of perfumed and approachable wines is now emblazoned across the range. Two versions of Soave Classico are made as well as the generic DOC wine from Ronca: the more structured Pigno is partly barrel fermented while Monte Tenda is lighter and more fragrant in style. The Durello wines remain at the forefront of their denomination, including 4,000 bottles of '120 mesi' which spends up to ten years on its lees.

Vicentini

Via Cesare Battisti, 62, 37030 Colognola Ai Colli VR
+39 045 7650539
www.vinivicentini.com

Agostino Vicentini makes Soave from vineyards at Colognola ai Colli: the crisp, floral and citrussy Terre Lunghe contains around 25 per cent Trebbiano di Soave while Superiore Il Casale is pure Garganega and a fuller, richer wine. Agostino also produces two versions of 'old-style', barrel-fermented Valpolicella from his vines near San Zeno. His larger than life personality is reflected in a range of wines that seem proud to be a bit different!

VALPOLICELLA

Stefano Accordini

Localita Camparol, 10 - 37022 Fumane, VR
+39 045 7760138
www.accordinistefano.it

The brothers Tiziano and Daniele Accordini (see also Cantina di Negrar) transferred the business from their cramped cellars in Pedemonte to a new winery in a commanding position just below Cavolo in 2010. They produce consistently reliable wines with the emphasis on freshness, ripe fruit flavours and expansive aromas. Around 180,000 bottles a year are produced from 25 hectares of vineyard mainly in the Fumane valley but also in Marano and Sant'Ambrogio. The basic Valpolicella Classico is a dependably good example and is backed up by two wines (Ripasso and Amarone) named Acinatico after the ancient Roman name for wines made from semi-dried grapes. The single vineyard Amarone Il Fornetto, aged in new barriques, is produced in top vintages only.

Aldrighetti Lorenzo e Cristoforo

Via del Muratore, 3, 37020 Marano di Valpolicella VR
+39 349 6369755
www.aldrighettivini.it

From their tiny cellars in Marano and with just 4 hectares of vineyards, the Aldrighetti family produce Classico versions of Valpolicella, Ripasso Superiore, Amarone and Recioto. The first bottling was in 2013 and so far the wines have spread as far as Russia by word of mouth alone! The uncompromising Valpolicella, made in a lean and slightly austere style, should appeal to lovers of authentic, food-friendly versions of the genuine article.

Allegrini: Fumane - the crest of a wave

Via della Torre, 25, 37022 Fumane VR
+39 045 6832070
www.website.allegrini.it

When the Allegrini siblings inherited the family wine business following the death of their father Giovanni in 1983, the tide of Valpolicella's fortunes was beginning to turn. While Nicolas Belfrage was lamenting the rise of 'industrial Valpolicella' designed for mass market consumption in *Life Beyond Lambrusco*, a number of smaller-scale producers were already making waves. Bepi Quintarelli's reputation had come to the attention of a wider audience; Romano Dal Forno was at the start of his career as a winemaker; Burton Anderson had picked up on the excellent work carried out at the Le Ragose estate, another Veronelli favourite, in his book *Vino* and wineries like Masi and Tedeschi were making inroads into export markets with wines of unquestionable quality. Giovanni Allegrini, too, was a force to be reckoned with: he had increased the family's vineyard holdings in some of the area's most prestigious sites such as La Grola and Palazzo della Torre, and introduced Guyot as his preferred training system. Over the course of the next couple of decades his children were to benefit from his foresight and the 'prevailing wind', cementing the family name amongst the region's greats. There is much more behind the story than serendipity, however: they turned themselves into the perfect team. Walter had a real passion for viticulture while Marilisa applied her boundless energy and enthusiasm to sales and marketing. Franco admits that, with his background in agriculture, he started out making wine in the same way as he had seen his father do; he has since gone on to become one of Italy's most respected winemakers.

Now a sprightly sixty, Franco reflects on the changes that have shaped the new face of Valpolicella. 'We can't underestimate the importance of climate change – we can grow vines at up to 500 metres now whereas a few decades ago, 300 was probably the limit. In the last twenty years we've only had one vintage when the grapes didn't achieve full phenolic maturity, 2003. At the same time we've seen the consolidation of Corvina as our most important variety; Rondinella, for example, used to be far more popular because of its productivity and reliability. Corvina and Corvinone both have characteristics that remind me of the great wines of Burgundy with their fragrance and spiciness. Oseleta too is finding its role: though Corvinone works well in hillside sites and when yields are closely controlled, it has a high liquid to solid ratio and Oseleta helps to balance this out. Higher-density planting is making a big difference: with the old-fashioned pergola we had around 2,500 plants per hectare whereas the modern version allows us at least another 1,000 and with Guyot we can go up to 6,000 – and beyond, even. It all adds up to a steady march towards better quality.' In the cellar Franco has slowly updated the Allegrini style, introducing smaller barrels and cutting back on wood ageing to conserve aroma and fruit characters but his principal achievement has had massive implications for the area as a whole: the rethinking of the *appassimento* process. As the theme of his doctorate thesis at the University of Bologna, Roberto Ferrarini had researched a new system of drying grapes with the objective of preserving the quality of the raw materials by maintaining the integrity of the skins and ensuring that colour and tannins would not be compromised during the process. 'It's all to do with humidity,' maintains Franco. 'Keep that under control and even higher temperatures become less of an issue.' Putting Ferrarini's ideas into practice, Franco headed up the team who went on to found the Terre di Fumane, thus paving the way for the opening chapter of the international success story of Amarone.

Allegrini's success depends on a carefully constructed range of wines from their 120 hectares of vineyard. Over one and a quarter million bottles of DOC and DOCG reds are produced to enviably high standards including 500,000 of Palazzo della Torre, a thoroughly modern wine made from both fresh and semi-dried grapes. Franco is a staunch believer that the *ripasso* process is fundamentally flawed: 'Would you use a teabag twice?' he queries. Instead Palazzo is made primarily from fresh grapes and undergoes its secondary fermentation with the addition of the juice from grapes pressed in January at the end of *appassimento*. Other wines include the collector's item La Poja, made from freshly harvested 100 per cent Corvina grapes grown on the plateau on top of the La Grola hillside; the exemplary Amarone (150,000 bottles a year); and the single-vineyard version Fieramonte, from high up above Mazzurega and replanted in 2003, is due to be relaunched. The family continue to look for new opportunities, and 20 hectares of new vineyard in the high parts of the eastern side of the Fumane valley at Monte Noroni beyond Purano will become productive in the next few years.

Sadly the eldest of the Allegrini children, Walter, died in 2003 but not before he had tasted some of the burgeoning success both his family and the overall area was beginning to enjoy. Along with Marilisa, he helped to set up the acquisition of the 70-hectare Poggio al Tesoro estate at Castagneto Carducci in the Bogheri production area. Marilisa has since gone on to found another winery in Tuscany, the San Polo estate in Montalcino, in partnership with American wine merchant Leonardo Lo Cascio. Marilisa shows little sign of slowing down her incessant campaigning on behalf of quality Valpolicella and still seems to spend much of her life on aeroplanes. She also recognizes her wider responsibilities as an international ambassador for the wines of Valpolicella as her term as president of the Famiglie Amarone indicates: 'If we want to continue to prosper, we first have to learn how to manage our success.' If the Valpolicella area's future is managed with the same degree of professionalism as the Allegrini family have handled their own, then it should be a rosy one.

Albino Armani

Località Ceradello - Dolcè VR
+39 045 7290033
www.albinoarmani.com

This impressive winery high up in the Marano valley of recent construction successfully blends the modern and the traditional. The wines are of similar inspiration: most of the fruit is sourced from local growers around the village of San Rocco for a stylish and cleverly made range of reds, mainly from the Classico zone.

Antolini

Via Prognol, 22, 37020 Marano di Valpolicella VR
+39 333 6546187
www.antolinivini.it

The brothers Pier Paolo and Stefano Antolini farm some 9 hectares of vines around the family cellars at Prognol, at Moropio near Novaia, plus a few hectares in Negrar and San Pietro in Cariano. Oenologist Pier Paolo uses various types of wood for ageing – not only oak, acacia, cherry and chestnut, but even mulberry which is almost impossible to find these days. Ironically, despite its high porosity, Pier Paolo insists mulberry maintains great freshness. Artisanal-type methods (spontaneous fermentation, no clarification or cold stabilization) result in a range of characterful and aromatic wines which give full expression to the different terrains in which the fruit is grown.

Begali

Via Cengia 10, 37029 San Pietro in Cariano
+39 045 7725148
www.begaliwine.it

Lorenzo Begali and his two children run this unpretentious winery based at Cengia with vines close by and near the summit of Monte Masua in Marano. The wines are very much hand crafted and reflect the warm and friendly disposition of the family. Simple Valpolicella is a real classic and while Amarone Ca Bianca has often picked up the gongs, the generic version is not far behind. The family note a difference in style between the two vineyard areas: the Cengia wines are well structured while those from Masua show more fruit and finesse.

Bertani - back to where it all began

Via Asiago, 1, 37023 Grezzana VR
+39 045 8658444
www.bertani.net

When Giovan Battista and Gaetano Bertani founded the Cantina dei Signori Fratelli Bertani in 1857, the brothers were laying down the foundations for more than just a family business: the modern history of Veronese wines dates back arguably to that moment. Up until then, most wine was still sold locally, in barrel or demijohn, and was for the most part sweet. By the end of the century, bottled wine from Bertani was beginning to make a name for itself in the US and another fifty years on, a century after its foundation, the firm was to play a part in the creation of Amarone. For many years Bertani had remained the leading name in Veronese wines until Bolla's conquest of the American market with Soave in the 1970s. The original base was at Quinto di Valpantena but by the middle of the 1950s the firm had acquired the neo-classical eighteenth-century Villa Mosconi (or Villa Novare as it is also known) at the foot of the Negrar valley in the Arbizzano district. While the villa remains in the hands of the Bertani family, the Secco-Bertani brand, Grezzana-based winery, and many of the vineyards were sold in 2011 to Tenimenti Angelini who own a number of wine estates throughout Italy. These were united in 2014 under the 'Bertani Domaines' banner with headquarters at the Grezzana winery deep in the Valpantena valley.

While Bertani have in a way returned to their original home, it would be an easy assumption to expect that everything there has now changed beyond recognition. It is fair to say that Bertani's reputation had slipped somewhat since those heady, early days but the current Operations Director of Bertani Domaines, Andrea Lonardi, is determined to restore some gloss to the name. Andrea was born in nearby San Pietro in Cariano and is a staunch defender of his local wines. Alongside a range of more commercially styled wines, he is looking to reaffirm time-honoured local values. He identifies three particular issues which have led to the current 'plight' facing Veronese wines as he sees it: 'Firstly, over the last twenty years, the reds of the Valpolicella have become "method" wines. Everything depends on *appassimento* and because we're looking to a process to define the fundamental characteristics of our wines, what we have is becoming increasingly easy to replicate elsewhere. Secondly the *tipicita* of our wines has been devalued by the arrival of international varieties, and thirdly we're compromising our identity even further with high residual sugar levels, which are simply ruining our wines.' Andrea's mission is therefore to return to what he believes are the true traditions of the area.

An improvement programme has begun in the vineyards. As well as introducing a modification to the company's mainly Guyot training system, a new method of controlling sugar levels in the ripening grapes has been formulated. Dubbed the 'Novare' method after the valley where the vineyards are located, the idea is that by partially breaking the bunch stems to prevent further nutrients reaching the grapes as harvest time approaches, the sugars are 'frozen' at the required level. The grapes are then left on the vines until the end of October to develop and intensify aromas. The 'first fruit' of the idea is Novare, a Verona IGT red wine made from 100 per cent Corvina grapes. Cement vats and wooden *tini* have been restored for fermentation. 'We just use stainless steel for Soave these days,' Andrea explains, 'and even then just a part – no more than 60 per cent usually.' While much of the wood maturation takes place in oak, Bertani are also experimenting with cherry and chestnut barrels, both commonly used in the past. The updated versions of the company's historic wines are gradually coming on stream: Soave Vintage is a reinterpretation of the 1930s wine, and through partial fermentation on the skins achieves a faintly tannic but almost unctuous and attractively oxidative style. 'It's a long way from the world of thiols,' says Andrea, smiling. The deliberately old-fashioned feel extends to the packaging, a recreation of the 1930s label. The same concept applies to the red counterpart, Secco Vintage, a blend of mainly Corvina with 10 per cent Sangiovese Grosso, plus smaller proportions of Syrah and Cabernet Sauvignon, aged in cherry and chestnut: 'The Bertani family were always lovers of great French wines and introduced French varieties in the early years. It's called Secco because that was what the family were always trying to achieve, a drier style of wine.' If the style of Secco Vintage seems rather out on a limb, Andrea's challenging views extend to the *appassimento* process as well. He believes that 'assisted' drying of the grapes (with dehumidifiers and giant ventilators) achieves little more than mere concentration of aromas and flavours and, moreover, that the duration of the process should be determined by the chemical composition of the grapes themselves rather than any set length of time. Bertani produce two versions of Amarone these days: the 'Classico' which keeps the same label design as the first vintage to be produced in 1958, and a new Amarone 'Valpantena' made in a more approachable, earlier-drinking style. Other wines include a wood-fermented, single-vineyard Soave Le Sereole, a youthful style of Valpolicella DOC which blends Corvina and Rondinella grapes from the Classico and Valpantena areas, a 'cru' Valpolicella Classico from the Ognisanti (All Saints) vineyard, a Valpolicella Ripasso, a more 'mainstream' version of Secco Bertani which blends Corvina and Merlot and finally a Recioto, aged in cherry wood, from grapes grown exclusively in the Valpantena and dried on traditional *arele* for around 150 days. The considered mix of consumer-friendly wines and challenging reinterpretations of traditional values would seem to suggest that Bertani is a name once again worth keeping an eye on.

Carlo Boscaini

Via Sengia, 15, 37015 Sant'Ambrogio di Valpolicella VR
+39 045 7731412
www.boscainicarlo.it

The Boscaini family own a 17-hectare estate in the south-facing amphitheatre at Sengia below San Giorgio, and a west-facing plot at nearby La Grola for their Ripasso Superiore Zane. A full range of good, honest and rather rustic Valpolicella is produced which reflects the good-natured and refreshingly unpretentious character of the proprietors. If you're looking for wines that are 'as friendly as the house of your brother', these might fit the bill.

La Brigaldara

37029 San Pietro In Cariano VR
+39 045 7701055
www.brigaldara.it

The Cesari family bought the Brigaldara estate back in 1929 though its origins date back to the 1400s. From 45 hectares of vines (some rented on long-term contracts), a broad range of wines includes Soave DOC, a Dindarella Rosé and the full range of Valpolicella, including three styles of Amarone. The house style leans towards spicy, generous and approachable wines. A total of 300,000 bottles a year are made. La Brigaldara is a member of the Famiglie Amarone group and is one of the founders of the Terre di Fumane Appassimento centre.

Buglioni

Via Campagnole, 55, 37029 Corrubbio VR
+39 045 6760681
www.buglioni.it

Though the Buglioni family began with just 5 hectares of vines in 1993, they have now amassed 48 hectares, mainly in San Pietro in Cariano and Sant'Ambrogio. A cleanly made and commercially styled range of all five DOC(G) wines is guided by the company policy to aim for elegance and drinkability. The company also own several *oseterie* and offer more serious fare and accommodation amongst the vines at the Locanda and Dimora di Bugiardo.

Bussola

Via Mulino Turri, 30, 37024 Negrar VR
+39 045 7501740
www.bussolavini.com

Tommaso Bussola and family grow vines in the mixed clay, volcanic and limestone soils around San Peretto on the eastern slopes of the Negrar valley. A full range of Valpolicella is produced including several different cuvées of Amarone. Apart from the more youthful Valpolicella Classico, the wines receive plenty of barrel ageing and are made in a rich, burly, somewhat rough and ready style.

Ca dei Maghi

Via Ca' dei Maghi, 5, 37022 Fumane VR
+39 045 7702355
www.cadeimaghi.it

From less than 5 hectares in Fumane, young Paolo Creazzi began making wine in 2009 and first bottled in 2013. The results are promising: two clean, perfumed varietal IGT whites from Trebbiano Toscano and Garganega and a delicious Valpolicella Classico form the basis of production. Superiore and Ripasso spend plenty of time in wood, but the pick of the bunch is the elegant and aromatic Amarone. The wines are sold at the family restaurant; a small hotel is also part of the set up.

Ca La Bionda – a measured approach

Via Bionda, 4, 37020 Marano di Valpolicella VR
+39 045 6801198
www.calabionda.it

Alessandro Castellani is the third generation to work the land around the family winery just below the well-known Ravazzol vineyard. Their 29 hectares of mainly east-facing vineyards lie on the western side of the Marano valley midway between the villages of Valgatara and Marano itself, at varying altitudes between 150 and 300 metres; this is quite a sizeable property for the Valpolicella Classico district and Alessandro is relieved that he invested in new land when he did. His father already owned 3 hectares of vines but between 2000 and 2006 Alessandro susbstantially increased vineyard holdings – fortunately for the Castellani family just before the boom in price which has seen the cost of a hectare of land in Classico rise to a current high of over €700,000.

He is a great believer in the unique potential of Valpolicella and a staunch defender of the points of difference which single the wine out from its peers. Hence the family favour traditional terraced vineyards even though they are much more costly to maintain: the walls help to retain the warmth of the sun and Alessandro has noticed how the fruit lying closest to them ripens particularly successfully. The vineyards are planted to the four classic varieties of the area: Corvina, Corvinone, Rondinella and Molinara. He is convinced that the true character of the wines comes from a mixture of these varieties in the vineyards as well as the finished wine, conferring a certain homogeneity of style and at the same time reinforcing the sense of place. When Alessandro first took over the business he started to introduce the Guyot training system, having seen the benefits it could bring during his work experience in both Bordeaux and Australia as well as vintages at Vajra in Barolo and Isole e Olena in Chianti Classico. He still feels Guyot can work well for Valpolicella Classico but prefers to rely on the time-honoured pergola for the wines deriving from the *appassimento* process these days. Great Amarone depends on a certain acidity level in the grapes which is more easily conserved with the pergola, he insists. For both systems he also believes that sensibly controlled yields – cropping at somewhere between 80 and 100 quintals per hectare – provide the best results. Similarly when it comes to drying the grapes, the company continues to store the fruit in humidity-absorbing wooden crates to ensure a slower and more linear maturation.

Nowadays Alessandro is the president of the local branch of FIVI (the Federation of Independent Vinegrowers). On behalf of the members, he is pushing for the issue of the *zonazione* of the Valpolicella district to be linked to both crop size and individual denomination. He foresees a vineyard hierarchy designed to maintain the style, identity and authenticity of the various wines with limits to crop size extending from 60 quintals per hectare at higher altitudes, to between 80 to 100 in the mid-hillside sites, and as far as even 120 quintals on the loamier and more fertile soils of the plains. At the same time strict limits should be imposed on the percentage of the crop to be put aside for *appassimento* in each sector. A sensible, measured approach to both production and the wider issues confronting Valpolicella is clearly necessary if the area is to remain on an even keel.

The wines at Ca La Bionda do not disappoint, reflecting Alessandro's studied production regime and respect for *tipicita*. Some 150,000 bottles are produced annually of the classic wines of the Valpolicella, mainly from limestone-based vineyards lying close to the winery. The Valpolicella Classico (30,000 to 35,000 bottles a year) is an excellent example of the Marano valley style – bright, ripe, fleshy and full of fruit with good balancing acidity. Casal Vegri is a single vineyard Valpolicella Classico Superiore made from Guyot-trained vines in a full and rich style. Malavoglia is a particularly impressive example of Ripasso: by spending just forty-eight hours on a mixture of Amarone and Recioto lees, it avoids the pitfalls of the often rather clichéd and oxidative mini-Amarone version and instead is typical of the house style of full, ripe and balanced wines. Malavoglia is a relatively recent addition to the range (the first vintage was 2008) but with just 3 g/l of residual sugar, shares with the two versions of Amarone the distinction of maintaining a drier, more obviously food-friendly character. While the regular Amarone (25,000 bottles a year) is made in an elegant fruit-forward style, the single vineyard Ravazzol – from 50- to 70-year-old vines grown in the family's 7-hectare site – is a much more intensely structured wine which needs time to show its full potential. In good vintages (2004, 2005, 2008, 2013 and 2015 are the most recent bottlings) Ca La Bionda also produces a few thousand bottles of a 100 per cent Corvina IGT wine which demonstrates the ageing potential that the variety undoubtedly possesses. A bottle from the 2005 vintage tasted over a decade later in spring 2016 was still in excellent shape. The range is completed by a simple but very drinkable example of Recioto della Valpolicella.

Their wines have found favour across the world and the export market now accounts for around 90 per cent of sales. As well as the classic European markets, Ca La Bionda's wines are available in Japan, China and Russia. Some eight years ago the company began exporting their wine to Australia, which has since become a good market for them. Alessandro smiles as he recalls the tasting that followed the initial enquiry: his new customers couldn't get over just how fresh the wines were. It is pleasing to note how that very quality – so often so undervalued – is gaining ever wider recognition.

Campagnola

Via Agnella, 9, 37020 Marano di Valpolicella VR
+39 045 7703900
www.campagnola.com

This *negoziante* winery produces an annual total of some five million bottles, a million of which are from Valpolicella. Campagnola own some 5 hectares of vineyards, otherwise sourcing fruit from growers in the Marano valley where the winery is based. The wines are cleanly made in a simple, commercial style.

Cantina di Negrar - strength in numbers

Via Ca' Salgari, 2, 37024 Negrar VR
+39 045 6014300
www.cantinanegrar.it

For many of the small vineyard owners in Valpolicella Classico, making and selling their own wine is not a realistic option and the logical solution is to join the local cooperative. Though honest and simple wines may represent a large part of production, Cantina di Negrar has a great deal more to offer members than a guaranteed source of income from their grapes. Some of those few hectares, or even few rows of vines, are located in the area's prime positions and the cooperative has one of the area's most respected winemakers in head oenologist and general manager Daniele Accordini. Indeed Daniele maintains that it is the larger companies, both private and cooperative, who are best positioned to innovate – simply because they have the resources to do so. An ideal example of this potential can be found in the Cantina's groundbreaking 'Espressioni' range of Amarone, first made under their Domini Veneti label in 2005. Fruit from vineyards in the five different communes of Valpolicella Classico follows the same production path of lengthy maceration times, low fermentation temperatures and five years in large *botti*. The results allow tasters to appreciate for themselves the effect that the varying soil types, microclimates and altitudes (from 150 metres in the Castelrotto vineyards of San Pietro in Cariano up to 510 metres in the San Rocco area of Marano) have on the finished product. Two of the five received the maximum 'Three Glass' rating in the 2015 edition of Italy's influential Gambero Rosso guide.

Daniele is from a family of local growers and graduated from Conegliano in 1982, joining the cooperative in 1988. Not only has he intimate knowledge of the various different areas of Classico but with thirty years' experience, is also well placed to reflect on the changes in both growing conditions and winemaking practices in recent years. In tandem with the effects of climate change, he has watched Amarone grow from a high-alcohol wine which often lacked body to today's sleeker version where alcohol, body and sugars are more finely balanced. Though the fashion for barriques helped to bring greater accessibilty and roundness at an earlier stage in the wine's development, he notes a definite swing back towards use of the traditional *botte*. In his view the wines show greater *tipicita* as a result, are easier to drink and match better with food. This riper, rounder style has come about through better vineyard management as well as the effects of climate change. While the autumn fog that used to hamper the *appassimento* process has all but disappeared these days and, thanks to warmer mean temperatures, the harvest will take place up to a month sooner than it used to, the famous *contadino* mentality of the smallholder who grew up in more difficult times is beginning to change too. 'Of course you can produce good Amarone in the lower-lying vineyards, they just need to be managed properly. The higher the yields, the less fruit you set for *appassimento*. My aim is to encourage each individual grower to take responsibility and make the right decisions,' he says. Managing the vineyards properly means not only working with reduced yields but also ensuring that the local varieties are treated with care and attention. 'Corvina is not the most robust of grapes: it can only be harvested by hand as the skins are delicate, particularly when yields are excessive. The lower the yield, the thicker the skin, and the more resistant the fruit will be to attacks of botrytis. Similarly in cooler vintages you need to strip back some of the foliage to help the grapes ripen but in hotter years the leaves are left on to shade the grapes from too much sun.'

As part of an ongoing programme to encourage members to aim for a sustainable approach to grape growing, the Cantina has introduced a range of measures to ensure healthy growing conditions such as the use of cover crops and integrated pest-management systems. The culmination of their efforts is the release of a couple of organic wines – Valpolicella and Amarone – under the main Cantina di Negrar label from certified organic vineyards in Negrar and Fumane. The cooperative also maintains an experimental vineyard where 'forgotten' varieties such as Spigamonte are kept alive using different rootstocks and training systems to guide their members' choices. Though such rarities may never play a major role in the future of Valpolicella, they 'still speak the same local language,' according to Accordini. 'And they still taste of cherries!'

Cantina di Negrar has 230 members farming 600 hectares of vineyard mainly in Classico but also in the DOC area and around Lake Garda. A number of product ranges are used to manage the different levels of quality. The premium wines are marketed under the Domini Veneti label (the name refers to lands which belonged to La Serenissima, as the Republic of Venice was known in its heyday during the fifteenth century). A number of wines from specific vineyard areas are the highlights of the range. There is an Amarone Vigneti di Jago and a Ripasso Vigneti di Torbe, for example. From the La Casetta estate of long-time President Ettore Righetti a second Ripasso is fermented on the lees of Recioto only. The more 'innovative' side of the story is represented by Verjago (from the traditional name of the Negrar valley), a 'Super Valpolicella' made from fruit semi-dried for forty days and aged for twelve months in the traditional *botti*.

Accordini laments the fact that the more simple Valpolicella seems to be slowly disappearing: 'It doesn't pay at the moment yet it's the wine that will tell you the most about our *terreno*.' He hopes that a solution can be found by setting the appropriate limits on *appassimento*. 'We need to look at our area as a whole and not just what is right for the individual winery. Our problem here in Valpolicella is that we lack a "team mentality".'

Cantina San Mattia

Via Santa Giuliana, 2, 37128 VR
+39 045 913797
www.giovanniederle.it

Young Giovanni Ederle runs this tiny winery up at Torricelle and produces a charming and supple Valpolicella Superiore and promising Amarone from 4 hectares of vines. The on-site *agriturismo* offers wonderful views over the historic centre of Verona.

Cantina Valpantena

Via Colonia Orfani di Guerra, 5, 37142 Quinto VR
+39 045 550032
www.cantinavalpantena.it

For many years perhaps the main reference point for the wines of the valley, this hard-working cooperative produces olive oil as well as wine at its headquarters at Quinto. Founded in 1958, there are now 250 members who own 750 hectares of vineyard. A well-run cooperative led by director and winemaker Luca Degani, Cantina Valpantena has taken on board its responsibility to the area and its members by introducing a number of measures to help steer growers towards both looking after their environment and improving the quality of their grapes. These include a 'Quality Project', various ways in which biodiversity may be promoted in the vineyards and a careful study of growing conditions to identify the best areas for the production of Amarone grapes. In the well-equipped cellars, particular care and attention is paid to winemaking practices and the wines are consistently clean and well made. A number of different labels are produced: the best known is probably Torre del Falasco which covers a full of Veronese wines and a selection from the Lake Garda area. The wines are made in a highly polished and commercial style though are perhaps a little over-reliant on small barrels and rather generous levels of residual sugar for the purist.

La Collina dei Ciliegi

Località Erbin, 36, 37023 Grezzana VR
+39 028 7158048
www.lacollinadeiciliegi.it

Owner Massimo Gianolli has ambitious plans and a slick marketing strategy for a wide range of wines from the Veneto under the Collina dei Ciliegi brand, though the heart of the enterprise is high up in the Valpantena above Grezzana. Wines from the 19-hectare estate surrounding the winery include the classic five red wines of Valpolicella, made by oenologist Luca Degani (see also Cantina Valpantena), in a clean, highly-polished and super-commercial style. Accommodation is available.

Corte Rugolin

Loc. Rugolin 1, 37020 Marano di Valpolicella VR
+39 045 7702153
www.corterugolin.it

Twins Elena and Federico Coati run this small estate at Valgatara – founded in 1998 – with vineyards in Sant'Ambrogio, San Pietro in Cariano and close to the winery near the bottom of the Marano valley, some 12 hectares in total. Good simple Valpolicella Classico, a promising Classico Superiore from the Conca d'Oro vineyard and two versions of Amarone form the backbone of production. Monte Danieli is a notably elegant and aromatic style of Amarone.

Corte Sant'Alda – living in harmony

Via Capovilla, 28, 37030 Località Fioi, Mezzane di Sotto VR
+39 045 8880006
www.cortesantalda.com

In 1985 Marinella Camerani took on the semi-abandoned property her father had bought, feeling she had to prove herself. Having outgrown her role as accountant in the family's car battery business, she was seeking a new challenge. Some thirty years later her Corte Sant'Alda estate serves as a model to aspiring new producers seeking to make wines that demonstrate a strong sense of place and a deep-rooted respect for the environment that produces them. Marinella cites her meeting in 2002 with Nicolas Joly, one of the leading figures behind the biodynamic wine movement, as a defining moment in her life as a wine producer.

Her voyage of discovery began, of course, in the vineyards: she has gradually introduced Guyot as the preferred training method, building up a much greater plant destiny per hectare than other systems allow. Having tried out *alberello* (bush training) too with the local varieties she found that they did not respond well and simply wouldn't produce fruit consistently. Since 2010 her vineyards have been certified to Demeter biodynamic standards but her search for the perfect system continues: she has surrounded herself with people who share her convictions and are prepared to put in the effort to see them through to fruition. One vineyard, for example, is worked entirely by hand, involving the use of no machinery whatsoever. The estate covers some 40 hectares on both sides of the slopes overlooking the small village of Mezzane di Sotto in the Mezzane valley. Approximately half of the land is planted to vines while the rest is wooded. Marinella grows other fruit too: the local Duroni cherry and various olive cultivars including the rare Grignano, a variety that originates in the Veronese. Most of the vines lie on the eastern slope of the narrow valley (facing from south through to west-south-west, therefore) where the soils are composed mainly of a greyish white limestone mixed with reddish clay, and lie at altitudes of between around 200 and 400 metres. There are just 2 hectares of vines on the western slopes which are more heavily wooded and where Marinella keeps her horses, chickens, pigs and cows. She has grown into her lifestyle and now feels totally at home in this tranquil rural environment. The road to her 'conversion' proved to be longer than she had expected, though: after first going organic, she undertook the necessary steps to achieve biodynamic certification for her vineyards. It was only then that she found out that biodynamic principles applied to winemaking as well.

In the cellar the basic principles of vinification follow simple 'natural' guidelines – fermentation without temperature control and certainly without the addition of any 'technical' aids. Thereafter every possible option is put through its paces. Stainless steel is only used for the fresh and juicy, citrus-scented Soave which contains some 20 per cent Trebbiano di Soave; the fermenting Soave can also function as a *pied de cuvée* for the red wines when required. The other white is a Chardonnay made as an 'orange' wine which starts off fermentation in cement pyramids (some lined, some not) before being transferred into demijohns. The Rosato 'Agathe' is produced using terracotta amphoras; made from 100 per cent Molinara grapes, Agathe shows an intriguing contrast between sweetness of aroma and the classic saline and mineral flavours of the variety on the palate. There is much more of a 'standardized' procedure for the estate's red wines, and these form the nucleus of her production. All are fermented in upright wooden *tini* and maturation takes place in large barrels of either oak or cherry. Marinella insists on using larger *botti* these days; as for the type of wood, cherry starts out as quite aggressive but improves with age while French oak remains a reliable favourite. Such attention to detail demonstrates Marinella's search to understand and give full expression to the true identity of her wines.

The gradual refinement of methodology is certainly bearing fruit – the wines have improved significantly over the years. No doubt the experiments with concrete and amphorae will bring new insights but the reds display a sureness of touch that was not always apparent in earlier vintages. The range is made up of a juicy and balanced but lively 'basic' Valpolicella DOC Ca Fui through the fresh and perfumed Ripasso Campo Magri (which undergoes a light secondary fermentation lasting just a few days) to the Valpolicella Superiore Mithas from the oldest vines on the estate, and finally the two wines from the *appassimento* process, Amarone and Recioto. A very clear house style is evident. The wines have tremendous freshness: the aromas are primarily black cherry, orange pomander and spice (notably black pepper) and there is an understated structure based on balanced acidity and sweet, ripe tannins. It is difficult to imagine Marinella ever resting on her laurels – or even wanting to – not least because every vintage represents a new challenge. There will no doubt be further developments in the Mezzane valley in due course.

Valentina Cubi

Via Casterna, 60, 37022 Fumane VR
+39 045 7701806
www.valentinacubi.it

The 13-hectare estate at the bottom of the Fumane valley at Casterna borders on San Pietro in Cariano. Valentina, its charming owner, is a great believer in the potential of the Corvina grape and using the most 'natural' methods of production possible (the vineyards have been certified organic since 2014). The pale, rather austere yet aromatic wines are made with great conviction but so far lack consistency.

Romano Dal Forno

Località Lodoletta, 1, 37031 Cellore d'Illasi VR
+39 045 7834923
www.dalfornoromano.it

Romano Dal Forno breaks into a broad grin as he describes his first encounter with the wines of Bepi Quintarelli. 'We must be talking about 1981 or

1982. I got married when I was 22 and by the time I was 26, I had three kids to look after and a business to run. The wines I was making back then (in the early 1980s) weren't bad but with a family to find for I had to come up with some way of marking my mark. At the time I was on the lookout for a decent cork supplier and a friend had recommended somewhere in Parona. It was rather a dingy place and there I was twiddling my thumbs while the man behind the counter was counting out the corks ...', he pauses for effect. "'... Ninety nine, one hundred ...". I happened to notice some rather odd-looking bottles tucked away to one side. The labels were covered in what looked like spidery handwriting. "What are those?" I asked. The clerk went into raptures. I'd never heard anyone talk with such passion and enthusiasm about one of our local wines before. There and then I knew I had to meet this Bepi Quintarelli.'

Dal Forno had to be patient. Finally the opportunity to meet the man who had so piqued his curiosity came about: through fellow Illasi-born Celestino Gaspari, then the fiancé of one of Quintarelli's daughters, he managed to arrange an introduction. 'I was thirty years younger than him and I have to admit I started out with so little knowledge. I think Bepi took me under his wing rather. You have to remember that he was born in 1927 and people's ways of thinking were a lot different back then, the mentality of the times was often quite backward. I'm not sure Bepi knew how his daughters would cope on their own, so I became a sort of protegé for him. Maybe he saw something in me of the son he never had. I listened to everything he had to tell me and tried my level best to understand what he was doing and learn as much as I could from what he had to say. What I came to realize above all seems so obvious now but it wasn't back then: to put the best possible quality at the heart of everything I did. I was attracted to modern ideas,' he continues, 'and I had to find my own way. Tradition is important, of course, but each successive generation adds something new. I expect my three sons to do the same.'

The firm was established with just 3 hectares of vines at Monte Lodelletta just above the village of Cellore some 3 kilometres north of Illasi. By 1990 Dal Forno was confident enough to begin to implement the full extent of his vision with the start of construction of one of the country's most remarkable wineries. It was not until 2008 that the building work was finally finished, and the results are extraordinary. The vinification area is a sculpture in stainless steel – tanks of all shapes and sizes ring the perimeter. A bank of smaller ones lines part of the back wall, not for microvinifications as might be expected, but to replace the traditional demijohns used for the process of *colmatura* or the frequent topping up of any wine lost to evaporation. Overhead, what at first looks like a model racing track is in fact a series of steel runners connecting the tanks for the passage of automatic cleaning equipment and the sets of mechanical pistons which perform *follatura*. The sight of such advanced technology is at least some preparation for the *fruttaio* located on the floor above. The space remains empty until harvest time and the beginning of the *appassimento* operation. The crates of fruit are stacked in rectangular blocks separated by aisles. Directly above more runners in the ceiling is an indication of what comes next: open-sided steel cabinets each containing three large fans, one on top of another, emerge from their housing in the walls and pass between the ranks of grapes. Tubes at the sides of the frame ensure that air is blown out from both above and below as well as from the side. They move slowly between the rows blasting out air. There is no control over either temperature or humidity and the *appassimento* is managed solely through air flow. The windows, also fully computerized, open and shut automatically depending on prevailing atmospheric conditions. Amarone meets Star Wars.

Vineyard holdings are now up to 13 hectares all planted to the traditional local grapes (including small quantities of Croatina and Oseleta). The only training system practised is, of course, Guyot, with a density of 13,000 plants per hectare. Vinification follows the classic school of thought with scrupulous – almost fanatical – control over exposure of the wine to oxygen restricted to the *follatura* phase; a recent change in wood-ageing policy (from 2011 onwards) has seen the period of ageing for all styles cut from three years to two while bottle ageing has been extended from two to four years – so the wine spends at least six years at the winery before release. The wine is aged in new barriques only (mainly French oak with some American), full replacement stock being bought in every year.

The Dal Forno family produce just three styles of wine: Amarone, Valpolicella and a Passito Rosso IGT Vigna Sere. This last wine has been made in only six vintages during the last thirty-four years, and a not dissimilar policy of 'selectivity' is applied to the Amarone which was not produced in 2005, 2007 or 2014: 'Though I did make some great Valpolicella in those vintages!' Romano says. The different wines are made from fruit at different stages of their individual *appassimento* process: Valpolicella from fruit which has been dried for approximately six weeks whereas the Amarone grapes go 'full term' and are pressed around the turn of the year. The Passito Rosso fruit is left longer still, typically up until nearly Easter. Despite such an overwhelmingly modern view of Veronese red wines, Dal Forno has another surprise in store. 'Amarone? I don't drink it during the summer and I don't drink it with food. I'd rather have a glass of Valpolicella if I'm eating something,' he explains. Such a position reinforces the classical view of Amarone as a 'Vino da Meditazione' – a wine to be sipped and reflected upon rather than one to accompany food. The Dal Forno wines are remarkable by any standards and Romano's point of view is not hard to appreciate: he describes Amarone as a 'supreme athlete' (or one able to take on all comers) and his wines are renowned for their sheer power, intensity and potential longevity. Romano feels that his Valpolicella may even take longer to 'come around' than the Amarone: 'Amarone is born with a natural balance between its component parts, principally acids, tannins and alcohol, even so I think my wine needs at least twenty years to arrive at its peak. Thereafter …' he leaves the question hanging; indeed, who knows how long a wine this well structured might last?

The next generation seems equally ambitious. As Michele, the eldest son who studied economics (Marco and Luca are oenologist and agronomist respectively), explains: 'We're going to keep the same product range. It will take time but we need to work towards receiving the same sort of plaudits for our wines as the French do. We want to create a symbol for the area at that level. We're not looking to be anything but a niche producer.' His father nods approvingly.

La Dama

Via Quintarelli Giovanni, 39, 37024 Negrar VR
+39 045 6000728
www.ladamavini.it

The new winery based at Moron (the lower slopes of Monte Masua) in Negrar with 10 hectares of vineyard received organic certification in 2015. The range consists of rather quirky wines which nonetheless show good freshness and acidity: Classico Superiore Ca Besi, from a dedicated vineyard (so the best grapes are not creamed off for Amarone) shows particular promise.

Damoli

Via Jago di Mezzo, 5, 37024 Negrar VR
+39 340 8762680
www.damolivini.com

The tiny cellar at Jago with vines close by and up at Mazzano is run by the brother and sister team of Daniele and Lara Damoli. The house style is for full-bodied and extracted wines across the range of classic Veronese reds; just a few thousand bottles are made.

Fumanelli – San Pietro in Cariano

Tenuta di Squarano, 37029 San Pietro in Cariano VR
+39 045 7704875
www.squarano.com

The Marchesi Fumanelli have been growing grapes in Valpolicella since 1470 at the Tenuta Squarano estate on 28 hectares of vines surrounding the villa which sits on top of a small conical hill on the outskirts of San Pietro, and at nearby Quar. Traditionally the estate mainly sold off grapes and bulk wine, a neat illustration of the division of roles typical of the traditional Veronese wine industry. However, the current proprietor, ex-Italian trade attaché Armando Pierola, has decided to reawaken this sleeping giant and increase production of bottled wine. Aiming at sales to high-end restaurants, the wines are carefully made in an elegant, balanced and slightly austere style.

Gamba

Via Gnirega, 19, 37020 Valgatara VR
+39 045 6801714
www.vinigamba.it

The Aldrighetti brothers produce an annual total of around 70,000 bottles from vineyards around the family winery at Gnirega on the western flanks of Monte Masua and, since 2012, a further 7 hectares of vines at Monte Solane above Mazzurega. Two ranges, Campedel and Le Quare, are distinguished mainly by different ageing regimes: Campedel mainly in barriques while Le Quare matures in larger and older Slovenian oak. Though these authentic wines can seem a little angular, the simple Valpolicella Classico is very good indeed.

Gruppo Italiano Vini

Via Belvedere, 37011 Villa VR
+39 045 7235772
www.gruppoitaliano.vini

As the largest producer of wine in Italy it is unsurprising that Gruppo Italiano Vini (GIV) should have substantial interests in Soave and Valpolicella. Though headquarters are at Bardolino near the shores of Lake Garda, GIV own two important Veronese houses, one of which – Bolla – has played a major role in the history of the area's wines. (The group's third winery in the Veneto, Lamberti, is more involved with the production of Garda wines and spumante.) The other – Santi – has recently undergone a major transformation. Founded in 1843 in Illasi the firm was primarily a *negoziante* house (though owning some vineyards too) which had been acquired in the early 1970s by Antinori. With the firm's subsequent decision to focus on the wines of Tuscany, GIV stepped in and bought Santi at the beginning of the 1980s. Meanwhile Bolla, founded in 1883, had long been associated with Soave and, in particular, the American market where it became an important brand in the 1970s. Indeed Bolla was bought up by the Brown-Forman corporation in the 1990s, before GIV took ownership in 2008.

GIV's new strategy is to develop Santi as their premium brand of Veronese wine from the restored palace in Illasi where the main *fruttaio*, vinification and ageing cellars will be located. Renowned local oenologist Cristian Ridolfi, who has worked at both Bertani and Masi, has been appointed to mastermind production. The revamped Santi range will focus more on niche wines from all three areas of Valpolicella, using fruit from vineyards in the Illasi and Valpantena valleys, and Marano, San Pietro in Cariano, and Negrar in Classico. The 'new' winery is impressively equipped with extensive stainless steel, cement and wood storage facilities. Bolla will remain as GIV's logistical centre and the motor behind the overall plan as the current most successful brand in the company's portfolio with sales accounting for a sizeable chunk of annual turnover.

While Ridolfi's influence will become more apparent once the dust has settled, the current Santi range contains a number of wines from Soave and Valpolicella amongst a broader selection from across the Veneto. The Soave Classico Monteforte is cleverly made in a balanced and commercial style. In Valpolicella, the Superiore Ventale from vineyards in Illasi undergoes an unusual wood-ageing regime composed of a mixture of oak, chestnut and cherry barrels while the Ripasso Classico Superiore Solane is another decently made example of its type. Two versions of Amarone, a generic and Il Proemio from the Gnirega vineyards in Marano, follow the same path of an 'updated' *tipicita* made with technical proficiency. Similarly the Bolla wines are being updated, aiming for a modern drinkable style. The wide range includes the more traditional Soave Classico 'Retro' made in conjunction with the Cantina di Monteforte, a simple Valpolicella Classico d'annata 'Il Calice' and two versions of Amarone. 'Rhetico' is made with fruit sourced mainly from Torbe while the more classically-styled Riserva Le Origini comes from vineyards in Marano.

GIV brings a level of professionalism and technical competence not always apparent amongst the proliferation of houses who favour either a more intuitive, hand-crafted approach or a more aspirational and experimental style. With such a diverse array of choices available to the consumer, something clean-cut and 'off the peg' can be a reassuringly safe option.

Guerrieri Rizzardi – Bardolino

2, Via Campazzi, 37011 Bardolino VR
+39 045 721 0028
www.guerrieririzzardi.it

The noble Guerrieri Rizzardi family own the Pojega estate with its delightful gardens and surrounding vines in Negrar, plus vineyards in Soave Classico at Costeggiola and Monte Rocchetta. A range of good-quality reds includes Valpolicella Classico, Ripasso Pojega and two excellent versions of Amarone, Villa Rizzardi and Calcarole. Soave Classico Ferra (from Rocchetta) is fermented in cement and aged in old *botti*; the more modern style Costeggiola contains 30 per cent Chardonnay yet remains recognizably Soave.

Manara

Via Don C. Biasi, 53, 37029 San Pietro in Cariano VR
+39 045 7701086
www.manaravini.it

This family-run business produces some 120,000 bottles a year from 11 hectares of vines at San Pietro, Marano and Negrar. The Manara brothers make the full range of Veronese reds in a simple and rustic style; the very traditional Amarone Corte Manara stands out.

Marion

Via Borgo 2, Marcellise 37036, San Martino Buon Albergo VR
+39 045 8740021
www.marionvini.it

Stefano and Nicoletta Campedelli bought the Marion estate on the edge of Marcellise in 1986 through his father's real estate business; the previous owners, the Conti Marioni, had owned the property since the 1500s. 'We were really fortunate: it's the *terreno* that counts, especially for red wine,' Stefano remarks. Their 16 hectares of vineyard (another 10 hectares are rented locally) are planted on limestone and clay soils which face due south. At first they sold the grapes off to the local cooperative at Colognola ai Colli as Stefano, new to the world of grape farming, learnt what he could from his fellow growers about selecting the right clone and the right rootstock for the right conditions.

Stefano cites his meeting with Celestino Gaspari in the mid-1990s as his light-bulb moment: 'We'd still be selling our fruit off to the co-op if it hadn't been for him.' They worked together for fifteen years. These days the firm produce around 80,000 to 90,000 bottles of stylish, aromatic and balanced wines made to a simple formula with the use of manual *follatura* and ageing in tonneaux and *botti* of mainly Slavonian oak. Valpolicella Borgo Marcellise, a fragrant and balanced example, is the point of departure. The Superiore includes around 30 per cent of later-harvested fruit which is then left for a further three or so weeks before pressing – a rounder wine with full, sweet fruit and abundant spicy notes. Stefano likes to give his Amarone plenty of barrel age and then, ideally, time at the winery in bottle; again aromas of cedar, clove and in particular black pepper come through strongly. Also of note are two varietal reds made from Cabernet Sauvignon and Teroldego. The Cabernet retains a distinctively Veronese freshness despite the evident power of the ripe-fruit aromas and flavours, while the Teroldego, made from a proportion of fruit which has undergone light *appassimento*, is again uniquely Veronese in style.

Masi - the Masi dynasty

Via Monteleone 26, 37015 Gargagnago di Valpolicella VR
+39 045 6832511
www.masi.it

'We should raise a statue to Sandro Boscaini!' Such recognition coming from a local winemaker and frankly, competitor, is to say the least uncommon amidst the rivalry that often bubbles just under the surface in Italy's important wine production areas. No one has done more to put Veronese wines on the map than the current president of Masi. Sandro has worked tirelessly to get his wines better known, and the opening up of new markets across the world to the idea of fine Veronese red wines owes much to his endeavours. Innovation has played a key role and two examples, among the many, stand out. The emergence of Ripasso (a major force behind the area's new-found prosperity) can be traced back to Masi's groundwork with Campo Fiorin in the mid-1960s. The current Veronese love affair with Oseleta might never have flourished without Boscaini's foresight. He first spotted its potential some forty years ago and planted an experimental vineyard at Valgatara; Masi now have 8 hectares of the variety. The foundation stone of the success story, however, has been Amarone. Masi's range of no fewer than five different cuvées has helped to lend the wine far greater credibility than could possibly have been imagined as little as half a century ago and introduced its unique aromas and flavours to the world at large. Between the Amarone Classico 'Costasera' and the more recent Riserva version, Vaio Armaron from the vineyards of the Serego Alighieri estate and the two seminal 'cru' wines Mazzano and Campolungo di Torbe from Negrar, Masi produce almost 900,000 bottles a year of unquestionably high quality. Sandro's sobriquet, Mister Amarone, says it all.

By his own admission, Raffaele Boscaini has some big shoes to fill. 'I never made a conscious decision to join the wine trade but it's something that's always been with me. A lot of my early memories are to do with wine. I remember drinking *acqua rosa* [water with a drop of red wine] when I was a child. Or Silvio Penna's father who worked in our cellars: he didn't even have a watch. When he wanted to know the time he'd glance up at the sun. And he was usually spot on! If there was a determining moment it came when I was 10 or 11. My parents were on holiday and I was helping my grandfather in the vineyard.

We left the car under a pergola while he went to check the ripeness of the grapes. He didn't need a refractometer, he just had to hold the grapes in his hand for a moment or two to know they needed another week on the vine.' Raffaele studied surveying and economics but joined the family winery in the year 2000 after a thorough grounding in the wine trade in the UK, working first in a wine shop and then as a sales representative. He says 'My father never put any pressure on me to follow in his footsteps, he just gave me some very simple advice: to do what I wanted to, to enjoy it and to do things my way.' After learning his way around the business, Raffaele took up his present position as marketing and communications director in 2010. His sister Alessandra works alongside him as Masi's commercial director, looking after sales, and is regional delegate of the national Donne del Vino association.

Raffaele is keen to minimize the gap between producer and consumer as so much of what Masi do to put the best possible wine in the bottle seems to disappear along the supply chain. The Masi Experience attempts to ensure the message is not lost: there are organized visits to their cellars at Gargagnago and Serego Alighieri and in 2014 the Masi Wine Bar and restaurant was opened in Zurich, with plans for further outlets in Singapore and Stockholm. The new Tenuta Canova near Lake Garda, however, takes the idea a stage further. Adjacent to the wine bar and restaurant where the firm's wines can be matched with typical local dishes is the barrel storage facility. Here Campo Fiorin is aged and customers can taste the wine directly from the wood.

Masi's experiments continue to uncover the underlying science behind decisions once based on inherited knowledge. Different varieties of yeast naturally present in their cellars and the idea of *appassimento* on the vine, ever more feasible owing to climate change, have been under the microscope recently: there is little danger of the Boscaini family resting on their laurels. The product range has been carefully honed and is based on almost six million bottles of Veronese wines. Under the supervision of winemaking director Andrea Dal Cin levels of quality are laudably high, and rather than being 'standardized', the selection is a mix of both classic and more authorial wines. Valpolicella Classico Bonacosta (800,000 bottles) is a reassuringly good and typical example. The Classico Superiore Toar, containing 10 per cent Oseleta, is a balanced wine of real substance while a second Classico Superiore Monte Piazzo from the Serego Alighieri estate is made from fruit which undergoes light *appassimento* and is then partly aged in traditional cherry-wood barrels. A supercharged version of Campo Fiorin 'Brolo' precedes the range of Amarone and Recioto which is a trip around the world of *appassimento* in itself. With the fleshy and opulent Vaio Armaron from lower-lying vines at Gargagnago and the more austere and aromatic Mazzano grown at nearer 400 metres, there is the perfect illustration of the relevance of altitude, for example. The three versions of Recioto include the Amandorlato, Mezzanella.

Masi have taken the concept of *appassimento* beyond the confines of the Veronese to neighbouring Trentino and Friuli where, in collaboration with the Bossi Fedrigotti and Stra' del Milione estates, the technique is used with the red grapes of the two areas. Much further afield, in Argentina, the firm's Arboleda estate at Tupungato in Mendoza's Valle de Uco produces red wines from a blend of semi-dried Corvina grapes with local favourite Malbec. With his position as President of the national Federvini association confirmed until at least 2019, Sandro's children now play increasingly important roles as international ambassadors for Masi's 'Venetian Values'.

Massimago

Via Giare, 37030 Mezzane Di Sotto VR
+39 045 8880143
www.massimago.com

The winery and Relais is run by ex-agronomy student Camilla Rossi at her family's 28-hectare property just below San Cassiano in the Mezzane valley. A sensibly small range of wines includes a good, simple Valpolicella, a more aspirational Superiore 'Profasio' and a promising Amarone from the highest vineyard of the estate called Le Macie. Camilla has plans to enlarge the tiny cellars and express herself more fully.

Roberto Mazzi

Via Crosetta, 8, 37024 Negrar VR
+39 045 7502072
www.robertomazzi.it

Stefano and Antonio Mazzi's grandmother was the sister of Gaetano Dall'Ora who, along with Count Giovanni Battista Rizzardi, helped to found the Cantina Sociale Valpolicella (which later became Cantina Valpolicella Negrar). Their small farm is constructed around the windmill which until the 1940s was used to process flour from the grain that was widely planted on the valley floor in amongst the vines. The brothers make a small range of Valpolicella from well-sited local vineyards in nearby San Peretto, Poiega, Calcarole and Castel'. Inspired by visits to Barolo in the 1980s (the vineyards are planted to Guyot and new wood used in the cellar), these homespun and authentic wines seem almost 'old school' these days. Accommodation is available.

Monte Dall'Ora – new beginnings
Via Monte Dall'Ora, 5, 37029 Castelrotto VR
+39 045 7704462
www.montedallora.com

Carlo and Alessandra Venturini discovered Monte Dall'Ora in 1995; the Monte Dall'Ora hillside takes its name from the afternoon ora wind which blows from the south upwards across Lake Garda in the spring and early summer. The vineyards had been badly neglected and the classic *marogne* (the dry-stone walls which frame many of the old terraced vineyards in the Valpolicella Classico area) had fallen into a sad state of repair. What they saw was potential: both came from farming backgrounds and the overgrown estate looked perfect for development. They decided to continue the work nature had begun during those years that the vineyards had been semi-abandoned, and employ methods of farming that placed healthy vines growing within an unspoilt environment at the heart of their story. They set about renovating the estate using locally quarried stone and finding alternative ways of tending their land, introducing different species of herbs, flowers and even cereals to encourage a favourable mix of microflora and fauna to maintain optimum growing conditions. Following organic certification in 2010, Alessandra and Carlo are currently converting to biodynamic methods as part of the Nicolas Joly-inspired Renaissance Italia group.

They currently own a total of 7.5 hectares of vines. Five of these lie at about 150 metres, facing mainly south-east, around the small winery at Castelrotto and are composed of fossil-rich, well-draining sandstone and limestone soils, with a higher tufa content on the south-west-facing parts of the hillside. There are a further 2 hectares of cherry and olive trees planted on the estate to keep alive two other local traditions increasingly under threat these days. They also have a small vineyard just a few hundred metres away on sand and clay soils known as Camporenzo in the Cariano and Monte vineyard area. The latest addition is a parcel of young vines near the village of San Giorgio di Valpolicella at 600 metres overlooking the Conca d'Oro. Though the new vineyards at San Giorgio were planted mainly to Guyot, the others lower down are all planted to pergola. The main grape varieties (Corvina, Corvinone, Molinara and Rondinella) dominate, though there is some Oseleta and Dindarella too and even a small amount of Croatina. The Venturini are Molinara fans and love the sapidity it gives their wines though they claim that the variety requires patience. 'Young Molinara vines don't do so well,' observes Alessandra. 'But from thirty years onwards they work much better. They bring this mineral element to the flavour of Valpolicella which gives the wine freshness and finesse and can even boost longevity.' The variety copes well with *appassimento* too, unlike Oseleta about which she voices the common complaint that the berries are too small to be of any use for the drying process, so Oseleta is always pressed when freshly picked. Regarding Dindarella, the variety is only planted at the end of a row as it requires such a lot of space – when planted in the middle it simply takes over. When fully ripe, Dindarella accumulates high sugar levels which is of particular interest for their Recioto Sant'Ulderico.

The cellars are small and run along simple lines. There are upright stainless steel fermentors for the fresh style of red wine, mainly the simple but delicious Valpolicella Classico which Alessandra feels displays the typical characteristics of Castelrotto – rustic wines with good acidity which need time in bottle to show at their best. Valpolicella Classico accounts for approximately half their annual output of just over 40,000 bottles. Their Ripasso is made in better vintages and refermented on Recioto lees only. A fairly brief period of seven to eight days for the secondary fermentation ensures that the wine maintains a ripe, rich and round character. Miniature conical wooden *tini* are used for fermenting the Valpolicella Superiore Camporenzo and Amarone Classico Stropa. The grapes for the Superiore are pressed mainly by foot during the early stages of their fermentation: the Venturini use freshly picked grapes only and believe, rather controversially, that semi-dried grapes have no part to play in this category. The wine spends a brief period in oak before bottling. A similar, only more protracted, fermentation policy applies with the Amarone which then spends up to four years or so in oak. Both wines are matured mainly in 2,500-litre oval barrels. Spontaneous fermentation with indigenous yeasts and the use of sulphur dioxide only following the non-induced malolactic fermentation are practices common to all their wines. The lunar calendar determines the timing of the various phases of the vinification process, such as racking, and even informs the decision of when to begin fermentation of the Amarone.

This small-scale operation is run by a couple whose commitment to and belief in a set of principles which respect both the environment and the authentic style of Veronese red wines is laudable. It is reassuring to note that the quality of their wines is on the whole equally impressive.

Monte dei Ragni

Località Marega, 337022- Fumane VR
+39 045 6801600
www.montedeiragni.com

Zeno Zinogli has chosen to live a simple way of life in harmony with his surroundings. He doesn't get angry any more and when it's too hot, he and his horse stop work as they're not enjoying themselves any more. (He had to get rid of the previous horse as it moved too quickly.) Zeno is completely guided by nature and the principles of biodiversity, farming the other traditional crops, cherries and olives, as well as vines. He makes just a few thousand bottles a year of Ripasso and Amarone, half of which is pre-sold. He likes to receive visitors too (by appointment) though rarely has much left to sell. That should come as no surprise: his wines are luscious, velvety, perfumed and serenely gentle.

Musella

Via Ferrazzette, 2, 37036 S. Martino Buon Albergo VR
+39 335 7294627
www.musella.it

The Pasqua family farm 24 hectares of Demeter-certified biodynamic vineyards surrounded by lush woodland at this little oasis just north of San Martino Buon Albergo. In addition to light and fresh Drago Bianco (Garganega) and Rosé (Corvina), the range includes a promising, perfumed Valpolicella DOC, a pretty, refreshingly lighter style of Ripasso and several versions of Amarone also made to highlight aroma and balance. The estate doubles up as a country Relais. Maddalena Pasqua runs the property with passion and a real sense of style.

Nicolis Angelo e Figli

Via Villa Girardi, 29, 37029 San Pietro in Cariano VR
+39 045 7701261
www.vininicolis.com

Bottling since 1978, the Nicolis family makes good volumes of voluptuous and perfumed wines from 42 hectares of vineyard spread over the Classico district though mainly in San Pietro and Sant'Ambrogio. The Valpolicella Classico from lower-lying sites is all cherry, raspberry and violets though backed up by good acidity; the Ripasso Classico Superiore and single-vineyard version Seccal continue the theme, and two versions of Amarone, the 'generic' and Ambrosan, are also impressive.

Novaia – Valpolicella forever sings

Via Novaia, 1, 37020 Marano di Valpolicella VR
+39 045 7755129
www.novaia.it

'With a wine like this, I'm optimistic about our future.' Marcello Vaona, winemaker at Novaia, is talking about his Vapolicella Classico *d'annata,* a wine from the most recent vintage, not Amarone, not Recioto, nor even Ripasso. Marcello's version is made from freshly picked grapes harvested when they are perfectly ripe, vinified in stainless steel and then bottled the following spring: 'No *appassimento*, no wood, no tricks. It's a simple wine but it's not banal and it tells you everything you need to know about the territory. It's the soul of Valpolicella.' The wine is delicious: a pale, almost crimson, ruby; the nose is extremely fresh and slightly nervy – ripe red cherries brushed with sage and a note of black pepper. It dances across the palate: fresh, pulpy cherry fruit with a pulse of brisk acidity and floral-toned red fruit notes to the long, sapid and faintly tannic finish. It is the perfect illustration of the classic 'food wine' the Veronesi are so good at making. Marcello believes that too many growers these days shun the simple *d'annata* wine and prefer to focus on Ripasso for which there is a much higher demand and which sells for between 30 and 50 per cent more a bottle. He thinks this doesn't necessarily make a lot of sense: 'I'm no economist but Valpolicella for me means cash flow. The other wines need ageing in wood sometimes for three years and more and obviously there are costs involved. I make and sell my Valpolicella within a year or so. By November 2016 I'd sold all of my Valpolicella 2015. And that's nearly half of my annual production.' If some producers argue that no one wants to buy the youthful style of Valpolicella any more, perhaps they should think again.

Novaia is a small estate situated on the mainly west-facing slopes of the Marano valley at between 300 and 400 metres. The Vaona family has lived here for several centuries though it wasn't until the early twentieth century that they began selling wine. 'It was all Recioto and Vino Santo back then, sweet wines. We still make them to keep the tradition alive,' says Marcello. Seven hectares are planted to the traditional local varieties, Corvina, Corvinone and Rondinella. 'We have a few rows of Oseleta and Turchetta, even some Molinara in the older vineyards,' he adds. There are a few olive and other fruit trees and the rest of the 10-hectare property is woodland. The Vaona family received certification for the production of organic wine in 2014. The farm is the traditional construction of a cluster of buildings grouped around an internal courtyard; the dovecote tower dates back to the fourteenth century while the others were built in the seventeenth. The family focus is on a traditional style of wine: in addition to the regular Valpolicella, they produce a Valpolicella Ripasso Classico Superiore, two bottlings of Amarone, a Recioto from their older vines and a single vineyard Classico Superiore called 'I Cantoni' from their highest plot at 400 metres on tufaceous soil. They are classic examples of the style for which Marano is known: fresh, perfumed, balanced and sapid, brimming over with ripe cherry fruit.

Nor, Marcello believes, is he ploughing a lonely furrow these days. Other small producers are beginning to put more focus on Valpolicella with similar success. 'That's the way it should be,' he claims. 'It's not that hard to make a thousand bottles of great wine – Amarone, say – and persuade people you're a decent winemaker. If the basic wine is a good one, then you can begin to see what the winery is all about. Valpolicella Classico is our calling card.' He is very proud of it, and rightly so.

Pasqua - Verona

Via Belvedere, 135, 37131 Verona VR
+39 045 8432111
www.pasqua.it

The Pasqua family founded a Verona-based *negoziante* business some ninety years ago selling mainly their local Pugliese wines; today the company produces around 15,000,000 bottles of wine from all over Italy. In 2007, offices and production were transferred to new premises at San Felice Extra at the foot of the Valpantena. Veronese wines are made partly from their own vineyards in Mizzole, San Pietro in Cariano and the Val d'Illasi and are marketed under a number of different labels – Villa Borghetti, for example. The Famiglia Pasqua selection is a range of modern-style wines and Cecilia Beretta is more traditional, while the new MAI DIRE MAI wines (Valpolicella Superiore and Amarone) from vineyards at Monte Vegro in the Val d'Illasi are positioned as 'Icons'.

Piccoli Daniela

Strada dei Monti 21/a, 37124 Parona di Valpolicella VR
+39 045 8890195
www.piccoliwine.it

The sisters Veronica and Alice follow the Magis system for sustainable production at this 15-hectare property above Parona. The wines see plenty of wood (even a proportion of the basic Valpolicella) but nonetheless are made in an aromatic and full-flavoured though quite gentle style. The intense, wood-aged Recioto is more demanding.

Quintarelli – where the magic begins

Via Cere, 1, 37024, Negrar VR
+39 045 7500016

In an obituary published on 17 January 2012, two days after his death, Verona's daily newspaper *L'Arena* reported Giuseppe 'Bepi' Quintarelli's valedictory wish: 'When I die I hope God will ask me to carry on making wine in paradise: it's the only thing I know how to do.' Quintarelli's passion for wine began at an early age. He was born at Valgatara in 1927 into a *mezzadria* family who originally worked land on and around the nearby Figari hillside in the Marano valley. Silvio Quintarelli, already a winemaker of some renown, had recently acquired an estate at Monte Ca' Paletta at Cere in Negrar. He had initially been attracted by the large cypress trees that surrounded the property, reasoning that if such beautiful trees could take root and flourish, anything else would too. Bepi grew up there working the land alongside his father, watching and learning from him constantly. The family led a simple life, dedicated to their work: in the fields Silvio would lead the ox while his wife guided the plough and it is not difficult to imagine a young Bepi trotting along behind them. The family had always made wine and grapes were still fermented in the traditional, large, old wooden *botti*.

His two elder brothers found work at the local agricultural consortium but, following military service, Bepi returned to the family cellars in the early 1950s to carry on the family's way of life and working methods he had learnt from his father. As viticulture became more and more important and demand for wine continued to grow, the family replaced many of their cherry trees with vines but Quintarelli still sold wine in demijohns as his father had done. Slip labels date the earliest remaining bottles back to the late 1950s, and the first 'officially labelled' wines were produced with the 1961 vintage.

Over the course of the next few decades his wines were to propel Quintarelli to legendary status. The man from this simple, humble background who never sought the limelight might seem a rather unlikely hero, but it was his unswerving commitment to quality that gradually brought him to the attention of such luminaries as Mario Soldati and Luigi Veronelli. Quintarelli worked with only the most carefully selected fruit, discarding bunches in vineyards and cellars alike that did not meet his exacting standards, with his wife Franca (the strong woman behind the modest man) helping out alongside him. He was a fanatical believer in the values of *appassimento*. Citing the example of Recioto, Quintarelli maintained that the process determined the defining features of Veronese red wines. The top floor of the winery was wholly given over to the drying of the grapes and Bepi resolutely checked progress, getting rid of any grapes that began to show any sign whatsoever of infection by botrytis. Grapes were dried mainly on the old-fashioned wooden *arele* but some were also suspended vertically from netting in the most traditional manner of all. More grapes would be set aside in better years and fewer in less favourable vintages. Near neighbour Antonio Mazzi remembers how rigorous he was in his selection of fruit: 'Quintarelli knew great fruit when he saw it and only the best would do.'

His approach to winemaking built on his early experiences of working with his father. Up until the 1980s the wines were still all fermented in wooden *botti* using indigenous yeasts, followed by a long ageing period in *botte* of between five to ten years depending on the wine style. Aside from his over-riding priority of working with great fruit, this lengthy ageing in cask made his wines stand out from the competition. Quintarelli's aim was to release wines only when he felt they had achieved the right stage in their development, notwithstanding their capacity to continue to carry on improving in bottle. It is a measure of the man's patience and dedication that he was prepared to wait until such time as he was satisfied that what his customers would receive was the best that he could offer. In his own way Bepi was also an innovator, planting varieties such as the two Cabernets, Chardonnay, Merlot, Nebbiolo and Sauvignon Blanc in the 3 hectares of Guyot-trained vineyards surrounding the winery, but at the same time he could be obdurate: he resisted for many years the idea of a using a bottling line and everything was done by hand until as recently as the 1990s.

The Quintarelli range is a surprisingly broad one given an annual average production of around 60,000 bottles from the family's 11 hectares of vineyard – a further 8 hectares (all pergola trained) are split between Marano, San Giorgio di Valpolicella and a smallholding near Montorio. A number of both red and white IGT wines made with a mix of international and local varieties show off the more authorial side of his nature; they include the famous Alzero, inspired by Cabernet Franc and made from semi-dried fruit, and Rosso del Bepi produced in years which Quintarelli deemed not to meet the levels he demanded for Amarone. However, his reputation is mainly based around his versions of the classic local reds, Valpolicella, Amarone and Recioto. The Valpolicella was made from the classic local grapes some of which undergo partial *appassimento*, and use of the *ripasso* technique before wood ageing. Amarone saw Quintarelli at full throttle and the wine would spend around eight years in wood before bottling. From the very best vintages, the Amarone Riserva – made in lots of just a few thousand bottles – would remain in cask for a decade.

Fame did not go to Quintarelli's head when thrust upon him and he remained a humble, patient and god-fearing man throughout his entire life. The winery is now run by his daughter Fiorenza and her sons Francesco and Lorenzo (who has recently graduated as an oenologist). They have vowed to maintain Bepi's legacy and his cherished beliefs, trusting that the world will continue to beat a path to their door.

Le Ragose

Località Le Ragose, 37024 Arbizzano di Negrar VR
+39 045 7513241
www.leragose.com

Marco and Paolo Galli carry on the pioneering work of their parents who established Le Ragose as an important name in Valpolicella, having started from scratch in 1969. From 18 hectares of vineyard, mainly in the south-facing amphitheatre adjacent to the winery, the brothers produce the full gamut of Veronese reds, in an authentic and characterful style. Delicious Valpolicella Classico smells and tastes of barely ripe strawberries laced with black pepper and aromatic herbs. Two versions of Superiore and a Ripasso are approachably ripe and seductive. A range of *appassimento* wines including the rare Ammandorlato (sic) and different cuvées of Amarone are given plenty of time to mature at the winery before release.

Recchia
Via Ca' Bertoldi, 30, 37024 Negrar VR
+39 045 7500584
www.recchiavini.it

Another brother and sister team: Enrico takes care of production and Chiara administration at this enterprising winery in the higher part of Jago. The family own over 40 hectares of vines there, carefully pieced together by their canny father, while the acquisition of the imposing Villa Bertoldi further down the hillside is a long-term restoration project. Enrico is helped in the cellar by Silvio Penna, for many years *cantiniere* at Masi who has a lifetime's experience of working with *appassimento*-style wines. Two ranges of Valpolicella are produced: the more traditional Masua di Jago wines and a number of 'limited edition' bottlings including Ripasso Le Muraie (refermented on Recioto lees) and single-vineyard Amarone Ca' Bertoldi.

Roccolo Grassi – self-portrait
Via S. Giovanni di Dio, 19, 37030 Mezzane di Sotto VR
+39 045 8880089
www.roccolograssi.it

If a wine reflects the personality of the person who makes it, then Marco Sartori is a case in point. The spacious modern family winery is located just a few hundred metres before the village of Mezzane di Sotto driving northwards along the valley, though the estate dates back to the early 1970s when it was still a mixed farming operation. Marco's father Bruno started off producing wine *sfuso* and then in *damigiane* before trying his luck with bottles. 'Even then he only ever made *vini d'annata*,' explains Marco, 'Dad liked an empty cellar.' In 1995 the family bought the Roccolo Grassi vineyard on the hillside further down the valley and decided to rename the business. Marco began a couple of years later having completed his studies in oenology at first in Conegliano and then at the University of Milan. Romano Dal Forno was already beginning to draw the world's attention to the potential of the Valpolicella DOC area for producing great red wines and Marco was on a mission to make the best Amarone he possibly could. His sister Francesca joined the team in 2003 to carry on the family tradition. Today they own almost 14 hectares of vines in the valley, an amount Marco feels is sufficient to meet their needs. Two hectares of Garganega lie close to the winery on the valley floor. The soils here are based on limestone and drain well, though the high nitrogen content encourages productivity and the vines require a high degree of maintenance. The red grapes are all grown on hillside sites as Marco believes that is where they perform best. 'We have two other people helping us in the vineyard and that's it. We want to remain where we are and focus on what we can accomplish here in Mezzane,' he says. All their vineyards are trained to the Guyot system which, though less productive, gives better quality in Marco's view. Roccolo Grassi produce a small range of just two whites (Soave and Recioto di Soave) and three reds (Valpolicella Superiore, Amarone della Valpolicella and Recioto della Valpolicella), around 50,000 bottles in total.

Marco's restless search for improvement continues in the cellar where he is constantly fine-tuning his methods, letting his experiences guide him. With Soave, for example, where he used to rely on new French oak barriques to achieve the concentration and potential longevity he was looking for, nowadays he ferments the wine in cement and prefers older, larger barrels for both fermentation and storage. Tasted back in 2015, though his Soave 2007 had held up well, the oak was still very evident. The wood element has been better integrated in more recent vintages and 2013 was arguably his best effort so far, though Marco continues to experiment: 'At first I preferred the glass-lined tanks, but retasting the wines after six months I preferred the wine from the unlined tanks, it had improved so much.' Cement, like wood, is porous enough to admit small quantities of oxygen which will benefit yeast activity. So he decided to use half glass-lined cement and half left in its natural state with the 2015.

His approach to making red wine is rather more standardized. He ferments in stainless steel, uses temperature control, avoids any 'technical aids' (tannins), etc., and likes a fairly lengthy maceration period of around fifteen to twenty days. Malolactic takes place in wood and the wines then refine for between eighteen and twenty-four months in barrel, the Valpolicella Superiore in a mixture of *botti* and (mainly used) barriques and the Amarone in barriques only. He matures the Amarone in bottle for at least another twenty-four months. Tiny amounts (a couple of thousand half bottles of each) of the two sweet wines complete the range. He uses what he defines as 'natural' methods of *appassimento* only, using ventilators but no dehumidifiers: air circulation is the key to success, he believes. He does not discourage the presence of a small amount of noble rot for the Recioto style wines. While the entire range shows poise and balance these days, there is no shortage of evidence of intensity and focus either. For wine lovers who appreciate full-bodied, richly flavoured wines with plenty of ageing potential, Roccolo Grassi will not disappoint.

Rubinelli Vajol

Via Paladon 31, 37029 San Pietro in Cariano VR
+39 045 6839277
www.rubinellivajol.it

The Rubinelli family produce around 60,000 bottles of textbook Valpolicella from 9 hectares of vineyard surrounding the winery in the south-facing amphitheatre known as Vajol. From the delightful, youthful Classico through to the sweetly aromatic Amarone, the range shows excellent *tipicita* and sensibly constrained levels of residual sugar (for example, normally no more than around 4.5 g/l in the Amarone); these are classic examples of the approachable San Pietro style.

Le Salette

Via Pio Brugnoli, 11, 37022 Fumane VR
+39 045 7701027
www.lesalette.it

This family-run business produces a range of eminently drinkable Valpolicella: regular Classico, a Ripasso refermented on the lees of Recioto and several different versions of Amarone which can age extremely well. With well-sited vineyards in Fumane, San Pietro in Cariano and Sant'Ambrogio, Le Salette is one of the area's most consistently reliable producers.

Tenute SalvaTerra

Via Cengia, 85, 37029 Cengia VR
+39 045 6859025
www.tenutesalvaterra.it

Tenute SalvaTerra is based at the splendid Villa Giona below Castelrotto and has vineyards high up at Prun in the Negrar valley. The firm is owned and run by a group of entrepreneurs who also produce wines in other areas across the Veneto. A carefully studied approach to production favours a highly polished and commercial style of wine.

San Cassiano

Via San Cassiano, 17, 37030 Mezzane di Sotto VR
+39 045 8880665
www.cantinasancassiano.it

Until the end of the 1970s the higher reaches of the Mezzane valley were used as pasture for grazing the local breed of sheep known as Brogna. Indeed Mirko Sella's grandfather practised mixed farming, looking after livestock and growing crops. The pastures are all planted to olive trees and vines now and Mirko's San Cassiano estate produces both oil from the local Grignano variety and Valpolicella. His rich, ripe and perfumed wines are made from 10 hectares of vines on the mainly limestone soils around San Cassiano and Monte Guala.

Casa Vinicola Sartori

Via Casette, 4, 37024 Arbizzano-Santa Maria VR
+39 045 6028011
www.sartorinet.com

Like so many of Verona's merchant houses, the Sartori family connection with wine began in the 'on trade' as restaurant and hotel owners who later diversified and bought up cellars. Many have since disappeared, usurped by the spread of the cooperative movement, yet today some sixteen million bottles of Sartori wine are still sold around the world. Thanks to a link up with the Colognola ai Colli cooperative, who now own 40 per cent of the company, Sartori has 'serious anchorage' and a guaranteed source of supply. Soundly made, commercially styled wines are made in part from vineyards still owned by the family. The current owner, the engaging and worldly wise Andrea Sartori, doubles up as president of the Valpolicella growers' consortium.

Tenuta Santa Maria di Gaetano Bertani

Via Novare 4, 37024 Arbizzano di Negrar VR
+39 045 6028802
www.tenutasantamaria.wine

When Bertani sold off the brand name and part of their vineyards to Tenimenti Angelini, the family retained ownership of the Villa Mosconi Bertani at Arbizzano. Today the elegant and well-preserved villa is the centre of their new venture in the world of wine. The small range is made from a mix of local and international varieties and all retain a decidedly Veronese character; good Soave from the Lepia vineyard and reds made in an 'uber-traditional' style.

Tenuta Santa Maria Valverde

Località Gazzo, 4, 37020 Marano di Valpolicella VR
+39 347 0908763
www.tenutasantamariavalverde.it

Perched above the excellent Gazzo vineyard, the tiny, quaint winery of Tenuta Santa Maria Valverde is owned and run by Nicola and Ilaria Campagnola. The couple produce just 10,000 bottles of wine from terraced vineyards at up to 500 metres. Their Valpolicella Classico Superiore, in particular, shows great purity of style and, like the Ripasso Classico Superiore and Amarone Classico, reflects the spicy, aromatic and slightly austere character of Valpolicella grown at high altitudes. The wines are not easy to find unless you're a cyclist who likes climbing steep hills; the winery is an accredited 'bike station' where people can rest and carry out minor repairs.

Santa Sofia

Via Ca' Dede', 61, Pedemonte, San Pietro in Cariano VR
+39 045 7701074
www.santasofia.com

Based at Villa Serego, which dates back to 1560, the Santa Sofia winery was founded in 1811 and is currently run by the Begnoni family. The broad range of Veronese wines sometimes struggles to live up to the splendour of the setting.

Azienda Agricola Scriani - *vignaiolo* by dedication

Via Ponte Scrivan, 7, 37022 Fumane VR
+39 045 6839251
www.scriani.it

'Spring is my favourite season: it's a new beginning after the vines have shut down over the winter. There's so much to do!' By his own admission Stefano Cottini lives to work. 'If you're a *vignaiolo* it really is a full-time job, so you have to have a passion for it. And work only stops when they put you in the wooden overcoat!'

This year Stefano has bought new vineyards and, after ripping up the old Guyot-trained vines, is busy replanting using pergola, a system he is adamant is the most suitable for the local vines in Valpolicella. Spring is when preparation for the new growing season begins and Stefano is up at dawn, anxious to be out on his tractor: 'We need to add manure to the ground to nourish the vines as they come round from their winter slumber.' He will also add minerals where necessary, especially calcium, iron, magnesium and potassium. His 13 or so hectares of vineyard are mainly in the Fumane valley below the hamlet of Cavalo, lying at between 250 and 500 metres above sea level. The soils here are mainly calcareous and the vines absorb the iron content quickly in order to strengthen the wood. 'They need to be resistant in these conditions so we give them a hand by maintaining the right balance in the soil,' he says. Vines, he feels, are like people and need help to stay in good health and that means looking after them by administering the right treatments. 'That's why I like the 2016 vintage so much.' He smiles. 'Good quality and good quantity. The growing season was so favourable, I was able to cut right back on treatments; it saved me a lot of money! But it's too late trying to put things right once the fruit has changed colour, the grapes need protection.' This means spraying the leaves with copper and sulphur to fortify them against attack from peronospera or, worse, oidium, and making sure the new shoots which will be the fruiting canes for the following season are kept free from infection. 'Peronospera is a seasonal malady,' he explains. 'Oidium is much trickier as the problem is still there the next year and the vines need to be treated in February before the vegetative cycle begins again.

'We carry on like this until May or June and flowering time when infection from grey rot is at its most dangerous. We have to spray with copper to help toughen up the stems of the grapes as they start to form. When the foliage is at its peak, the grapes are at their most vulnerable: the plant has put so much of its energy into producing leaves. An infection at this point could destroy as much as half the crop.' Stefano mentions an old proverb, a real favourite amongst local *vignaioli,* which maintains that whether the season begins early or late, the fruit knows to ripen and the climate has a way of balancing itself out. July is a critical month when growth will either speed up or slow right down. If temperatures climb too high (above 34°C) the vines start to close down, an auto-defensive action to protect themselves against the heat. 'The plants seem to know what to expect,' he says. 'If there's a sudden spurt of growth you can guarantee there's heavy rain on the way – the vine is making sure that it can conserve humidity. That's why an old plant produces better fruit, through its experience; it knows what's coming.'

Once colour change has taken place in the first half of August there are forty days left before harvest time. The main worry for the *vignaiolo* now is hail which can easily wreak havoc with the ripening fruit, but it's a risk that simply cannot be prepared for as its arrival is so unpredictable. 'You can maybe go on holiday in August if all you do is produce red grapes. But I've got Pinot Grigio to harvest at Sona [over the other side of the Adige to the west of Verona] and I need to start making wine.' Even so work continues in the vineyards. 'Mal d'Esca is a worry, especially with any new shoots off the main trunk: if the infection gets into the graft you've had it.' The tender green shoots are vulnerable because of their high moisture content and need to be stripped off; the trunk itself is protected by the tougher bark.

The Valpolicella harvest begins in September and can continue up to late October. Some varieties – Sangio'eto and Teroldego, for example – need harvesting quickly but the local grapes, although ripening in the strict order of Corvina, then Rondinella and finally Corvinone, can be left on the vine a little longer if necessary as Stefano believes they go into 'stand by' mode. While full attention turns now to the cellar, the later 'field' work will take place when the leaves have fallen. The plant shrinks back before dropping its foliage and then shuts down with the cooler temperatures as winter sets in. This is the time for pruning, an activity normally measured in terms of the number of buds left for the next vintage. Stefano prefers to be guided by the age and health of the individual vine but in any case always leaves one or two more than will eventually be required as the odd bud or two will usually be 'lost or damaged in transit' during the course of the season. 'Growers need to bring in a certain quantity of fruit each year in order to survive, so I like to make my decisions in winter for the year ahead. I'm not a great fan of *diraddamento*. You might need to lose a little fruit in order to meet the legal requirements on yields but you can only do that properly once the grapes have changed colour. Otherwise, I decide early: "*diraddamento*" is a word invented by marketing people.'

Stefano's view of organic grape growing is equally sceptical: 'A grower needs to protect his vines. Measures for organic production are based on average values taken over a five year period; it's simply not enough.' Previous generations have impoverished the soil and done a lot of damage by pumping it full of chemicals, he thinks. 'The current generation has to do what it must to survive. I like to think my kids might be able to look at biodynamics though you need to create the right conditions first and that takes a long time. And you have to think holistically – the car you drive, the energy you burn. It's a lifestyle choice. So either you make sacrifices or you salvage what you have.'

The main thrust of the Scriani production focuses on the wines of the Valpolicella. Some 80,000 bottles are divided between the principal styles: Valpolicella Classico, a Superiore version, a Valpolicella Ripasso Classico Superiore, Amarone, Recioto and a varietal Corvina which undergoes partial *appassimento* before fermentation in wood. Ageing in various sizes of oak (French) is practised on all the range apart from the youthful Valpolicella Classico *d'annata*. As might be imagined, the wines are well-crafted in a positive, direct and slightly uncompromising style that reflects both their Fumane patrimony and the forthright character of a man with his feet very firmly on the ground.

Secondo Marco

Via Campolongo 9 - 37022 Fumane di Valpolicella VR
+39 045 6800954
www.secondomarco.it

Marco Speri made a break from the important Speri family of Pedemonte to set up his own cellars in 2008 and has built up a reputation as something of a maverick producer. He produces a sensibly small range of wines from 11 hectares of vineyard at Cengia and in Fumane. Recent experiments have seen him fermenting out Amarone to around 2 g/l of residual sugar with an extended maceration time of ninety days in 2014 and even a hundred days in the 2015 vintage. The effects on the wine, as well as making it taste drier and therefore more food friendly, are that the aromas have less impact and the sensations of volume and substance are decreased; at the same time, however, the wine appears cleaner and takes on a more ethereal character. Marco's aim is also to conserve good acidity and keep pH levels low in order to promote stability and increase longevity. The other wines are also quite singular in style: Valpolicella Classico (approximately 24,000 bottles a year) spends some six months in old *botti* before its release as a pale but floral and perfumed red with crisp acidity and good length. Marco's desire to make a statement is also evident in his version of Ripasso (20,000 to 25,000 bottles); in his view this style is better served as being a serious or super-charged Valpolicella rather than a mini-Amarone. As such, it shows good freshness and vitality with precise acidity and interesting salty/minerally flavours. For the moment there is just one version of Amarone in production (fewer than 20,000 bottles a year) and the selection is completed by a tiny amount of spicy and bittersweet Recioto.

Speri

Via Fontana, 14, 37029 San Pietro in Cariano VR
+39 045 7701154
www.speri.com

Making wine in a clean and commercial style which is pleasing to the consumer without losing sight of *tipicita* is a tricky balancing act. Few accomplish the feat with such aplomb as the family-run Speri winery based at Pedemonte di Valpolicella; they have been involved with grape growing for seven generations. Freshness and elegance are hallmarks of the Speri range, and quality of fruit the determining factor. 'Wine is a part of our DNA by now,' says Giampaolo Speri, acknowledging the wealth of experience earlier generations of the family have passed on to the current one. 'When my grandfather Sante went off to war he made sure he left behind a list of places from where to buy the best grapes. It's basically all about the *terreno* and the exposition. Perhaps the greatest patrimony of all is the mix of grape varieties that's been handed down to us. There's real magic in our *uvaggio* and each year has its own story to tell: the raw materials are everything. Our aim is make the best of what we've got and that basically means Corvina, Rondinella and Molinara: that's where the elegance of Valpolicella comes from.'

Speri identifies clonal research as one of the most important issues in their continuous pursuit of making better wine. 'Everything used to be determined by sugar levels: the *contadini* would readily sacrifice extra aroma for more sugars. We're looking at various older biotypes which have good aromatic expression even though they're less productive.' The search applies across the board and not just to the noble variety Corvina; Speri is not a huge Corvinone fan though believes that Rondinella has more potential than generally recognized, Molinara too. 'So we select vines which have the characteristics we're looking for, take cuttings and propagate them ourselves.'

The family own around 60 hectares in Valpolicella Classico, certified organic from the 2015 vintage. Giampaolo believes this is a major step forward: 'Our generation has to make its contribution too and leave the vineyards in the best possible condition: we've seen definite improvement in the quality of the fruit as a result.' Total production is currently around 350,000 bottles a year and focuses on the five classic reds of Valpolicella from across the family's holdings in Fumane, Negrar and San Pietro in Cariano, and all Pergoletta Veronese trained. Fermentation at relatively low temperatures in stainless steel and cement ensures that little aromatic impact is lost. The youthful Valpolicella Classico is a burst of fresh fruit aromas and flavours sustained by good acidity while the Ripasso spends around a week on the lees of Amarone and alcohol levels are not exaggerated. Two wines are produced from their finest vineyards located at up to 300 metres on Monte Sant'Urbano where they own almost 20 hectares. Fruit for the Valpolicella Classico Superiore Sant'Urbano undergoes *appassimento* for three to four weeks before pressing, while Amarone grapes remain in the *fruttaio* for the full term of a hundred days or so. Both wines are capable of sustaining many years of bottle age, the Amarone in particular. Lastly, Recioto La Roggia is another single vineyard wine from around Villa Giona in the Castelrotto area of San Pietro in Cariano.

Tedeschi – family values

Via Giuseppe Verdi, 4/a, 37029 Pedemonte di Valpolicella VR
+39 045 7701487
www.tedeschiwines.com

At 84, Renzo Tedeschi is still a keen cyclist. Whether reminiscing about the forty-two steps he used to climb carrying a *gerla* full of grapes to be set aside for drying in the family *fruttaio*, recalling how proud he felt the first time his Recioto della Valpolicella Classico Monte Fontana appeared on the shelves at Harrods in London or reflecting upon how much life has changed in both the vineyards and the cellars over his lifetime, this softly-spoken and unassuming man is a gold mine of information about the formative years of Valpolicella. He likes to ponder over the traditional and almost mystical union of the four principal red grapes of Valpolicella (including, therefore, Molinara). Not only were they once planted alongside each other in the same vineyard but then, as if by magic, would find their way back together again in the cellars and create a whole much greater than the sum of its parts.

The next generation has a deep well of experience to draw on and all three children have followed in their father's footsteps. Antonietta looks after domestic sales while Sabrina, as well as managing export markets, has taken on the challenging role of president of Famiglie Amarone. Riccardo has inherited his father's insight and considerable skill in the cellars and vineyards and is in charge of production. The family produce an impressive selection of Valpolicella from across the entire DOC territory. The youthful Classico, Lucchine, from vines in San Pietro in Cariano, is an excellent introduction to the range while Ripasso Capitel San Rocco has been in production since the 1970s (originally as a *Vino da Tavola)*. The La Fabriseria wines from 7 hectares of vines high up on the border between Fumane and Sant'Ambrogio are particularly distinctive. But the most ambitious project yet is largely Riccardo's brainchild. In 2006 Tedeschi acquired the 84-hectare Maternigo estate above Mezzane to carry out some, quite literally, ground-breaking work. The property had not previously been planted to vines so Riccardo carried out an in-depth study of growing conditions to help him make the right choices to get the best of the new property, particularly given his initial concerns that the fruit might struggle to ripen fully at such relatively high altitudes. Around 30 hectares were reshaped and planted to three different training systems: Guyot, pergola and 'lyre' or the 'U' shaped trellis system common in New World vineyards, which in theory allows for good air circulation through the canopy and partial shading. So far he leans towards Guyot: not only is the canopy easier to manage to ensure full phenolic maturity, but the fruit achieves a higher concentration of sugars and gives wines of better structure. With climate change an increasingly important consideration, however, he has decided not to commit himself fully yet. Now the vines are beginning to approach maturity, the first results show the wisdom of their choice as well as the enormous potential of the DOC territory. Valpolicella Superiore Maternigo is made from low-yielding vines where the grapes have undergone a period of *sovramaturazione* on the plant. The wine combines freshness, breadth of aroma and intensity with a structure that promises good ageing potential, a combination that few reds other than 'serious' Valpolicella manage quite so well.

Amarone is a key part of the Tedeschi range with several different bottlings. The generic version (130,000 bottles a year) is a full, ripe and fleshy wine with good tannins (one of the hallmarks of the house style) while two small vineyards are used to produce Riserva wines. La Fabriseria is a big, structured Amarone designed for the long haul while Capitel Monte Olmi, a 2.5-hectare plot on the lower slopes of Monte Mausa, made its debut with the 1964 vintage. Monte Olmi is more approachable and shows off the seductive side of Amarone; nonetheless it ages well too.

Sabrina is convinced that the many different interpretations of Valpolicella on the market today are something to be celebrated though, at the same time, is concerned that the wines maintain their integrity. Like many other producers, she worries that with Amarone, minimum alcohol levels are too low and maximum sugar levels too high: 'We prefer not to pander too much to current trends and focus on a classic style which respects *tipicita*.' Riccardo agrees: 'The classic attributes of our wines – acidity, freshness and elegance – are not necessarily incompatible with good structure and colour, etc. Our great fortune is that we're able to make wines which incorporate all of those aspects.'

Terre di Leone

Via Valpolicella, 6/b, 37020 Località Porta, Marano di Valpolicella VR
+39 045 6895040
www.terredileone.it

Chiara and Federico Pellizzari farm vines grown in the basalt and tufa soils below the Santa Maria Valverde church, and rent others close by. Winemaking methods follow a simple, reductive, gravity-fed system and ageing in various sizes of oak barrel. Carefully made wines maintaining great freshness are presented under two different labels: the more forward Re Pazzo wines and the more ambitious, structured and polished Terre di Leone range including the bizarre Dedicatum, a blend of up to fourteen different varieties. Their youthful Valpolicella and both styles of Amarone are particularly good.

Terre di Pietra

Via Arcandola, 4, 37036 San Martino B.A. VR
+39 328 0849020
www.terredipietra.it

Making just 17,000 bottles a year from vines at the property and in Torbe in the Negrar valley, Terre di Pietra could almost be described as a micro-winery! The artisan-style wines show great character, some being made with indigenous yeasts, etc. Two versions of Superiore provide a fascinating contrast: Vigna delle Peste (from Marcellise), fermented and aged in cement, is unflinchingly pure, lively and scented while Mesal from Torbe is softer and more luscious, thanks in part to a lengthy period of oak ageing. Sadly the owner, Laura Albertini, passed away at the beginning of March 2017 leaving Cristiano Saletti to pursue his late wife's dream of becoming a successful wine producer.

Tezza

Stradella Maioli, 4, 37142 Verona VR
+39 045 550267
www.tezzawines.it

The brothers Federico, Flavio and Vanio fly one of the few flags for the smaller, family winery in Valpantena. Production from 27 hectares runs to 200,000 bottles a year of soundly made wines. Of particular interest is a range of no less than four Ripasso wines: Corte Majoli is refermented on Amarone lees, while Ma Roat ('red moon' in the ancient Cimbrian language) is a unique interpretation, made without the use of wood. The other two are both labelled Valpantena Superiore: the 'classic' version is made with a one-to-one ratio of base wine and Amarone lees, while premium Brolo delle Giare is refermented on Recioto lees.

Agricola Tommasi Viticoltori – keeping it in the family

Via Ronchetto, 4, 37029 Pedemonte di Valpolicella VR
+39 045 7701266
www.tommasiwine.it

Italy's sharecropping system was still widely in operation until the 1950s and '60s, albeit by then in modified form in Verona. The farmers or *mezzadri* customarily kept a part of what they cultivated, but their main objective was to produce as much as possible from the land they worked. The idea of a high-quality crop of grapes from much-reduced vineyard yields would have been a fantasy. When the *mezzadria* system finally collapsed, vineyards were often abandoned as the next generation sought jobs in factories or offices as an alternative to the tough physical labour of the fields. Some families, through sheer hard work, careful management of their resources and good business sense were able to buy out their landlords when the opportunity arose.

In 1902 the 25-year-old Giacomo Tommasi had married into a family who practised mixed farming on a few hectares of land near Torbe. Seeing the demand for wine in Verona's plentiful *osterie* continue to grow despite the devastation of phylloxera, Giacomo decided to devote himself to wine production. In 1919 he was granted sharecropping rights to their land in and around Pedemonte di Valpolicella by the noble Campostrini-Bocolli family, owners of one of the region's most important estates, Santa Sofia, which then stretched for over 300 hectares between Santa Maria di Negrar and San Pietro in Cariano. While the Tommasi family were still farming all manner of fruit and vegetable crops, they came to an agreement with their landlords over the full rights to the wine they made from the vineyards. Soon afterwards they began to extend their interests in the food and drink trade with the purchase of an *osteria* in Parona. From then on the business has grown exponentially and the family now owns several hotels and restaurants in Verona and has built up a portfolio of wine estates not only in the nearby Bardolino and Lugana denominations but also in Treviso for Prosecco, Lombardia (Oltrepo Pavese), two properties in Tuscany in Maremma and Montalcino, and an estate in Manduria for the production of Pugliese wines. The entire enterprise is owned and run between nine members of the fourth generation of the Tommasi family.

With over 100 hectares of vineyard in Valpolicella Classico in San Pietro in Cariano and Sant'Ambrogio plus a further 10 hectares of land in Soave, Veronese wines remain very much at the heart of their empire. The vineyards include 'Rafael' just above the winery at the foot of Monte Masua, and Ca' Florian with subsequent additions at the Conca d'Oro and La Grolleta, a part of La Grola. Meanwhile their estate in Soave, Tenuta Le Volpare, consists of two plots on Monte Foscarino.

For early consumption, Tommasi produce a Rosso Veronese IGT called Terra dei Ciliegi, a blend of Corvina, Rondinella and around 10 per cent Pelara. However, the company's main thrust these days is a range of more 'serious' red wines. It is an interesting reflection of exactly where the market for Veronese wine lies at the moment that, where they produce some 35,000 to 40,000 bottles of Terra dei Ciliegi a year, they make three times that amount of their Valpolicella Classico Superiore Rafael from a second selection after the grapes to be set aside for *appassimento* have been harvested. The fruit may take some *sovramaturazione* from being left to hang on the vine but this worthy red is made from freshly gathered fruit. Production moves up to around 300,000 bottles a year of Valpolicella Ripasso Classico Superiore: the base wine spending around a week in contact with the remaining lees before being transferred to oak for up to fifteen months. They claim the wine to be a reinterpretation of what their grandfather's Valpolicella would have been like; their first vintage of the modern version was 1995. The wines are produced at the large, functional winery in Pedemonte, their traditional headquarters, and the cellars contain what the family claim to be the largest barrel in the world. Made from some 5000 kilos of selected oak, 'La Magnifica' (the magnificent one) holds 333 hectolitres of wine (almost 45,000 bottles) and is still used for maturing Amarone. As one of the wine's leading producers, it is clearly Amarone upon which Tommasi's reputation has been founded.

The family produce a total of around 250,000 bottles of Amarone divided between four different labels. The 'basic' Amarone Classico is made in lots of around 200,000 bottles a year, between 35,000 and 40,000 bottles of Amarone Il Sestante (the sextant), a further 7,000 to 9,000 bottles of Amarone Classico Riserva Ca' Florian, bottled only in the finest vintages and which benefits from several additional years' bottle age at the winery, and finally a new release, Amarone Classico Riserva from the company's vineyards at La Groletta. Like the other Tommasi wines, they are all carefully made in a robust, traditional style which can improve over the years in bottle.

The Tommasi approach to the *appassimento* process is a pragmatic one. While old style *arele* are used for drying grapes for the Ca' Florian Riserva, smaller, plastic crates are favoured for the other examples. The grapes are dried in the main facility in Pedemonte di Valpolicella, managed by simply either opening or closing windows (or in extreme cases switching on giant fans) to move the air around. They have recently taken over a new *fruttaio* at Sant'Ambrogio which will allow them a little more control over the process as it is being equipped with dehumidifiers for use when the health of the fruit is at risk. Such a level-headed approach allows them to keep their options open, no doubt one of the main reasons why the company has gone from strength to strength.

Tenute Ugolini

Strada Bonamico, 37029 San Pietro in Cariano VR
+39 045 7703830
www.tenuteugolini.it

No expense has been spared by the Ugolini family in setting up this 22-hectare estate overlooking Castelrotto. What was originally a Benedictine monastery has been carefully restored along with some 12 kilometres of *marogne* to create an imposing setting for a highly individual interpretation of the wines of Valpolicella. Oaky, substantial and alcoholic, they are likely to divide opinion.

Venturini

Via Semonte, 20, 37029 San Pietro in Cariano VR
+39 045 7701331
www.viniventurini.com

A family-run business established in 1963, with 12 hectares under vine mainly at Monte Masua and spacious new cellars constructed in 2014. Around 90,000 to 95,000 bottles a year are made in a full and solid, unrestrained style including a well-structured Classico Superiore and three different cuvées of Amarone: a generic version, tiny quantities of Riserva and around 8,000 bottles of the excellent Campo Masua. Venturini is a member of the Famiglie Amarone.

Villa San Carlo

Via della Segheria, 25/A, 37141 Montorio, VR
+39 392 9814592
www.villasancarlo.wine

The Pavesi family have owned the elegant seventeenth-century Villa San Carlo for some sixty years. Originally the 70-hectare property was tended by six *mezzadri* families who gradually left to work in factories, offices, and the like, and until 2008 the grapes were all sold off. From today's 23 hectares of vineyard the family vinify the grapes from just 5 hectares, selling the rest either as fruit or 'bulk' wine. The selection policy enables them to focus on small quantities and a limited range of wines: a delightful, fuller-style Valpolicella, a persuasive Ripasso Superiore not over-reliant on sugar levels, and a well-balanced and authentic-tasting Amarone. An Amarone Riserva is produced in more successful vintages. This is a winery to watch.

Villa Spinosa

Via Colle Masua, 14, 37024 Negrar VR
+39 045 7500093
www.villaspinosa.com

From 20 hectares of vineyard divided between Jago di Sotto, where the winery is based, Figari on the other side of Masua in Marano, and Costa del Buso near Le Ragose on the eastern slopes of Negrar, Enrico Cascella Spinosa produces a range of stylish and individual wines guided by oenologist and ex-Ferrarini acolyte Gianmaria Ciman in the cellar. Spinosa's vision is to recreate the style of wines produced thirty or forty years ago before technology 'took over'. The wines might not appeal to all tastes but purists will appreciate the lean, austere yet elegant and aromatic Valpolicella Classico and Superiore Figari in particular. A distinctive, drier style of Ripasso and several versions of Amarone, named after the families who used to work the vineyards, complete the offer. A name that too often passes under the radar.

Viviani

Via Mazzano, 8, 37024 Mazzano VR
+39 045 7500286
www.cantinaviviani.com

Claudio Viviani produces around 80,000 bottles of the full range of Valpolicella from 10 hectares of vines at Panego and Mazzano high up in the Negrar valley. A restless perfectionist, Claudio leaves no stone unturned in his pursuit of excellence. While favouring Guyot for Corvinone (which, he believes, performs particularly well up at Mazzano), he is yet to be convinced that this is the right system for Corvina in a world beset with climate change. He has even experimented with planting diagonally across the hillside rather than either following contours or the *ritocchino* system. His commitment continues in the cellar and shines through in a selection of juicy and aromatic wines which marry power and precision: Classico Superiore Campo Morar and regular Amarone are exceptional examples of the classic Negrar style.

Zanoni Pietro

Via Are Zovo, 16/D, 37125 Verona VR
+39 045 8343977
www.pietrozanoni.it

Pietro Zanoni produces the full range of Veronese reds from his 6.5 hectares of vineyard mainly at Zovo around the family winery in Quinzano and in the neighbouring valley of Avesa. Good, reliable Valpolicella, a more ambitious Superiore from the Campo Denari vineyard in Avesa which ages well, and an impressive Amarone from vines grown around the winery are especially convincing.

Corte Zardini

Via Val Verde 1, Località Pezza, 37020 Marano di Valpolicella VR
+39 045 7755304
www.cortezardini.it

Based at Pezza above Marano, Corte Zardini is a small firm producing just three types of wine from 10 hectares of vines at around 450 metres below the Santa Maria Valverde church. Though homespun, the wines are nonetheless valid, approachable and cleanly made from good-quality raw materials.

Zenato

Strada San Benedetto, 8, 37019 Peschiera del Garda VR
+39 045 7550300
www.zenato.it

Though perhaps best known for their Lugana, the Zenato family also own some 35 hectares of vineyards in Valpolicella Classico above and below the village of Sant'Ambrogio in Costalunga and Montindon. As befits the company's reputation, the wines are carefully made in a highly polished and commercial style and include a full range of Valpolicella (apart from the youthful *d'annata* style) plus a couple of IGT wines.

Zyme

Via Cà del Pipa, 1, 37029 Località Mattorona, San Pietro in Cariano VR
+39 045 7701108
www.zyme.it

Celestino Gaspari spent many years as a highly respected consultant oenologist (working with Marion, Buglioni, Tenuta Sant'Antonio, Monte Dall'Ora, etc.) before setting up his own winery in the Mattonara area of San Pietro in Cariano. The eye-catching cellars were once a quarry where the local tufa and sandstone were extracted to be made into bricks, and tunnel deep into the ground. The wines are no less imaginative: the 'classic' range spans a lovely simple, fresh Valpolicella to Amarone La Mattonara which can spend as much as nine years in wood, while the experimental wines include the bizarre Kairos and Harlequin both made from a blend of around fifteen different varieties! If winemakers were painters, then Celestino would be Salvador Dali.

THE WORK OF THE *CONSORZI*

Though there might be room for all of the many different styles of Valpoli-cella, ensuring that production does not develop into a free for all is, to put it mildly, a tricky business. The rules that govern the various denominations are maintained by the local growers' consortium, the Consorzio Tutela Vini Valpolicella. Olga Bussinello, who studied international law before becom-ing the consortium's director, has the unenviable task of keeping open a dialogue with both the producers and the markets they serve: 'Our objec-tive is to encourage members to make wines which respect the territory and its traditions, and meet the needs of the consumer.' Carrying the message to the world at large involves taking part in trade fairs and organizing tastings to help the wine become better known – though closer to home the consortium's role as mediator is especially challenging. She acknowledges that the decisions made by the committee which determines policy might not always be popular. A brake is being applied to contain the momentum of the current *appassimento* frenzy by imposing stricter limits on the amount of grapes being dried. The stated intention is to help maintain standards of quality: for example, in the potentially excellent 2016 vintage the maximum amount was reduced to 40 per cent. Political interests ensure that any such restriction is applied across the board – that is, in all vineyards of the geographical sub-zones: a position that some find at best questionable. The administration committee represents the three different categories of winery that make up membership, the 'vertical' producers who make and bottle their own wine, the 'industrial' producers or larger-scale bottlers which includes the *negoziante* houses, and the 'simple' producers who grow grapes, ensuring that a form of democracy holds sway. Conflicts of interest between the different factions are alarmingly apparent, yet Olga somehow remains cheerfully buoyant about her responsibilities: 'As long as everyone's unhappy, then I know I've done my job properly,' she says.

Aldo Lorenzoni, director of the Consorzio Tutela Vini Soave, is faced with a different set of problems, not the least of which is trying to ensure that Soave receives more of the attention it deserves in both domestic and foreign markets. A series of initiatives designed to get Soave talked about more often has been founded on an in-depth study into the growing conditions of the area and their effect on the style of the wines. Begun in the mid 2000s, the *zonazione* project mapped out in a remarkably clear fashion the vineyards of Classico and pinpointed areas of particular note in the 'regular' DOC area, examining the relevance of soil types, altitudes, topography, etc., in both. Further studies including the effects of climate change have led to the inauguration of the 'Volcanic Wines' campaign and the annual Soave Preview, a press and public event which marks the release of the new vintage. Tastings in key export markets have followed the informative and carefully-researched work *Il Soave: Origine, Stile e Valori*, published in 2015 in a valiant attempt to drive the message home. Aside from such prodigious efforts and at a structural level the two sub-denominations, Soave Colli Scaligeri DOC and Soave

Superiore DOCG, designed to give growers more freedom of expression have foundered recently though Aldo will doubtless continue to press for a solution which receives more enthusiastic support from growers.

In both instances some of the load has been taken off consortial shoulders with the ratification of Siquria in 2012 by Mipaaf, the Ministry which determines governmental policy on agriculture, foodstuffs and forests in Italy. Siquria manages the quality control and traceability of agricultural produce in the Veneto allowing the *consorzi* to spend more time fighting fires or devising new ways to promote their products.

ALTERNATIVE ASSOCIATIONS

If membership of the *consorzio* – which remains optional – does not appeal, growers can consider the option of joining one of two other growers' associations active in the area. The Italian Federation of Independent Winegrowers (FIVI) is the parallel body in Italy to various similarly constituted groups across Europe, such as Vignerons Indépendants de France. The common aim is to represent the interests of the smaller winery, one that grows vines and bottles the wine from them, at an institutional level. Many who belong will also be a part of the local *consorzio* to make sure the voice of the small grower is heard. The aims and objectives are broader based than mere political lobbying, and promote ways of producing wine without 'sophistication' in the cellars and using sustainable viticultural practices. FIVI operates in both Soave and Valpolicella. The other possibility could be seen as a 'splinter group' of the Valpolicella Consorzio though the Famiglie Amarone would probably dispute the use of the term. 'We don't want to be seen just as polemicists but we do want to be part of the discussion about the future for the area's wines,' insists Sabrina Tedeschi, the current president. 'Our worry is that Amarone is being treated as if it were a commodity by the big players who hold the balance of power at our local level.' The families' policy is to put the interests of the overall territory at the heart of the debate and to maintain Amarone as the iconic wine of Valpolicella. Founded in 2009, thirteen historic family-owned and run wineries make up the current membership: Allegrini, Begali, La Brigaldara, Guerrieri Rizzardi, Masi, Musella, Speri, Tedeschi, Tenuta Sant'Antonio, Tommasi, Torre d'Orti, Venturini and Zenato. They organize events in key markets such as Scandinavia and North America (parts of the emerging

Asian market are possible future destinations), and purchased Verona's famous restaurant-cum-wine bar La Bottega del Vino in 2011 to showcase their products.

A NEW PROFESSIONALISM

As new markets began to open up in the period following the Second World War, a more considered approach to production methodology prompted the emergence of a new breed of professional winemaker. Figures like Lamberto Paronetto and Nino Franceschetti pointed the way forwards and, more recently, Roberto Ferrarini became a figure of indisputable importance whose ideas were to revolutionize the *appassimento* process. During his time as Professor of Oenology at the University of Verona, Ferrarini also acted as adviser to Quintarelli and other wineries of note such as La Brigaldara and Guerrieri Rizzardi. He died in late 2014. While many of today's older generation of producers learned much of what they know about winemaking from their fathers, their sons and daughters have gone on to become qualified oenologists. The presence of a consultant oenologist to help guide and administer production is often considered a useful insurance policy, particularly when starting up a new venture. While Celestino Gaspari and Flavio Pra, for example, have gone on to focus mainly on their own wineries, they have also helped to steer a number of emerging estates through the early stages of their development. Others, such as Paolo Grigolli and Beppe Caviola, continue to provide a useful service particularly to wineries with an eye on lucrative export markets. Larger wineries, including the cooperatives, will invariably employ both qualified oenologists and agronomists to look after the day-to-day running of the cellar and ensure vineyards are well managed. Founded in Friuli in 2003, The Pruning Guys Simonit&Sirch offer practical courses on the importance of pruning methods in maintaining a healthy vineyard. While all these services may come at a cost they all speak of a new professionalism throughout the vineyards and cellars of Verona.

7

LOOKING AHEAD

THE STRUGGLE FOR THE SOUL OF VALPOLICELLA

Over the last decade, the amount of wine produced directly from the *appassimento* process in the Valpolicella area has risen by nearly 50 per cent and now accounts for approximately a quarter of the entire DOC/ DOCG red wine production. This is mostly Amarone and the proportion of Recioto continues to dwindle. Of perhaps greater significance is that in the same period – from 2007 to 2016 – the proportion of their derivative, Ripasso, has gone from 14 per cent of total production to 45 per cent. As a consequence, quantities of 'simple' Valpolicella have plummeted from 70 per cent in 2007 to 30 per cent in 2016. However, the figures for Valpolicella also include the Superiore category, an increasingly high proportion of which is made from at least some semi-dried fruit (100 per cent in certain cases) as well. While these grapes do not always undergo the full term of *appassimento* (and frequently are set aside for just a month or so) they are nonetheless no longer freshly gathered fruit. The most gloriously drinkable and uncomplicated wine of the area has a huge question mark hanging over its immediate future. In fact the amount of Amarone and Recioto produced over the last decade seems in the short term at least to be sustainable and the 'cold reality' is that the Ripasso category has become a runaway gravy train.

Concerns amongst growers about the quality of some of the Amarone on the market today are also becoming more widespread, in particular with regard to the wine produced from lower-lying vineyards. Groups like the Famiglie Amarone and FIVI point to a clause in the contentious

Article 4 of the production discipline which states that Amarone grapes should not be sourced from vineyards planted in 'cooler' or poorly draining conditions on the plains or the valley floor. They both maintain a fairer solution would be to impose different limits to different sets of growing conditions and have put forward proposals for staggered yields closer to the maximum 65 per cent of the crop allowed under the law for more elevated hillside sites, with smaller proportions for less favourable positions. 'Amarone was born in the hills of Valpolicella and must return to its rightful home' is a commonly expressed view. Alternative proposals such as the creation of an 'Albo Vigneti', which would limit the production of Amarone grapes to designated vineyards only, flies in the face of vested interests despite its inexorable logic.

The widely acknowledged effects of climate change present a different problem in terms of how they are factored into the production regime. Some growers take the sanguine view that climate cycles come and go. A small but growing number argue that as achieving a harvest of fully-ripened grapes is no longer the lottery that it used to be, the *appassimento* process may not be the only solution. They believe that the appropriate biotypes of the local varieties, freshly gathered, are in fact capable of producing the sort of 'serious' red wine with the structure to age well and indeed improve in bottle that many aspire to. Examples so far of the Valpolicella Superiore category made along these lines only support the view and offer a potentially exciting alternative to those that rely on a proportion of semi-dried fruit to provide body and structure. While one school of thought may follow the Bepi Quintarelli dictum that *appassimento* is the source of Valpolicella's distinguishing characteristics, another maintains that to allow the overall identity of the wines to be defined by the process is too dangerous a course. Wines made with freshly gathered fruit speak first and foremost of the unique growing conditions that produce them: when tasting an *appassimento*-derived wine, the process and not the place provides the over-riding olfactory and gustatory sensations. The alternative option of leaving grapes a little longer on the vines to gain a degree of *sovramaturazione* is beginning to gain wider credibility as the true relevance of the *appassimento* process is called into question. The reinvention of the traditional standard bearer for Veronese wines has brought not only success, but a whole new set of problems too.

As the wines of Valpolicella have 'grown up' over the last century, the tendency has consistently been for growers to follow market demands in order to ensure that what they produce gets sold. The manner in which this has been achieved has often been ingenious, as the 'reinvention' of the *ripasso* process so aptly demonstrates, though absolute quality may not always have been at the head of the checklist. Yet well-made, commercially styled wines, which both meet market requirements and satisfy the need to maintain *tipicita*, do not necessarily cover all the bases. Other examples follow the guiding light of 'terroir' in order to attract the more demanding wine lover to the rarified delights that an individual vineyard with its own distinct growing conditions can offer. Natural, biodynamic and organic wines which champion biodiversity are an increasingly appealing option for smaller growers seeking to demonstrate commitment to their territory. A sustainable approach to viticulture, however, also requires a framework of production that puts the overall health of the denomination at the heart of the debate. The Valpolicella Superiore denomination needs to be carefully thought through and *appassimento* applied more prudently if the wines that do not depend on the process are to be allowed to shine. While *appassimento* guarantees a certain richness and roundness in the finished product it also brings high levels of alcohol and residual sugar, making the wines difficult to match with food. For now the wines have found a receptive market but putting all your eggs in the one basket is a foolhardy long-term strategy. Fashions come and go, but if style is indeed permanent then food-friendly Valpolicella with its incomparable freshness and elegance will also have its day.

SOAVE: UNITY OF PURPOSE

To revisit Angelo Gaja's paradigm of the quality pyramid briefly, Soave differs from Valpolicella in that it does not have a wine at the apex to lend greater credibility to the so-called lesser lights below. Where Amarone is a beacon which draws consumers to the Valpolicella denomination, Soave has forged ahead on its own merits alone. Overall standards of quality have become remarkably consistent over the last couple of decades as two distinct styles of the dry version have emerged. Modern technology has paved the way for a new generation of fresh, crisp and aromatic wines of real elegance while extra lees ageing has given an updated twist to the more traditional, richer and fuller-bodied style. In Soave the use of *appassimento* is still centred on the production of Recioto, though experiments with using a proportion of semi-dried fruit to enrich the drier wines are being undertaken. So far results seem to endorse the view that this is simply unnecessary though some believe a little *sovramaturazione* may enhance aroma and flavour profiles of the more ageworthy versions. Similarly the use of wood has been carefully modified and plays much more of a supporting role in the make up of the new Soave. The various denominations still require some fine tuning and Trebbiano di Soave remains undervalued; otherwise, Soave looks to have the world at its feet, held back only by the last vestiges of that old 'cheap and cheerful' image.

ALL TOGETHER NOW

While both areas have issues to be resolved, they are not insurmountable. In the eyes of influential producers such as Dal Forno and Masi, the true value of Amarone is as a niche wine. Restoring it to this status and halving the double Ripasso rule would go a long way towards bringing some much needed stability to the overall Valpolicella denomination. The unpalatable truth for producers, from the simple grape grower through to the elite estates, is that everyone will need to make sacrifices to foster the common good and ensure long-term prosperity. However, the building blocks for a bright future are in place. In terms of grape varieties, vineyard sites, technical know-how, a readiness to embrace sustainable production methods and, as further bait to attract the wine tourist, a delightfully picturesque setting as a backdrop, Soave and Valpolicella have the raw materials to take on the world. In the vine-clad hills that lie just beyond the city, the restoration of Verona as a centre of wine producing excellence, a reputation it has not enjoyed since Roman times, is under way.

GLOSSARY

Acinatico. Late Roman term meaning 'made from grapes', here signifying the use of grapes which have been semi-dried.

Agriturismo. A working farm that offers accommodation.

Allevamento. In viticultural terms, the training/pruning system used for growing vines, such as Guyot.

Amarone. Veronese wine speciality: a dry red wine made from semi-dried grapes – literally 'big bitter one'.

Appassimento. The process of drying grapes before they are pressed and made into wine.

Arele. Wooden racks used for storing grapes as they dry, once used in the silkworm-farming industry.

Autoclave. Pressurized fermentation tank for the production of sparkling wine.

Azienda Agricola. Usually a small company producing wines from fruit grown in their own vineyards.

Azienda Vitivinicola. A company producing wine from partly bought-in grapes or wine.

Barrique. A 225-litre wooden barrel, usually of French but sometimes American or even Austrian oak.

Botte. Large wooden storage cask.

Cantina. Cellars.

Cantina Sociale. Cooperative cellars.

Cantiniere. Cellarmaster.

Colmatura. Topping up casks with wine.

Conferenti. Members of the cooperative who 'confer' their grapes to the organization.

Consorzio. Producers' consortium.

Contadino. Peasant farmer/agricultural worker.

Crio maceration. The 'cold soak' of crushed grapes at temperatures below those at which fermentation will begin.

Damigiane. Glass demijohn, usually containing 50 litres.

D'annata. From the latest vintage.

Diraddamento. Summer pruning or removal of whole bunches of grapes to improve the quality of those that remain.

DOC. *Denominazione di Origine Controllata*, or the official classification of a wine controlling origin, grape varieties, yields, etc.

DOCG. As above plus *Garantita* indicating that a wine has been approved by a tasting panel as a typical example of its type.

Famiglie Amarone. The 'Amarone Families' – a group of producers dedicated to maintaining traditional quality standards for Amarone.

FIVI. *Federazione Italiana Vignaioli Indipendenti* or the Italian Federation of Independent Vinegrowers.

Follatura. Breaking up of the cap which rises to the surface of the fermenting must.

Frazione. A small hamlet or part of a village (literally 'fraction').

Frizzante. Fizzy (a lower atmospheric pressure than sparkling).

Fruttaio. A room dedicated to the storage of drying grapes.

Gerla. A basket used to carry grapes.

Graspia. A weak version of 'wine' made by adding water to lees.

Lessinia. A mountainous area to the north of Verona, partly a national park. *Bassa Lessinia* refers to Lower Lessinia.

Localita. A smaller version of a *frazione,* i.e. a small geographical area.

Long charmat method. The fermentation of sparkling wine in tank with extended lees contact.

Marogna. Veronese term for a dry-stone wall, usually seen its plural form, *marogne*.

Metodo Classico. The bottle fermentation of sparkling wine (the equivalent of *méthode champenoise*). Also the name for the bottle-fermented wine.

Mezzadria. The feudal tenancy or sharecropping system whereby the farmer gave half the crop to the landowner.

Muffa Grigia. Grey rot.

Muffa Nobile. Noble rot (*Botrytis cinerea*).

Negoziante. Negociant producer, who purchases grapes or wines from growers.

Oidium. A fungal disease of the vine caused by powdery mildew.

Osteria. A tavern or hostelry selling food and wine.

Pagus arusnatium. The Roman name for what equates approximately to today's Valpolicella district, though there is no precise definition of the territory.

Passito. Wine made from semi-dried grapes (usually sweet).

Peronospera. A disease which affects the vine, also known as downy mildew.

Quintal. A measure of weight equivalent to 100 kilos.

Recioto. Sweet wine produced from semi-dried grapes in either Soave or Valpolicella.

Resa. Vineyard yield. '*Resa in vino*' is the proportion of wine that can be produced from a certain quantity of grapes.

Retico. Rhaetian or Raetic.

Ripasso. A Veronese speciality produced by refermenting a young wine on the *vinacce* of a Passito.

Ritocchino. A row of vines planted vertically – up and down – a hill rather than following its contours.

Saltari. An archaic term referring to vineyard guardians.

Sapidity. A pleasant savoury or salty taste; sometimes used as an alternative to 'minerality'.

Sfuso. 'Bulk' or loose wine, i.e. not bottled.

Sovramaturazione. Over or extra ripening, whereby grapes are left on the vine to gain extra ripeness which can mean a light shrivelling.

Spumante. Sparkling wine which meets the minimum 3 bars of pressure.

Superiore. 'Higher quality' wine that has a higher alcohol content and has been aged for longer.

Tendone. An old-fashioned vine training system using a pergola, common around Verona.

Terreno. 'Land' or 'terroir'.

Tini. Upright conical wooden tanks often used for fermentation.

Tipicita. Typicity or degree of authenticity.

Tonneau. A 900-litre wooden barrel; as barrique, usually of French but sometimes American or Austrian oak. It is frequently used in Italy to describe a 500-litre barrel (or double barrique).

Uvaggio. A mixture of grapes either as they are planted in the vineyard or as components of a blend.

Vajo. A Veronese term referring to a valley or gorge, plural *vai*.

Veronese. This is used as either an adjective meaning from the Verona area or a noun referring to the area comprising the two DOC territories of Soave and Valpolicella.

Veronesi. The people of Verona.

Vigna. Or *vigneto* – vineyard.

Vignaiolo. Vine grower.

Vinacce. The solids remaining from the fermentation process consisting mainly of grape skins and pips.

Vino da Tavola. 'Table wine' – the lowest classification of Italian wine.

Vino Santo. Literally 'holy wine', a term used to refer to a sweet wine often produced from semi-dried or later-harvested grapes.

Viticoltore. Vine grower; see also *vignaiolo*.

SELECT BIBLIOGRAPHY

Anderson, B., *Vino*, London, 1982

Avesani, B. et al., *Valpantena dal Vinum Raeticum all'Amarone*, Verona, 2013

Batt, C. A. et al., *Encyclopedia of Food Microbiology*, London, 2014

Battista, F. and Tomasi, D., *I Segreti del Territrio, dei Vigneti e del Vino Amarone della Cantina Valpantena,* Verona, 2014

Belfrage, N., *Life Beyond Lambrusco,* London, 1985

Bertolazzi, M., *Il Vino Santo di Brognoligo*, Verona, 2008

Black, C., *Early Modern Italy: A Social History*, London, 2001

Bode, C. G., *Wines of Italy*, London, 1956

Carlesso, M. V., *Dalla Fillosera alla Zona Classica del Soave*, Verona, 2013

Carrier R., *Food, Wine and Friends*, London, 1981

Cosmo, I. and Sardi, F., *Principali Vitigni da Vino Coltivati in Italia*, Vol. 3, Rome, 1964

Curi, E., *Gaetano Pellegrini e la Nascita dell'Enologia Veronese*, Verona, 2006

D'Agata, I., *Native Wine Grapes of Italy*, London, 2014

Jackson, R. S., *Wine Science: Principles and Applications*, London, 2008

Lorenzoni, A. et al., *Il Soave: Origine, Stile e Valori*, Verona, 2015

Paronetto, Lamberto, *Verona Antica Terra di Vini Pregiati*, Verona, 1970

Paronetto, Lamberto, *Viti e Vini di Verona*, Verona, 1991

Paronetto, Lamberto et al., *Storia Regionale della Vite e del Vino Italiano Veneto*, Milan, 1996

Paronetto, Llanfranco et al., *Appassimento and Amarone – The Essence of the Venetian Art of Winemaking*, Verona, 2014

Peynaud, E. and Blouin, J., *The Taste of Wine: The Art and Science of Wine Appreciation*, second edition, London, 1996

Ribereau-Gayon, P., Dubordieu, D., Doneche, B. and Lonvaud, A., *The Handbook of Enology*, Chichester, 2006

Various authors, *Valpolicella dal Visibile alla Scoperta dell'Invisibile*, Verona, 2012

Various authors, *Terra, Uomini e Passioni nel Mito del Recioto e dell'Amarone*, Verona, 2013

INDEX